The Collected Works of
Marie-Louise von Franz

MLvF

Volume 8

General Editors

Steven Buser

Leonard Cruz

Marie-Louise von Franz
1915-1998

Volume 8

The Interpretation of Fairytales

An Introduction to the Interpretation of Fairytales
and
Animus and Anima in Fairytales

Marie–Louise von Franz

Translated by Barbara Davies
Edited by Michaela Kopp-Marx
Revised by Alison Kappes-Bates

CHIRON PUBLICATIONS • ASHEVILLE, NORTH CAROLINA

Logo of the Foundation of Jungian Psychology, Küsnacht Switzerland:
Fons mercurialis from Rosarium Philosophorum 1550 (Fountain of Life).

An Introduction to the Interpretation of Fairy Tales,
previously published by Spring Publications, ©1970
Psychologische Märcheninterpretation, previously published
by Stiftung für Jung'sche Psychologie, ©2012

Translated from French to German by Barbara Davies
Revised and adapted English version by Alison Kappes-Bates
Edited by Michaela Kopp-Marx
Cover Image by Martina Ott
Interior and cover design by Danijela Mijailovic

Animus and Anima in Fairytales,
previously published by Inner City Books, © 2002
Animus und Anima im Märchen,
in print by Stiftung für Jung'sche Psychologie, © 2023

Translated and revised from English to German by Michaela Kopp-Marx
Adapted new English version by Alison Kappes-Bates
Cover Image by Martina Ott
Interior and cover design by Danijela Mijailovic

◊

A Note on the Compilation of
The Collected Works of
Marie-Louise von Franz

Marie-Louise von Franz was blessed with a keen intellect and an outstanding memory. As a classical philologist with a doctorate in Latin and Greek, she was familiar with the writings of the ancient philosophers. She was exceptionally well read. Her private library alone contained over 8,000 books and writings. She was also both diligent and conscientious in her work. She met C.G. Jung in her youth and found him to be an excellent teacher and mentor. She went on to become a close confidant and collaborator, particularly in his work on alchemy. Jung's psychological observations and the conclusions and hypotheses he drew from them about the structures of the unconscious psyche increasingly coincided with her own observations. Marie-Louise von Franz was imbued with an inexhaustible creativity that inspired her well into her old age. She devoted her last lecture to the rehabilitation of the feeling function, a subject that was of great importance to her and to C.G. Jung. Her unconditional devotion to the manifestations of the unconscious psyche was exemplary for all who met her during her lifetime, and for many who came to know her from her writings or their own dreams.

Only a few of her works survived in the form of finished manuscripts. Many of her books derived from transcriptions of her lectures, some of which were delivered in German, though most were in English. The English transcriptions were later translated into her native German. Her primary focus was always on the psychological context and background of her books, and less on their linguistic delivery. Some publishers therefore took the liberty of adding or changing certain things in her texts to make it easier for the reader, as they thought. After realizing what they had done, Marie-Louise von Franz indignantly insisted on her original text being used, claiming that what she had written was what she had wanted to express. Since then, many of her works have been translated into 23 languages, with editions of varying quality being used as the basis for translations into local languages.

In addition to the publishing rights, Marie-Louise von Franz left to the Foundation for Jungian Psychology a handwritten list in which she noted which editions of her books she considered to be the best and most accurate. After her death in 1998, the members of the Foundation decided to republish all of her works in German in accordance with her list. We have respectfully endeavored to remain as close as possible to her original tone, to correct obvious audio or transcription errors, to add footnotes to facilitate understanding, and to supplement texts when written records or tape recordings of her lectures were available. In some instances, this has resulted in greatly altered and revised publications, which we consider to be the basis for all new translations.

For the publication of the Collected Works of Marie-Louise von Franz by Chiron Publications, the Stiftung commissioned Alison Kappes-Bates, Hirzel, a professional translator who knew Marie-Louise von Franz for over 30 years and was a close companion until her death, to translate into English the newly-revised texts in German. Mark Kyburz, Zürich, an experienced translator of Jungian texts, re-edited the first three English volumes of Archetypal Symbols in Fairytales, translated Volumes 4 and 5, and will translate further volumes. The Foundation for Jungian Psychology is responsible for the content and the design, the latter having been created in close consultation with Chiron Publication, Asheville.

On behalf of the Foundation for Jungian Psychology,
Küsnacht, April 24, 2023
PD Dr. Hansueli F. Etter

"From the standpoint of Jungian psychology, we may say that fairytales do not recount consciously experienced human events, but that these 'pure forms' make visible *fundamental archetypal structures of the collective unconscious.* This accounts for the non-human ... abstract character of the figures; they are archetypal images behind which the secret of the unconscious psyche is hidden. By the collective unconscious, we mean that part of man's unconscious psyche which, regardless of all the differences between individuals, remains the same in all men and women, just as certain aspects of the anatomical structure of *Homo sapiens* are the same in all individuals precisely because they are human."

Marie-Louise von Franz, The problem of evil in fairytales, in: *Archetypal Dimensions of the Psyche*, Shambhala, Boston and London 1999, 76 (Intended as CW Vol. 27, 2028).

◇

Editorial Note

Marie-Louise von Franz gave her lectures without a written script — there is no original manuscript of her talk. The text at hand is based on the transcript of the seminar "Animus and Anima in Fairy Tales," which was held at the Los Angeles Society of Analytical Psychology, now the C.G. Jung Institute of Los Angeles, in February of 1953. The typescript of the lectures, prepared by Cassil Welch, was not edited for publication at the time; it later served as a model for the first English edition, *Animus and Anima in Fairy Tales* (Inner City Books, Toronto, Canada 2002). That edition was arranged by Daryl Sharp; it was heavily revised by the editor for publication and, at times, supplemented to include his own thoughts. For the new edition of this early work by Marie-Louise von Franz, the transcript of the original lectures from 1953 was used.

Any transfer from oral to written language requires a compromise between the imperative to retain the literal meaning along with the characteristic peculiarities of the original and the need for factual accuracy. Thus, the oral tone of this seminar — its spontaneous and partly associative style, along with the Germanic tinge in the sentence structure — was retained and, where necessary, slightly revised, keeping as closely as possible to "verbatim von Franz." All questions from the audience and answers or contributions to the discussion by Marie-Louise von Franz have likewise been included. Obvious errors and content-related misunderstandings have been silently corrected. For clarity, the text has been divided into chapters. Explanatory footnotes which might facilitate reading and understanding were added where they seemed helpful.

Von Franz herself described the spirit in which she held these first lectures on "Anima and Animus in Fairy Tales" when she revisited the C.G. Jung Institute in Los Angeles in 1976. Looking back to the 1953 seminar, she remembered: "We were a group of younger pupils [Rivkah Kluger, Aniela Jaffé, et al.], and when we had these invitations abroad, Jung always said to us, 'Now, remember that by being close around me and hearing so much' — we went to all the lectures and all the speeches and so on — 'you know more than these people. So don't be shy. Your task is to hand on what the people who can't come to Zurich want to learn about, what you have learned to hand on.' And that gave one a feeling of a function, that one had something to give."

(M.-L. von Franz: "Confrontation With the Collective Unconscious", in: *Psychological Perspectives*, 59: 295-318, 2016; lecture at the C.G. Jung Institute of Los Angeles, 1976).

◆

Foreword

Marie-Louise von Franz was already interested in fairytales as a young doctoral student in the main subjects Latin and Greek. At that time, she interpreted around 1,000 fairytales during several years of work. Her comprehensive interpretations are published by Chiron Publications in five volumes entitled "Archetypal Symbols in Fairytales" as part of the *Collected Works of Marie-Louise von Franz* (Vol. I/II/III/IV/V).

As Marie-Louise von Franz herself writes, the present book is based on the extensive experiences she has gained with her early work. It forms an instructive and accurate summary of the psychological interpretations of fairytales. The text is based on a lecture that Marie-Louise von Franz first gave in English in 1963 entitled "An Introduction to the Psychology of Fairytales." The first English edition was published by *The Analytical Psychology Club of New York* (Spring Publications, New York 1970). Later, French, and German translations were published. It was the wish of Marie-Louise von Franz to adapt the revised German edition of her book to the French version. Barbara Davies, Zürich, has taken on this demanding work. Michaela Kopp-Marx, Mannheim, was responsible for the careful editing and revision of the bibliography and the index. Alison Kappes-Bates, Hirzel, has prepared the revised English edition for publication in her habitual careful manner. We would like to thank all three women for their precious work.

The text for the new edition for "Animus and Anima in Fairy Tales" by Marie-Louise von Franz is based on the transcript of the seminar, which was held at the Los Angeles Society of Analytical Psychology, now the C.G. Jung Institute of Los Angeles, in February of 1953. The typescript of the lectures was not edited for publication at the time; it later served as a model for the first English edition of

"Animus and Anima in Fairy Tales," which came out four years after the death of Marie-Louise von Franz (Inner City Books, Toronto, Canada 2002). That edition was heavily revised by the editor for publication.

The oral tone of this seminar — its spontaneous and partly associative style, along with the Germanic tinge in the sentence structure — was retained and, where necessary, slightly revised, keeping as closely as possible to "verbatim von Franz." All questions from the audience and answers or contributions to the discussion by Marie-Louise von Franz have likewise been included. For clarity, the text has been divided into chapters. Explanatory footnotes which might facilitate reading and understanding were added where it seemed helpful. The respectfully revised English text of "Animus and Anima in Fairytales," including footnotes, bibliography, and index, was carefully prepared by Michaela Kopp-Marx, Mannheim. We owe her a great debt of gratitude.

The Foundation for Jungian Psychology decided to publish "Interpretation of Fairytales" and "Animus and Anima in Fairytales" together and are thankful to Chiron publications, Asheville, and all employees, for the accurate print of Vol. 8 of the *Collected Works of Marie-Louise von Franz*.

On behalf of the Foundation for Jungian Psychology, Zürich
April 24, 2022.

PD Dr. Hansueli F. Etter
President

◆

Table of Contents

Part 1

The Interpretation
of Fairytales

Updated and revised German edition (2012) / English edition (2017)

A series of lectures on "An Introduction to the Psychology of Fairy Tales" held by Marie-Louise von Franz at the C.G. Jung Institute in Zurich in 1963 were first published in German in 1986 by Kösel Verlag, Munich. It was Marie-Louise von Franz's own wish that the new edition of her book *Psychologische Märcheninterpretation. Eine Einführung* be adapted to reflect the French version *L'interprétation des Contes de fées* that was edited by Francine Saint René Taillandier-Perrot (Collection La Fontaine de Pierre, Paris 1978). Barbara Davies took on this challenging task, for which we are very grateful. We are also indebted to Michaela Kopp-Marx, in Mannheim, who assisted with proofreading, with questions on grammar and style in adapting the text, with revising the bibliography and with creating an index. For this new updated and revised English edition that is based upon the revised German edition of 2012, we thank Alison Kappes-Bates, Hirzel.

Acknowledgements
(for the original English edition 1970, 1973, 1996)

I wish to thank the many people who helped to see this seminar into print: Una Thomas for her faithful transcript upon which the text is based; Marian Bayes and Andrea Dykes for their help with my English; and Thayer Greene for helping to finance the original publication. I would also like to thank Patricia Berry and Valerie Donleavy for the first form in which this seminar appeared.

I also want to thank Alison Kappes-Bates for translating the additions made in the German version for this new revised English edition. My greatest gratitude goes to Dr. Vivienne Mackrell for helping me to organize this book, but mainly for her general support.

◆

Preface to the
German edition of 1986

1 This book resulted from lectures that I gave in English at the C.G. Jung Institute more than twenty years ago. Based upon a recording of the lectures, it was first published in English in 1970.

2 These lectures summarize my experience in fairytale interpretation and are based upon the contributions I made for Hedwig von Beit in *Symbolik des Maerchens* (1952). At that time there were some early studies from the Freudian school, along with some short essays by Alfons Maeder, Franz Riklin, and Wilhelm Leiblin; no interpretations of fairytales by Jungian authors were available. My primary intention at that time was to open up the archetypal dimension of fairytales to the students. For this reason, the ethnological and folkloric aspects are only touched upon, which is not meant to imply that they are unimportant.

3 Since the 1960s, there has been a real blossoming of fairytale interpretation from the standpoint of depth psychology. From the Freudian school, Bruno Bettelheim's book *The Uses of Enchantment: The Meaning and Importance of Fairy Tales* should be primarily mentioned. From the Jungian school, so many books have been published that I cannot name them all here. In this respect I would like to express a personal opinion: In many so-called Jungian attempts at interpretation, one can see a regression to a very personalized approach. The interpreters judge the hero or heroine to be a normal human ego, and his or her misfortunes to be an image of his or her neurosis. Because it is natural for a person listening to a fairytale to identify with the main character, this kind of interpretation is understandable. But such interpreters ignore what Max Luethi found to be essential for magical fairytales, namely, that in

contrast to the heroes of adventurous sagas, the heroes and heroines of fairy tales are abstractions — that is, they embody archetypes. Therefore, their fates are not neurotic complications, but rather are expressions of the difficulties and dangers given to us by nature. The problem of a personalized interpretation is that the very healing element of an archetypal narrative is nullified.

4   Let me give you an example. The hero-child in fairytales is nearly always abandoned. If one interprets his fate as the neurosis of the abandoned child, one ascribes it to the neurotic family novel of our time. If, however, one leaves it embedded within its archetypal context, it takes on a much deeper meaning, namely that the new God of an era is always to be found in the ignored and deeply unconscious corner of the psyche (the classic example being the birth of Christ in a stable). If an individual has to bear the neurotic suffering of being an abandoned child, he or she is called upon to turn towards the abandoned God within, instead of identifying with one's own suffering.

5   Hans Giehrl, (*Volksmaerchen und Tiefenpsychologie, 1970*) makes what I view to be a partially justified reproach of depth psychology interpreters, namely that they transfer their own subjective problems onto the fairytales, where they are not to be found at all. As in all scientific work, the subjective factor can never be entirely excluded. But I believe a very earnest mythological amplification can hold such subjectivism in check; it gives us, at least to some extent, the chance to reach a generally valid interpretation.

6   The second tool we can use to reach a certain level of objectivity is to consider the context. Here, Giehrl expresses criticism that I do not agree with. He believes that because variations sometimes include contrary motifs that are omitted for this reason, the objectivity of contextual research is thereby impaired. But if one goes into this more deeply, one sees that each contrary motif changes the whole context — proving the very opposite of Giehrl's reproach. The Russian fairytale "Beautiful Vassilissa," for example, tells the story of a girl's encounter with an ancient witch, which ends on a positive note. The German version, "Frau Trude," ends on a negative note. If

one scrutinizes both versions, one sees that the girl in the Russian version is kind, obedient, and has good common sense, whereas her counterpart in the German version is disobedient, impatient, and cheeky. This permeates the whole context, and because of this, one cannot interpret both fairytales the same way, despite the fact that both stories circle around the same archetype of an encounter with the Great Mother.

7 In what follows, I have endeavored to interpret a few classical stories — basic types of important fairytale plots, as it were — in order to help clarify for the reader the Jungian method of interpretation. If, as a result, some readers feel motivated to try their hand at interpretation and they have fun doing so, then the goal of this book will have been reached.

MARIE-LOUISE VON FRANZ
Kuesnacht, Switzerland
April 1986

Chapter 1
Some Theories of Fairytales

8   Fairytales are the purest and simplest expression of collective unconscious psychic processes.[1] Therefore their value for the scientific investigation of the unconscious exceeds that of all other material. They represent the archetypes in their simplest, barest, and most concise form.[2] In this pure form, archetypal images afford us the best clues to understand the processes going on in the collective psyche. In myths, legends, or any other more elaborate mythological material, we get at the basic patterns of the human psyche through an overlay of cultural material. Fairytales, on the other hand, contain much less specific conscious cultural material, and therefore they mirror the basic patterns of the psyche more clearly.

9   According to Carl Gustav Jung, every archetype is in its essence an *unknown* psychic factor, and therefore there is no possibility of translating its content into intellectual terms. The best we can do is to circumscribe it on the basis of our own psychological experience and from comparative studies, bringing up into light, as it were, the

---

[1] "The collective unconscious is a part of the psyche which can be negatively distinguished from a personal unconscious by the fact that it does not, like the latter, owe its existence to personal experience and consequently is not a personal acquisition. While the personal unconscious is made up essentially of contents which have at one time been conscious but which have disappeared from consciousness through having been forgotten or repressed, the contents of the collective unconscious have never been in consciousness, and therefore have never been individually acquired, but owe their existence exclusively to heredity." See C.G. Jung, *The Archetypes and the Collective Unconscious*, 2nd ed., vol. 9/I, *Bollingen Series XX: The Collected Works of C. G. Jung*, ed. Herbert Read, Michael Fordham, Gerhard Adler and William McGuire, trans. R. F. C. Hull (Princeton, NJ: Princeton University Press, 1980), § 88.

[2] "This collective unconscious does not develop individually but is inherited. It consists of pre-existent forms, the archetypes, which can only become conscious secondarily and which give definite form to certain psychic contents." See ibid., § 90. "The archetype in itself is empty and purely formal, nothing but a *facultas praeformandi*, a possibility of representation which is given *a priori*. The representations themselves are not inherited, only the forms. [...] With regard to the definiteness of the form, our comparison with the crystal is illuminating inasmuch as the axial system determines only the stereometric structure but not the concrete form of the individual crystal. [...] The same is true of the archetype. In principle, it can be named and has an invariable nucleus of meaning – but always only in principle, never as regards its concrete manifestation." Ibid., § 155.

whole net of associations in which the archetypal images are enmeshed. The fairytale itself is its own best explanation for its meaning is contained in the totality of its motifs that are connected by the thread of its story. So why do we not immediately understand them? The unconscious is, metaphorically speaking, in the same position as one who has had an original vision or experience and wishes to share it. Since it is an event that has never been conceptually formulated, one is at a loss for means of expression. When a person is in a position like this, he will try to convey his experience in different ways in order to evoke an echo in his listeners by appealing to their intuition and by drawing analogies to already known material. He will expound upon his vision until he feels that his listeners have some sense of the content of his thoughts. In the same way, we can put forward the hypothesis that every fairytale is a relatively closed system compounding one essential psychological meaning that is expressed in a series of symbolic pictures and events, and is discoverable in these.

10   After working for many years in this field, I have come to the conclusion that all fairytales endeavor to describe one and the same psychic fact, but a fact so complex and far-reaching and so difficult for us to realize in all its different aspects that hundreds of tales and thousands of repetitions are needed until this unknown fact is delivered into consciousness, rather like multiple variations on a musical theme that can never be exhausted. This unknown inexhaustible fact is what Jung calls the Self; it represents the psychic totality of an individual and also, paradoxically, the regulating center of the collective unconscious. Every individual and every nation has its own modes of experiencing this psychic reality.

11   Different fairytales give average pictures of different phases of this experience. They sometimes dwell more on the beginning stages, which deal with the experience of the shadow; later stages are then only briefly outlined. Other tales emphasize the experience of the animus and anima with the father and mother images behind them and gloss over both the preceding shadow problem and what follows. Still others emphasize the motif of the inaccessible or

unobtainable treasure and the central experiences that are involved. There is no difference of value between these tales because in the archetypal world there are no gradations of value. There are none because every archetype is, in its essence, only one aspect of the collective unconscious, while simultaneously also representing the whole of the collective unconscious.

12   Every archetype is a relatively closed energetic system whose energetic stream runs through all aspects of the collective unconscious. An archetypal image is not to be thought of as a merely static image, for it is always simultaneously a complete, organized process that includes other images in a specific way. An archetype is a specific psychic impulse whose effect is like a single ray of radiation, and at the same time it is a whole magnetic field that expands in all directions. Thus the stream of psychic energy of a "system," an archetype, actually runs through all other archetypes as well. Therefore, although we have to recognize the indefinable vagueness of an archetypal image, we must discipline ourselves to chisel sharp outlines that throw its different aspects into bold relief. We must get as close as possible to the primal, "just so" character of each image and try to express the very specific nature of the psychic situation that is contained in it.

13   Without laying any claim to it being comprehensive, I would like to go into some aspects of the history of fairytale research, along with some theories from the different schools of thought and their literature. We read in Plato's writings that old women told their children symbolic stories — *mythoi*. Even at that time, fairytales were connected with the education of children. In later antiquity, Apuleius, a philosopher and writer of the 2nd century, wove into his famous novel *The Golden Ass* a fairytale called "Amor and Psyche," a type of "Beauty and the Beast" story.[3] This fairytale has the same pattern as those one can still collect nowadays in Norway, Sweden, Russia, and many other countries. It has therefore been concluded that at least this type of fairytale (of a woman redeeming an animal lover) has existed almost unaltered for two thousand years. But

---

[3] Cf. Marie-Louise von Franz, *The Golden Ass* (Asheville: Chiron Publications, 2022).

fairytales go back even further — to Ancient Egypt where they have been found in Egyptian *papyri* and *stelai*.[4] One of the most famous is that of two brothers Anup (Anubis) and Bata. It runs absolutely parallel to the fairytales of two brothers that can be found in all European countries. So the written tradition goes back three thousand years, and it is striking to see that the basic motifs have not changed. According to Father Max Schmidt, certain fairytale themes go back as far as 25000 years B.C.[5] Until the seventeenth and eighteenth centuries, fairy tales were — as they still are in remote primitive centers of civilization — told to adults as well as to children. In Europe they used to be the chief form of wintertime entertainment that became a kind of spiritual occupation in agricultural populations.[6]

14   Scientific interest in fairytales began in the 18th century with Johann Joachim Winckelmann, Johann Georg Hamann, and Johann Gottfried Herder.[7] Others, like Karl Philipp Moritz, gave these tales a poetical interpretation. Herder thought such tales contained the remnants of old, long-buried religious beliefs, expressed in symbols. One recognizes an emotional impulse in such thoughts, i.e., neo-paganism that had already begun to stir in Germany at the time of Herder's philosophy in a not very pleasant way. At that time, dissatisfaction with the Christian teachings and a longing for a more vital, earthy, and instinctual wisdom had begun to stir in people. Later, we find the same tendency amongst, above all, the German Romantics.

15   It was this religious search for something that seemed to be lacking in official Christian teaching that also first induced the famous brothers Jakob and Wilhelm Grimm to collect folktales.[8] [9] Prior to the Grimms, fairytales suffered the same fate as the

---

[4] Emma Brunner-Traut, *Altägyptische Märchen*, Märchen der Weltliteratur, ed. Friedrich von der Leyen (Munich: Diederichs, 1989).

[5] Pater Wilhelm Schmidt, *Der Ursprung der Gottesidee* (Munster: Aschendorff, 1912–1955).

[6] On this, see Johann Georg Schmidt, *Die gestriegelte Rocken-Philosophie* (Chemnitz, 1705).

[7] Jan de Vries, *Forschungsgeschichte der Mythologie* (Freiburg: Alber, 1961).

[8] On this, see Johannes Bolte and Georg Polivka, *Anmerkungen zu den Kinder- und Hausmärchen der Gebrüder Grimm*, 5 vols. (Leipzig: Diederichs, 1913–1932).

[9] The first collection of fairy tales that became popular in France was the collection of Charles Perrault, *Contes de ma Mère l'Oye* (Brussels: Candide & Cyrano, 2017). [Note added by the translator of the French edition].

unconscious itself, which was taken for granted. People take it for granted and live from it, but do not want to consciously admit its existence. They make use of it, for instance, in magic, in superstitions, in advertising, and in art. Often a good dream is also exploited and is not taken seriously. These people do not look at a fairytale or a dream accurately, but distort it. Since it is not "scientific" material, one can just as well put a spin on it, and, it would seem, one has the right to pick what suits one and discard the rest.

16   This same strange, unreliable, unscientific, and dishonest attitude prevailed towards fairytales for a long time. This is why I place great importance upon examining the original. One can still get editions of the Grimm fairytales in which some scenes have been omitted and those from other fairytales inserted. The editor or translator is sometimes impertinent enough to distort the story without taking the trouble of adding a footnote. They would not dare do that with a Gilgamesh epic or a text of that kind, but fairytales seem to provide a free hunting ground where some feel free to take any liberty. The Brothers Grimm wrote down fairytales in a relatively literal fashion, just as people in their surroundings told them, but even they could sometimes not resist mixing a few versions, though in a tactful way. They, however, were honest enough to mention it in footnotes or in their letters to Achim von Armin. But even the Grimms did not yet have the scientific attitude that modern folklore writers and ethnologists try to have, namely, of taking down a story as it is told and leaving the holes and paradoxes in it, as dreamlike and paradoxical as they may sound.

17   The collection of fairytales published by the Brothers Grimm was a tremendous success. There must have been a strong unconscious emotional interest for other editions popped up everywhere, like mushrooms out of the ground. People everywhere began to collect their essential national fairytales. People were struck by the enormous number of recurrent themes. The same theme popped up in thousands of variations in French, Russian, Finnish, and Italian collections. Simultaneously, Herder's first emotional interest in the

search for the remains of some "old wisdom" or "religious belief" began to stir. Along with the Brothers Grimm, the so-called symbolic school came into existence, whose main representatives are Christian Gottlob Heyne, Friedrich Creuzer, and Joseph Goerres. Their basic idea was that myths are the symbolic expression of deep philosophical realizations and thoughts; they were believed to express some mystical teaching full of deep truths about God and the world.[10] Although these investigators had some interesting ideas, their explanations seem to me to be decidedly speculative.

Then came a more historical and scientific interest in fairytales; for example, an attempt was made to answer the question why there were so many recurring motifs.[11] As there was no hypothesis on a common collective unconscious or a common human psychic structure (although some investigators indirectly pointed to it) at this time, a passion arose to find out exactly where a fairy tale had originated and to follow the path of its migration. Theodor Benfey[12] tried to prove that all fairytale motifs had originated in India and had later migrated to Europe, while others like Alfred Jensen, Hartmut Winkler, and Eduard Stucken contended that all fairytales were of Babylonian origin and had then spread throughout Asia Minor and from there to Europe. One positive outcome of this research was the creation of the folklore center of the Finnish school, whose first representatives were Kaarle Krohn and Antti Aarne. These two men decided that it was not possible to discover a single country in which fairytales had originated, and instead they assumed that there must have been various places of origin. They made collections of the same types of fairytales with the idea that of all the "Beauty and the Beast" tales, of all the "Helpful Animal Tales," and so on, the best, the richest and the most poetical version had to be the original version from which all other versions were derived. In my view, this hypothesis is indefensible because today

---

[10] See Werner von Bülow, *Die Geheimsprache der deutschen Märchen* (Hellerau bei Dresden, 1925); and Philipp Stauff, *Märchendeutungen: Sinn und Deutung der deutschen Volksmärchen* (Leipzig: Dürr, 1935).
[11] On the history of fairytale research, Felix Karlinger, *Grundzüge einer Geschichte des Märchens im deutschen Sprachraum* (Darmstadt: Wiss. Buchgesellschaft, 1983) is of relevance; as well as the anthology edited by Karlinger, *Wege der Märchenforschung* (Darmstadt: Wiss. Buchgesellschaft, 1973).
[12] Theodor Benfey, *Kleinere Schriften zur Märchenforschung* (Berlin, 1894).

we know that fairytales do not necessarily degenerate but may just as well improve. Nevertheless, I believe the scholars of the Finnish school gave us a useful collection of motifs. Antti Aarne's main book, *Verzeichnis der Maerchentypen*, has meanwhile been published as *The Types of the Folktale*. This was the basis for Stith Thompson's well-received six-volume work *Motiv-Index der Volksliteratur*.[13]

19   At the same time a movement arose led by Max Mueller. He interpreted myths as paraphrases of natural phenomena such as the sun and its different appearances (solar myth by Leo Frobenius), the moon (lunar myth by Paul Ehrenreich), the dawn (Aurora by Eduard Stucken and Angelo de Gubernatis), the life of vegetation (by Wilhelm Mannhardt) and the storm (by Adalbert Kuhn). In the 19th century, a different direction was taken, and leading it was a man who is seldom remembered, although to my mind he has great merit: Ludwig Laistner.[14] His hypothesis was that the basic fairytale and folklore motifs derive from dreams. He concentrated chiefly on nightmare motifs, trying to show a connection between recurring typical dreams and folklore motifs. The material that he cites to support his hypothesis is most interesting.

20   At the same time, the ethnologist Karl von den Steinen[15] believed most magic and supernatural beliefs of primitives arose from dream experiences, insofar as the people in question considered dream experiences to be as valid as actual and real experiences. For instance, if someone dreamt that he was in heaven where he talked to an eagle, he was quite justified to tell this as a fact the next morning. This is how, according to Von den Steinen, the stories of these people originated.

21   Another significant scholar, Adolf Bastian, proposed the interesting theory that all basic mythological motifs are, as he called

---

[13] Antti Arne, *The Types of the Folktale: A Classification and Bibliography*, 2nd ed. (New York, 1971); and Stith Thompson, *Motif-Index of Folk Literature: A Classification of Narrative Elements in Folktales, Ballads, Myths, Fables, Mediaeval Romances, Exempla, Fabliaux, Jest-Books and Local Legends*, 6 vols. (Copenhagen, 1955–1958).

[14] Ludwig Laistner, *The Sphinx's Riddle: Elements of a History of Mythology*, 2 vols. (1889).

[15] Karl von den Steinen, *Unter den Naturvölkern Zentral-Brasiliens: Reiseschilderung und Ergebnisse der zweiten Schingu-Expedition 1887–1888* (Berlin: Severus Verlag, 2013).

them, "elementary thoughts" of mankind.[16] His hypothesis was that mankind has a store of "elementary thoughts" which do not migrate but rather are inborn in every individual, and that these thoughts appear in different variations in India, Babylonia, and even, for instance, in South Sea stories. He called such locally specific stories *Voelkergedanken* (national thoughts). His idea clearly approaches Jung's idea of the archetype and the archetypal image, with the archetype being the structural basic disposition to produce a certain mythologem, while the specific form in which it takes shape being the archetypal image. The "elementary thoughts," according to Bastian, are a hypothetical factor, meaning they are not visible, but the many national thoughts point to the existence of one basic thought underneath. My only disagreement with this is his description of the motifs as "thoughts." Bastian was a very philo-sophically minded man, obviously a thinking type,[17] and he tried to interpret some elementary thoughts by associating them with ideas of Kant and Leibniz. For us, the archetype is not simply an "elemental thought," but also an elementary poetical image and fantasy, an elementary emotion and even an elementary impulse towards some form of action. So we add to it a whole substructure of feeling, emotion, fantasy, and action that Bastian did not include in his theory. The hypothesis of Ludwig Laistner and later of Georg Jacob,[18] who wrote a book on the fairytale and the dream in much the same way as Laistner, had no influence. Their approach was unsuccessful, and the suggestions made by Karl von Steinen were also not accepted. Adolf Bastian was also ignored by the general scientific world for it adhered more to the English and Finnish books on folklore.

22   Besides the collections of fairytales and their variations, there were also the efforts of the so-called literary school. In a purely formal way, it was interested in the differences between the various types of tales: between myths, legends, amusing stories, animal

---

[16] Adolf Bastian, *Beiträge zur vergleichenden Psychologie: Die Seele und ihre Erscheinungsweisen in der Ethnographie* (Berlin: Nabu Press, 2010).
[17] C. G. Jung, *Psychological Types*, vol. 6, *CW* (Princeton, NJ: Princeton, 1971).
[18] Georg Jacob, *Märchen und Traum* (Hannover: H. Lafaire, 1923).

stories, trickster stories, and what one might call the classical fairytales.[19] Their comparative studies — for example between the heroes of legends with the heroes of classical fairytales — brought some interesting results to light, and I highly recommend these works. A further modern movement was made up of a group of ethnologists, archaeologists, and specialists in mythology and the comparative history of religion. They have some knowledge of Jung and his psychology but only make indirect use of his discoveries by trying to interpret mythological motives whilst omitting Jung's hypotheses. They write books with titles such as *The Great Goddess* or *The Threefold Godhead* or *The Hero*. Their starting point is not the human individual and his psychic structure that has produced these symbols; instead, they choose to sit in the middle of the archetype, as it were, and let it amplify itself, poetically and "scientifically." Raffaele Pettazoni and Julius Schwabe belong to this mythological school, and, at times, Mircea Eliade.[20] Mention should also be made of Otto Huth, who works on fairytales in this way, Robert Graves, and, in some ways, Erich Fromm and Gilbert Durand.

23   The unscientific and illegitimate approach of these authors induces them to fall into a trap they did not foresee. As soon as one approaches an archetype in this way, everything becomes everything. If you start your research, for example, with the world tree, you can easily prove that every mythological motif leads to the world tree in the end. If you start with the sun, you can easily prove that everything is finally a solar motif. One gets lost in the chaos of interconnections and overlapping meanings that all archetypal images have with one another. If you choose the Great Mother or the world tree or the sun or the underworld or the eye or something else, as a motif, you can pile up comparative material forever, but you have completely lost your Archimedean standpoint from which to interpret.

24   In his "Memories," Jung pointed out that it is a great temptation for the intellectual type to proceed in an abstract way because

---

[19] Max Lüthi, *The European Folktale: Form and Nature* (Bloomington: Indiana University Press, 1986).
[20] Julius Schwabe, *Archetyp und Tierkreis: Grundlinien einer kosmischen Symbolik und Mythologie* (Basel: Schwabe, 1951).

intellectuals overlook the emotional and feeling factor, which is always connected with an archetypal image.[21] An archetypal image is not only a thought pattern (as a thought pattern, it is connected with every other thought pattern); it is also an emotional experience — *the* emotional experience of an individual. Only if it has an emotional and feeling value for an individual is it alive and meaningful. As Jung said, you can collect all the Great Mothers in the world and all the saints and everything else, and what you have means absolutely nothing if you leave out the feeling experience of the individual.

25   The tendency of research into fairytales today is to illuminate the underlying structures, for example day and night cycles. To date, this undertaking by academics like Gilbert Durrand[22] or Vladimir Propp[23] has been in vain. As the choice of subject is, at bottom, random, one can, as, for example, Claude Lévi-Strauss did, set off with one theme and end up on the shore of all others.[24] This happens because the individual experience is not included in the system. Archetypes cannot be described if one leaves out their relationship to man. Similarly, one cannot exclude Depth Psychology if one is trying to investigate the living maternal earth out of which all archetypal images spring. Although myths are of a collective nature, they are through and through connected to man. Any abstraction that omits to consider the individual, his structures, and his psychic needs will lead to a chaotic collection of random meanings and to an impoverishment of the content. This danger is great for our academic training tends to discard this feeling factor. Think of how the natural sciences are taught at college: When a teacher shows a crystal, girls particularly tend to cry out, "Oh what a beautiful crystal," whereupon the teacher says, "We are not now admiring its beauty, but want to analyze the structure of this object."

---

[21] C. G. Jung, *Memories, Dreams, Reflections,* ed. Aniela Jaffé, trans. Richard and Clara Winston (New York: Vintage Books, 1989).

[22] Gilbert Durand, *The Anthropological Structures of the Imaginary* (Brisbane: Boombana Publishing, 1999).

[23] Vladimir Propp, *Morphology of the Folktale* (Austin: University of Texas Press, 1975).

[24] Claude Lévi-Strauss, *The Raw and the Cooked,* trans. John and Doreen Weightman (Chicago: University of Chicago Press, 1996).

From the outset, students are trained to repress their personal emotional reaction and to train their mind to be what we call "objective."

26   I agree with this up to a point, but we cannot proceed this way in psychology. Connected to this problem is the difficult position psychology has as a science, for, in contrast to all other sciences, psychology cannot afford to overlook feeling. It has to take into consideration the feeling tone and emotional value of outer and inner factors, including the observer's feeling reactions as well. As you know, modern physics accepts the fact that the observer and the theoretical hypothesis he has in his mind, on account of which he has set up his experiment, plays a role in the result of his investigation. What is not yet accepted is that the emotional factor *in* the observer may play a role. But physicists will have to rethink that for, as Wolfgang Pauli has pointed out, we have no *a priori* reason to reject it.[25] Most certainly we can say that in psychology we *have* to take feeling as an effective factor into consideration. The reason why so many academic scientists call Jungian psychology unscientific is because it takes feeling into consideration, a factor that has hitherto been habitually and intentionally excluded from the scientific outlook. It is not acknowledged that inclusion of this emotional factor is not done upon a whim or a childish acting out. We know from conscious scientific insight that these feelings are necessary and belong in the method of psychology, if you want to get at the phenomenon in the right way.

27   Psychological interpretation of fairytales has recently become very widespread.[26] Bruno Bettelheim's *The Uses of Enchantment: The Meaning and Importance of Fairy Tales,* written from the Freudian

---

[25] C.G. Jung und Wolfgang Pauli, *The Interpretation of Nature and the Psyche* (New York: Pantheon Books, 1955). This book includes the essay by Jung *"Synchronicity: An Acausal Connecting Principle."*

[26] Mention should be made of the important non-Jungian contributions on comparative mythology research by Franz Vonessen, „Sich selbst bestehlen – von der symbolischen Natur des Eigentums," in *Symbolon, Jahrbuch für Symbolforschung*, vol. 5, ed. Julius Schwabe (Basel: Schwabe, 1966); and Heino Gehrts, *Das Märchen und das Opfer: Untersuchungen zum europäischen Brüdermärchen* (Bonn, 1967). On both these authors, see also *Vom Menschenbild im Märchen* (Kassel: Roth-Verlag, 1980). Of the Depth Psychology literature, one must mention Herbert Silberer's work, *Problems of Mysticism and its Symbolism*, trans. Smith Ely Jelliffe, Moffat, Yard and Company (New York, 1917) that also contains dream and fairy tale interpretations from the standpoint of psychoanalysis.

viewpoint, was widely read in the USA and France.[27] Further works can be found in Wilhlem Laiblin's collected volume *Märchenforschung und Tiefenpsychologie.*[28] Jung's own theories are for the most part to be found in his early work, *Symbols of Transformation*[29] and in his later work, *Science of Mythology: Essays on the Myth of the Divine Child and the Mysteries of Eleusis.*[30] Jung wrote about fairytales primarily in *The Phenomenology of the Spirit in Fairytales.*[31] Interpretations of archetypal motifs can, however, be found throughout his entire collected works. In Germany, the three volumes of *Symbolik des Märchens* ,which was published under the name of Hedwig von Beit, but the whole psychological interpretations are my own work.[32] Mention should also be made of the works of Wilhelm Laiblin.[33] Further interpretations from the Jungian standpoint followed, amongst others, the works of Hans Dieckmann[34], Sibylle Birkhäuser-Oeri,[35] Emma Jung,[36] A. Jaffé,[37] as well as my own contributions.[38] [39]

---

[27] Bruno Bettelheim, *The Uses of Enchantment: The Meaning and Importance of Fairy Tales* (New York: Vintage Books, 1975–1976). Also from the Freudian standpoint, Ottokar Graf Wittgenstein, *Märchen, Träume, Schicksale* (Munich: Kindler, 1973).

[28] Wilhelm Laiblin, *Märchenforschung und Tiefenpsychologie*, 5th ed. (Darmstadt: Primus-Verlag, 1997).

[29] C.G. Jung, *Symbols of Transformation,* vol. 5, *CW* (Princeton, NJ: Princeton University Press, 1967).

[30] C.G. Jung and K. Kerényi, *Science of Mythology: Essays on the Myth of the Divine Child and the Mysteries of Eleusis* (London: Routledge and Kegan Paul, 1985).

[31] Jung, *Archetypes and the Collective Unconscious*, Ch. 8., vol. 9/1, *CW*.

[32] Hedwig von Beit, *Symbolik des Märchens: Versuch einer Deutung*, 7th ed. (Bern: Francke, 1986).

[33] Wilhelm Laiblin, „Der goldene Vogel: Zur Symbolik der Individuation im Volksmärchen," in *Jugend gestern und heute* (Stuttgart: Klett, 1961), 137–87; as well as *Wachstum und Wandlung: Zur Phänomenologie und Symbolik menschlicher Reifung* (Darmstadt: Wiss. Buchgesellschaft, 1974).

[34] Hans Dieckmann, *Märchen und Träume als Helfer des Menschen* (Stuttgart: Bonz, 1968); as well as *Märchen und Symbole: Tiefenpsychologische Deutung orientalischer Märchen*, Psychologisch gesehen, no. 31 (Stuttgart: Bonz, 1999); *Der Zauber aus 1001 Nacht* (Krummwisch: Königsfurt, 2000); *Gelebte Märchen: Lieblingsmärchen der Kindheit* (Stuttgart: Kreuz, 1993); *Methods in Analytical Psychology: An Introduction* (Asheville: Chiron Publications, 1991).

[35] Sibylle Birkhäuser-Oeri, *The Mother: Archetypal Image in Fairy Tales* (Toronto: Inner City Books, 1988).

[36] Emma Jung, „Die Anima als Naturwesen," *Festschrift zum 80. Geburtstag von C. G. Jung* (Zurich, 1955); and *Animus und Anima: Two Essays* (New York: Spring Publications, 2004).

[37] Aniela Jaffé, *Bilder und Symbole aus E. T. A. Hoffmanns Märchen "Der goldene Topf"* (Einsiedeln: Daimon, 2003).

[38] Marie-Louise von Franz, "In the Black Woman's Castle" in *Archetypal Dimensions of the Psyche* (Boston: Shambhala, 1999); *Feminine in Fairy Tales* (Asheville: Chiron Publications, 2022); *The Psychological Meaning of Redemption Motifs in Fairytales*, (Toronto: Inner City Books, 1980); *Individuation in Fairy Tales* (Boston: Shambhala, 1990); *Shadow and Evil in Fairy Tales* (Asheville: Chiron Publications, 2022); *Golden Ass*.

[39] In general, I do not recommend dictionaries of symbols for they are most often superficial and misguiding. The one exception in my view is the Jean Chevalier and Alain Gheerbrant, *Dictionnaire des Symboles*, 20th ed. (Paris: Robert Laffont, 1982) that I can recommend for it contains excellent contributions on the otherwise little known mythology of Africa. Concerning individual books that are important for researching symbolism, I would primarily recommend the comprehensive work of

28   Freudian interpretation tries to fit every fairytale into the predefined Freudian schema. Jungian interpretation, on the other hand, tries to let the fairytale speak for itself. Through the method of amplification,[40] we aim at letting the fairytale explain itself, as it were. We do not approach it with a given, set theory. Rather, a mystery is in the foreground that some person once experienced and then later tried, as best he could, to communicate. By considering the content of each image as well as the connection that exists between the images, we try to uncover the specific meaning and the inner logic of a fairytale.

29   If an individual has an archetypal experience — for instance, an overwhelming dream of an eagle coming through a window — this is not only a thought pattern about which you can say, "Oh yes, the eagle is a messenger from God, and it was one of Zeus's messengers, and one of Jupiter's, and in North American mythology the eagle appears as the creator," and so on. This is quite correct intellectually for you are amplifying the archetype, but you are overlooking the emotional experience. Why is it an eagle and not a raven or a fox and or an angel? In mythological terms, an angel and an eagle are the same thing: an *angelos*, a winged messenger from heaven, from the Beyond, from the Godhead, but for the dreamer, it makes a lot of difference if he dreams about an angel with all that that means to

---

Manfred Lurker, *Bibliographie zur Symbolkunde*, Bibliotheca Bibliographica Aureliana XII (Baden-Baden: Heintz, 1964). In addition, I would recommend Richard Broxton Onians, *The Origin of European Thought: About the Body, the Mind, the Soul, the World, Time and Fate* (Cambridge: Cambridge University Press, 1951), which contains very interesting material about body parts and functions. On individual topics it is worth reading Arnold van Gennep, *Les Rites de passage* (Paris, 1909), as well as Otto Huth, *Das Sonnen-, Mond- und Sternenkleid (manuscript*, 1942); and *"Der Glasberg,"* in *Symbolon II* (1961), 15 ff. On the mythology of antiquity, I would recommend the works of Karl Kerényi, *The Gods of the Greeks* (London: Thames and Hudson, 2010); *The heroes of the Greek* (London: Thames and Hudson, 1974); as well as Mircea Eliade's work *Myths, Dreams, and Mysteries: The Encounter Between Contemporary Faiths and Archaic Realities* (London: Harper and Row, 1968); *Shamanism: Archaic Techniques of Ecstasy* (Princeton, NJ: Princeton University Press, 2020); *The Forge and the Crucible: The Origins and Structres of Alchemy* (Chicago: University of Chicago Press, 1978); and *The Myth of the Eternal Return: Cosmos and History* (Princeton, NJ: Princeton University Press, 2018). Equally important is Joseph Campbell, *The hero with a Thousand Faces* (New York: Joseph Campbell Foundation, 2008). Information on current new literature can be found in the *Journal of Folklore Fellows Communication* (Helskini/London) and *Fabula*, Zeitschrift für Erzählforschung (Berlin).
[40] Sources that are useful for amplification: *Handwörterbuch des deutschen Aberglaubens*, 10 vols., ed. H. Bächtold-Stäubli, reprint of the edition from 1927–1942 (Berlin: Verlag de Gruyter, 2000); as well as the ground-breaking work of Johannes Bolte and Georg Polivka, *Anmerkungen zu den Kinder- und Hausmärchen*; as well as Lutz Mackensen, ed., *Handwörterbuch des deutschen Märchens* (Berlin, 1930–1940). Parallel to this I can recommend the *Enzyklopädie des Märchens. Handwörterbuch zur historischen und vergleichenden Erzählforschung* (Berlin: Walter de Gruyter, 1975 ff.).

him, or if he dreams of an eagle with all one's positive and negative reactions that an eagle evokes. You cannot just skip the dreamer's emotional reactions, though scientists like Mircea Eliade and Otto Huth and Erich Fromm and others will simply say that both are messengers from the Beyond. Intellectually, it is the same thing, but emotionally there is a difference. Thus, we cannot ignore the individual and the whole setup into which such an experience falls.

30   The representatives of this outlook try to pull all the results of Jungian psychology backwards into the old setup of academic thinking and to push aside the most important factor which Jung introduced to the science of myths: *the human basis* from which such motifs grow. We cannot study plants without studying the soil on which they grow: Melons, for example, grow best on dunghills and not on sand, and if one is a good gardener, one has knowledge of the soil as well as of the plants. In mythology, *we*, the individual human beings, are, as it were, the soil of the symbolic motifs. This fact cannot be ignored, but for thinking types and intellectuals it is a great temptation to exclude this subjective background for doing so fits into their habitual attitude.

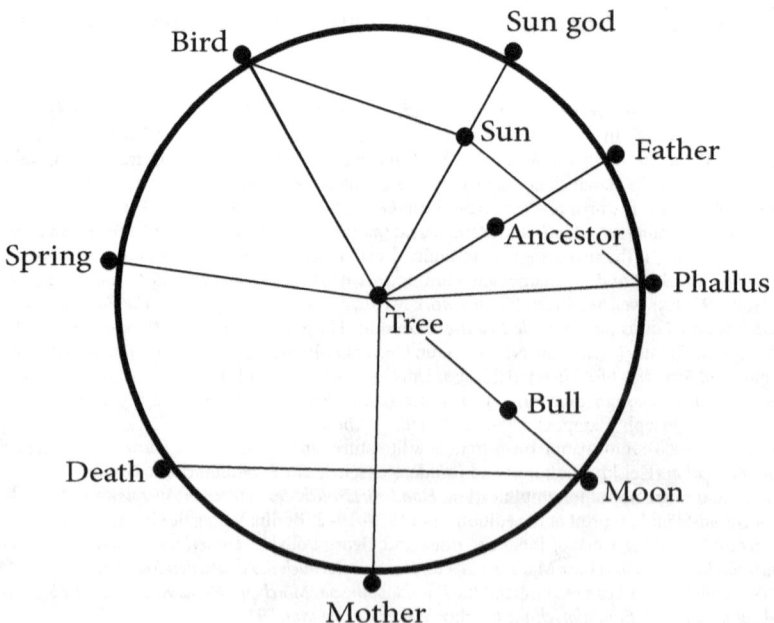

31   Let us assume that I am an investigator who has a tree complex, so I will start my research with the tree as my point of departure. Being emotionally fascinated by it, I might say, "Oh, the sun myth and the tree myth are connected for in the morning the sun is born in the east out of the tree." There is, for example, the Christmas tree, and every Christmas tree gives birth to the new light at the moment of the winter solstice. So all sun myths are in a way also tree myths. But the tree is also a mother. You know that in Saxony, even now, it is said that beautiful girls grow under the leaves of trees, and I could show you pictures that show how children come from trees; the souls of unborn children rustle under the leaves, and that is why there are trees in the center of all German, Austrian and Swiss villages. The tree is therefore the Great Mother. But the tree is not only the mother of life but also the death mother because coffins are made from trees, and there are tree burials. The shamans of circumpolar tribes and people in certain North Canadian tribes are buried in a tree. Babylonian Zikkurats and those columns on which the Persians put their dead are probably also a modification of the tree. And have you ever thought of the tree and the well? There is, for example, the world-ash Yggdrasil with the Urd well underneath. I can show you Babylonian seals on which there is a tree underneath the well of life. So all the motifs of the water of life are really associated with the tree. That is quite clear! Everyone sees that. But you can also bring in the moon. As the mother, the tree is feminine, but it is also the father because the tree is a phallic symbol; for instance, in the Aztec chronicles the word for the original land from where the Aztecs and Mayans emigrated represents a broken-off tree, a kind of tree trunk, and the trunk form is a phallic father-image. There are stories of a woman passing a tree and of a seed from the tree entering her womb. Therefore clearly, the tree is a father, and that links up with the tree being the sun, which is also a father figure. If you have a sun complex, then everything is solar, and if you have a moon complex, everything is lunar.

32   *In the unconscious all archetypes are contaminated with one another.* It is as if several photographs were printed one over the

other; they cannot be disentangled and sorted. This has probably to do with the relative timelessness and spacelessness in the unconscious. An archetype is like a package of representations that are all present simultaneously. If a conscious mind looks at the unconscious, it selects one motif because it puts its searchlight onto it. It just depends where one directs one's searchlight first, for in some way one always has the whole of the collective unconscious in view. Thus, for one scientist the mother is everything, for another everything is vegetation, and for yet another everything is a solar myth.

33   The amusing thing is that when such intellectuals see the connection — for instance between the tree and the sun or the coffin — they write, "of course" or "obviously" or "naturally." Thus, the tree is *obviously* the mother. I usually watch to see where the investigator uses these words. Because archetypal connections are obvious and natural, the writer says "naturally" or "obviously" and is sure that all his readers will agree with him. This is particularly true of people who are thinking types. Others revolt after a while for they realize that one thing could just as easily be another thing, and they return to the emotional differences in value between symbols.

34   One can interpret a myth or fairytale with any of the four functions of consciousness.[41] The thinking type will point out the structure and the way in which all the motifs are connected. The feeling type will order them according to their value (a hierarchy of values), which is also completely rational. A good and complete fairytale interpretation can be made with the feeling function. The sensation type will look at the symbols very exactly and amplify them. The intuitive will see the whole package in its oneness, so to speak; he will be most gifted in showing that the whole fairytale is not a discursive story but is really *one* message, split into its many facets. The more you have differentiated your functions, the better you can interpret because you are in a position to circumambulate a story as much as possible with all four functions. The more you have used and developed your conscious functions, the better and more colorful

---

[41] Cf. Jung, *Psychological Types*, vol.6, *CW*, §§ 621–740.

your interpretation will be. It is an art that requires practice. Apart from some general indications that I will try to give you, it cannot be learned. I always tell students not to memorize my lecture, but to try to interpret fairytales themselves, for that is the only way to learn. Interpretation is an art — a craft, actually — which finally depends on you yourself. Seminars at which everyone interprets the same fairytale are almost like a confession and a Rorschach test. This cannot be avoided. And it is right, for you have to put your whole being into it.

35 We must ask why in Jungian psychology we are interested in myths and fairytales. Jung once said that it is in fairytales that one can best study the comparative anatomy of the psyche. In myths or legends, or any other more elaborate mythological material, we get at the basic patterns of the human psyche through a lot of cultural material. But in fairytales there is much less specific conscious cultural material, which is why they mirror the basic patterns of the psyche more clearly. One of the things that other psychological schools throw at our heads is that we analysts see archetypes everywhere and that our patients apparently dream about archetypes every night, but their patients never produce such material. If the analyst does not know what archetypal motifs are, naturally he does not notice them; he interprets them personally by linking them up with personal memories of the patient. In order to be able to spot archetypal material, we have first to have a general knowledge of it — this is why we try to learn as much as possible about these motifs and their different setups.

36 But there is another reason that has proved even more important and leads to more essential problems. If someone has a dream and you already have the anamnesis — that is, his general outer and inner life story — even if you try to refrain from doing so, you have usually made a kind of general hypothesis about what the dreamer's problem is; that this is a mother-bound man or a father-bound daughter, an animus-ridden woman, or God knows what else. Suppose, for instance, you have the hypothesis that a certain analysand is greatly bothered by her animus. If she brings you the dream of a burglar,

which frightened her terribly, you have an "Aha! There we have it!" reaction. You do not notice that you have not interpreted the dream but have only recognized in it what you knew beforehand. You call the burglar an animus figure, and it looks like an objective interpretation. But you have not really learned to interpret the dream scientifically — in which case you would have had *no* hypothesis as to what might emerge from its motifs. What I want to say is that we should look at dreams as objectively as possible and only deduce a conclusion at the end. For a dream always brings a *new* message with it, one that neither the analyst nor the analysand knew beforehand. This objective method can best be learned by practicing with fairytale motifs for in fairytales you have no knowledge of the conscious situation to help you work on it.

37 But now let us consider the following: How does a fairytale originate? If we are realistic, we have to say that it originates at one particular moment: At a certain time a certain fairytale must have come into being. How could that happen? I have developed my own theory that I would like to share with you. Max Lüthi[42] shows that in legends and in local sagas, the hero of the story is a very human creature. A local saga is the sort of story which runs like this: "Do you see the beautiful castle up there? Well, you know, a story is told about it. There was once a shepherd who, on a hot midsummer day, tended his sheep around this castle when he was suddenly seized by curiosity. He thought he might go inside even though he had heard that there were ghosts there. So he opened the door with trembling hands and saw a white snake that spoke to him in human speech and said that the shepherd should come with it, and if he could endure three nights, he could redeem it…." — or something like that. Lüthi showed, with a great many examples, that in those local sagas the hero is a "real" human being whose feelings and reactions are told. For instance, it is said that the shepherd's heart beat violently when he opened the castle door and that he shivered when he was given the cold kiss of the snake, but that he was courageous and bore it all.

---

[42] Max Lüthi, „*Die Gabe im Märchen und in der Sage: Ein Beitrag zur Wesenserfassung und Wesensscheidung der beiden Formen,*" Dissertation (Bern, 1943).

The story is told as though an ordinary human being were having a supernatural or parapsychological experience. But if you take a classical fairytale, such as the Grimms' "Golden Bird," the hero there has no such feelings. If a lion comes towards him, he takes his sword and kills it. Nothing is said about his being frightened and shivering and then putting his sword down the lion's throat and scratching his head and asking himself what he had done. Because he is a hero, he just naturally kills the lion. So Lüthi says that the hero in a fairytale is an *abstract figure* and not at all "human." He is either completely black or completely white, with stereotypical reactions: He redeems the lady and kills the lion and is not afraid of the old woman in the woods, and so on — his deeds are completely schematic.

38   After reading Lüthi, I came across a story from a 19th century family chronicle that was published in a Swiss journal on folklore (1937). The family still lives in Chur. The great-grandfather had had a mill in some lonely village in the Alps, and one evening he had gone out to shoot a fox. When he took aim, the animal lifted its paw and said, "Don't shoot me!" and then disappeared. The miller went home rather shaken because speaking foxes were not part of his everyday experience. There he found the mill water racing autonomously around the wheel. He shouted, asking who had started the mill wheel turning. No one had done it. Two days later he died. In spiritualistic or parapsychological circles, this is a typical story. All over the world such things sometimes happen before someone dies: Instruments behave as if alive, clocks stop as if they were part of the dying owner, and various queer things occur.

39   Now the man who had read this story in the chronicles of this family went to the village and asked the people there about the mill. The mill itself was in ruins. A few people said, "Yes, there was a mill up there and there was something uncanny about it. It was haunted." One sees how the story had degenerated. They all knew that it had something to do with death and a parapsychological event, but they did not remember anything in particular. It would seem that the Finnish school are right in saying that things get poorer in the retelling, but then this same investigator found other old people who

said, "Oh yes, we remember the story. The miller went out to shoot the fox, and the fox said, 'Miller, don't shoot me. You remember how I ground the corn at Aunt Jette's.' And then at the funeral party a wineglass was broken, and Aunt Jette, the miller's aunt, went quite white. Everybody knew that she was the fox, and that it was she who had killed the miller."

40   There is a general belief that witches can take on the form of a fox. Witches are said to go out at night as fox souls, do much mischief in this form, and then return to their bodies that have lain as if dead on their beds meanwhile. This can be "proven" because sometimes a hunter comes across a fox, shoots him and wounds him in the paw. In the morning Mrs. So-and-So is seen sneaking about with her arm in a sling, and when she is asked what has happened, she will not say. Naturally, she was the ghost-fox going around making mischief. There is a general archetypal belief that you come across in the Alps and in Austria, as well as in Japan and China. It is that witches and hysterical women have fox souls. So a general archetypal motif has been associated with our special fox story. The fox is an enrichment of the story and makes it more coherent. It is as if the people found the story unsatisfactory — why did the fox talk to the miller just before he died? So it was enriched with a witch story and projected onto the miller's aunt, who promptly gave herself away at the wake. Another old woman in the village told the same story but added still another motif — that when the miller came home and saw the mill wheel turning, there was a fox running around on it.

41   This proved to me that Antti Aarne was wrong in thinking that stories always degenerate, for they can just as well improve, expand, and be enriched by the addition of archetypal motifs. My hypothesis is that probably the more original forms of folktales are local sagas and parapsychological stories, miraculous stories that have arisen from invasions of the collective unconscious in the form of waking hallucinations. Such things still happen; Swiss peasants experience them constantly, and they are the basis of folklore beliefs. When something strange happens, it gets gossiped about and handed on, just as rumors are handed on. Under favorable conditions, the

account gets enriched with already existing archetypal representations and slowly becomes a story.

42 It is interesting that in the fox story only one person remembered the miller's personal name. In the other versions, it was already "a miller." So as long as it is Miller So-and-So, it is still a local saga, but when it becomes "A miller once went to shoot a fox…," it begins to be a fairytale, a general story in a form in which it could migrate to another village for it is no longer bound to a particular mill and a particular man. So Lüthi's statement is probably correct: Fairytales are an abstraction. They are an abstraction of a local saga that has been condensed and given a crystallized form. Thus they can be handed down and are better remembered because they appeal to the people. Since I came across this idea that parapsychological experiences are at the bottom of local sagas, this same phenomenon has also been discovered and presented by J. Wyrsch,[43] as well as by H. Burkhard.[44] More on this can be found in the excellent work of Gotthilf Isler.[45]

---

[43] Jakob Wyrsch, „Sagen und ihre seelischen Hintergründe," *Innerschweizerisches Jahrbuch für Heimatkunde*, vol. 7 (Lucerne, 1943).

[44] Heinrich Burkhardt, „Psychologie der Erlebnissage," Dissertation (Zurich, 1951).

[45] Gotthilf Isler, *Die Sennenpuppe* (Basel: Schweizerische Gesellschaft für Volkskunde, 1992).

◊

Chapter 2
Fairytales, Myths and
other Archetypal Stories

43   I think it is likely that the most frequent way in which archetypal
stories originate is through individual experiences, either in a dream
or in a waking hallucination, by means of which some archetypal
content invades one's life. This is always a numinous experience.[1] In
primitive societies practically no secret is ever really kept — it is
always talked about; and it also becomes amplified by any other
existing folklore. Thus the story develops in the same way a rumor
spreads.

44   Such invasions of the collective unconscious into the field of
experience of an individual probably create, from time to time, new
nuclei of stories and keep alive the material that already exists. A
story like the one of the miller and the fox will locally reinforce the
belief in fox-witches. The belief existed before, but this story will
keep alive, modernize, or bring about a new version of the old idea
that witches, in the form of foxes, go about killing or bewitching
people. Psychological events that always reach an individual first are,
to my mind, the source and factor that keep the motifs in folklore
alive.

45   In this connection, it has been suggested that people know
certain fairytale motifs and stories that they then pin onto a local
situation. Let us say that there is a girl in a village who commits
suicide by jumping off the cliffs. Ten years later this suicide, which
took place because of an unhappy love affair, might be surrounded

---

[1] Numinous: a concept borrowed from Latin that expresses something divine, holy or supernatural.
Numen (Lat.): "Hint"; an indication of the divine will of a god, or divine being, through the nodding of
the head.

by a classical fairytale suicide motif. I think that this could easily happen, but I have not yet found any striking example where one could prove it. Probably we have to reckon with both possibilities. A story that is rooted to a specific place can mutate to a local saga. When a story wanders about, like a water plant cut off from its roots, it becomes more of an abstract fairy tale. If it were to later once more take root, it would again become more of a local saga. If one were to compare legends to a body, then fairytales would be the naked skeleton, the most basic and fundamental structure of the psyche — its eternal nucleus.

46   A similar controversial problem concerns the relationship of myth and fairytale. The classical scholar Eduard Schwyzer has shown that the Hercules myth is built up out of single scenes, all of which are fairytale motifs. He showed that this myth must have been a fairytale that was enriched and lifted to the literary level of a myth. Other researchers fight for the opposite theory contending that fairytales are degenerated myths. They believe that originally populations had only myths and that when the social and religious order of a population decayed, the remains of that myth survived in the form of fairytales. There is a certain amount of truth to this theory of the "decayed myth." Thus, in the volume of Greek fairytales, for instance, in *Die Märchen der Weltliteratur (The Fairy Tales of World Literature)* — a collection that has in the meantime grown to include 70 volumes[2] — one finds slightly distorted episodes of the *Odyssey*: A prince sails to an island where there is a big fish (or ogre), and he blinds that one-eyed man-eater. The prince hides under the belly of a big ram in order to be able to creep out of the monster's cave. This was how Ulysses escaped from the cave of the Cyclops. In this way, Homer's tales have been preserved in their folkloric form till today. I do not, therefore, think it far-fetched to say that this tale is a remnant of the Odyssey story. It has survived and has become an ordinary Greek folktale. The story has convinced me that basic motifs can survive as fairytale motifs and migrate or stay in the same country when the great myths die along with the

[2] Friedrich von der Leyen, ed., *Die Märchen der Weltliteratur* (Jena: Diederichs, 1912–2003).

culture to which they belonged. To me, the fairytale is like the sea: Sagas and myths are the waves upon it; a tale rises to be a myth and sinks down again to become a fairytale. Here again, we come to the same conclusion: Fairytales mirror the more simple but also more basic structure — something like the bare skeleton — of the psyche.

47   A myth, on the other hand, belongs more to a specific culture. If you think of the Gilgamesh myth, you think of the Sumerian-Hittite-Babylonian civilization, for Gilgamesh belongs there and cannot be put into Greece or Rome, just as the Hercules and Ulysses myths belong to Greece and cannot be imagined in a Maori setup. If one studies the psychological implications of myths, one sees that they very much express the national character of the civilization in which they originated and have been kept alive. They have a beautiful form because generally either priests or poets, and sometimes priest-poets, have endeavored to give them a ceremonious, poetic form. A myth represents a conscious addition to a culture, which makes its interpretation easier in some ways for certain things are said more explicitly. Gilgamesh, for instance, was said to have been favored by the sun god, Shamash; material can thus be collected about the sun god and included in the amplification, providing all that is necessary. Sometimes a fairytale hero also has solar qualities, but these may be indicated by only a small detail — for instance, that he has golden hair; no mention is made of his being favored by a specific sun god. So it can be said that the basic structure or archetypal elements of a myth are built into its formal expression, which links it up with the cultural collective consciousness of the nation in which it originated, and that therefore, in a way, it is closer to consciousness and to known historical material.

48   In some ways, it is easier to interpret a myth for it is less fragmentary. Because its form is often more beautiful and more impressive than that of a fairytale, one is more easily seduced into saying that myths are the bigger deal and all else in folklore are just miserable remnants. On the other hand, by lifting such an archetypal motif to a cultural and national level and by linking it with religious traditions and poetic forms, it more specifically expresses the

problems of that nation in that cultural period but loses some of its generally human character. Odysseus is the essence of the Hermetic-Mercurial Greek intellect and can easily be compared to trickster heroes of other nations. But the Odyssey myth as a whole is more specific and thoroughly Greek.

49   For us, the study of fairytales is very important because they depict the general human structure of the soul. They are especially important if one analyzes people "from the other end of the world"; if a Hindu or an Australian walks into the consulting room and one has only studied one's own myths, one will not be able to build a human bridge. If, however, the analyst has knowledge of basic human structures, he will find a way to relate.

50   I have read of a missionary in the South Sea Islands who says that the simplest way to find a connection with these people is by telling them fairytales. It is a language in which both parties can understand each other for basic material is being used in its simplest form. If one were to tell some big myth, it would not work so well. Because the fairytale is beyond cultural and racial differences, it can migrate so easily. Fairytale language seems to be an international language — it unites all ages and cultures.

51   Sometimes, when I do not understand a fairytale, I use myths as parallels because the greater closeness to consciousness of the mythic material often gives me an idea about the meaning. If one is amplifying a fairytale, one should not neglect corresponding myths. They can be used to make a bridge when you do not see what the fairytale material means — fairytales can be so terribly remote from one's conscious world. There needs to be a subdivision of religious myths for some are told in connection with a ritual while others are not. A myth is told on a certain day at a certain festival, and the song that belongs to a certain mythological event is sung. Or, in some traditions or schools — the Talmud school, for instance — there are holy texts that are read on certain occasions and are thereby built into a liturgy of some kind. But this is also true of religious myths that are not built into a liturgy — for example, the Gilgamesh epic. It was generally recounted at the king's court, but we do not know if

it was ever built into a liturgy. These religious myths that are not built into a liturgy and are not told at a certain ritual, and do not comprise sacred knowledge that is recounted either orally or in writing on certain occasions, can be classified as myths like the ones I mentioned earlier.

52   Liturgies or songs that are sung by certain priests and are built into religious rituals are a special type of myth. In my opinion, such liturgical myths are only different from other myths if they have been integrated into the body of conscious knowledge of a nation. This does not make them in any way secondary; it is only that they have been elaborated upon for a long time. Generally, such myths have been influenced by specific historical traditions; these sacred texts and songs are very often almost unintelligible for they merely allude to something known. Our Christmas carols are like this. If you were to dig them up two thousand years from now and knew nothing about Christianity, you would not be able to make head nor tail of them. In a German Christmas carol "Es ist ein Ros' entsprungen aus einer Wurzel zart" ("From a tender root a rose has blossomed forth"), there follow a few more remote allusions to an untouched virgin. Assuming that you knew nothing about Christianity and discovered this carol, you would say that here is something about a rose and a virgin, but its meaning would remain dark. The song is intelligible to us because it alludes to a mystery we all know. Christian teaching is so integrated into our culture that the many songs that refer to it require only mere allusions. Only archetypal motifs that have been meaningful to many people for many hundreds of years are treated in this fashion. If Christianity had been confined to a local sect in Asia Minor, it would have died with its myth and would not have attracted other symbolic material and would not have been elaborated upon. Extensive elaboration of the original material probably depends upon the impact that the archetypal key event has upon people.

53   It has been suggested that perhaps Christianity had its origins in a local saga that then developed into a more general myth. In his

book *Aion*,[3] Jung elaborates that the unknown and mysterious and impressive personality of Jesus of Nazareth, about whom we know very little, attracted an enormous number of projections — for instance, that of the fish, the lamb, and many other archetypal symbols of the Self that were well known in antiquity. Many of these are not mentioned in the Bible — for example, the peacock. It is an early Christian symbol of the resurrection and of Christ. A whole web of existing mythological ideas of late antiquity slowly crystallized around the personality of Christ. The specific features of Jesus of Nazareth are blurred to such an extent that we are mostly confronted by the symbol of the God-Man, which is amplified by many other archetypal symbols.

54   In this way the figure of Jesus is generalized, but in another way it is made specific, as can be seen in the fight of the early Church Fathers against the tendency of that time to say that Jesus Christ was just another Dionysus or another Osiris. The Christian Apologists were furious, saying that Jesus Christ was not to be compared with the ancient gods for the Christian message Jesus brought was a new message that had to be seen in a new light. It should not be regressively put down to those old myths. But the people who said of Jesus, "He is Osiris! He is our Dionysus! We have known and loved this suffering and dismembered god for a long time!" were also right for they saw in him an archetypal pattern. But the others were also right when they insisted that the message of Christ was a new cultural consciousness appearing in a specific and new form. The same kind of thing happened when the Conquistadores discovered the ritual of crucifixion amongst the indigenous peoples of South America. One Jesuit Father said that the devil must have put it into those people's heads to weaken the possibility of their conversion.

55   The hypothesis of the archetypal structure of the human psyche prevents unnecessary disputes about religious myths from even getting started. The different versions are the variations in certain

---

[3] C.G. Jung, *Aion: Researches into the Phenomenology of the Self*, 2nd ed., vol. 9/II, *CW* (Princeton, NJ: Princeton University Press, 1978).

aspects of an archetype. When an important archetypal content is constellated, it tends to become the central symbol of a new religion. When, however, an archetypal content is not specifically constellated, but rather is merely a part of the general human condition, it is handed on in the form of folklore.

56   At the time of Christ, the idea of the God-Man — which had existed since time immemorial — had become *the* eminently important message — the one thing that had now to be realized at all costs. That is why it became the new message, the new light. Its emotional impact gave rise to all that we now call the Christian civilization, just as Buddha's enlightenment created all that we now call the Buddhist religion. In his book *Primitive Culture* and with his theory of animism, Edward Burnett Tylor tried to prove that fairytales are derived from ritual, claiming that not only should they be regarded as the remains of a decayed faith, but that they are specifically the remains of an old ritual: When a ritual dies, its story survives in fairytale form.[4]

57   I, on the other hand, am more inclined to believe that the basis is not a ritual, but an archetypal experience. Rituals are so age-old that one can only guess at how they may have come about. I found the best evidence of my inclination in mythical stories, like, for example, the story that Black Elk, a medicine man belonging to the American Indian tribe of the Oglala Sioux, tells in his auto-biography.[5] As a boy, when Black Elk was suffering from a severe illness and was almost in a coma, he had a tremendous revelation. In his vision he was transported to the skies where many horses came to him from the four points of the compass. He met the Grandfather Spirits who gave him a healing plant for his people. Deeply shaken by his vision, the youth kept it to himself, as any normal human being would do, but later on he developed an acute phobia about thunderstorms, so that when even a little cloud appeared on the horizon, he would shake with fear. This forced him

---

[4] Edward Burnett Tylor, *Primitive Culture: Researches into the Development of Mythology, Philosophy, Religion, Art and Custom* (London, 1891).

[5] John G. Neidhardt, *Black Elk Speaks: Being the Life Story of a Holy Man of the Oglala Sioux* (Lincoln: University of Nebraska Press, 1988).

to consult a medicine man who told him that he was ill because he had kept his vision to himself and had not shared it with his tribe. The medicine man said, "Nephew, I know now what the trouble is! You must do what the bay horse in your vision wanted you to do. You must perform this vision for your people upon earth. You must firstly show the horse-dance for the people to see. Then the fear will leave you; but if you do not do this, something very bad will happen to you." So Black Elk, who was then seventeen, and his father and mother and some other members of the tribe gathered together the exact number of horses — a certain number of white, a certain number of black, a certain number of sorrel, a certain number of buckskin, and one bay horse for Black Elk to ride. He taught the songs that he had heard and the movements he had seen during his experience. The enactment of his vision had a profound — even therapeutic — effect upon the entire tribe. The blind could see, the paralyzed walked, and other psychogenic diseases were cured. The tribe decided to perform it again, and I feel sure that it would have continued as a ritual if the tribe had not been almost destroyed by the whites soon afterwards. This account gives us evidence of the way in which a ritual comes about.

58   I have found another trace of the origin of a ritual in an Inuit tale reported by Knud Rasmussen.[6] Certain circumpolar Arctic tribes celebrate what is known as the Eagle Festival. They send out messengers, with feathers glued onto their sticks, to invite other tribes to a big feast. The hosts build a large igloo, sometimes even a big wooden assembly house. Once a year, people come in their dog sledges. In the hall there is a stuffed eagle, and they dance, tell stories, exchange wives and trade. The Eagle Festival is a big half-religious, half-profane meeting of all the tribes, and it came about because of a lonely hunter who once shot an especially beautiful eagle. He took it home with him with, apparently, a rather guilty feeling, stuffed it, and kept it. From time to time, he even felt compelled to give it a little food-sacrifice. One day when he was out on his skis hunting, he was caught in a blizzard. He sat down and suddenly saw two men

---

[6] Knud Rasmussen, *The Eagle's Gift: Alaska Eskimo Tales* (Whitefish: Literary Licensing, 2011).

in front of him with sticks onto which feathers were glued. The men wore animal masks and ordered him to come along with them and to hurry. So he pulled himself up onto his feet in the blizzard. The strangers went very fast, and he followed them, feeling exhausted until, through the mist, he saw a village from which came an uncanny booming noise. He asked what the drum was saying, and one of the men said very sadly, "That is the beating of a mother's heart." They led him to a very dignified woman in black, and he suddenly realized that she was the eagle-mother of the eagle he had shot. The dignified eagle-mother said that he had treated her son very well and had honored him and she wished for this to continue. She wanted that her people (all the people were really eagles who had temporarily assumed human form) would now show him the Eagle Festival. He must try to memorize everything and then return to his tribe and report it to them. This festival should take place in just this way every year. After the human eagles had performed the Eagle Festival, suddenly everything disappeared, and the hunter found himself back in the snowstorm, numb and half-frozen. He dragged himself back to his village, assembled the men, and delivered the message. From then on, the Eagle Festival has been performed in exactly this prescribed way. In a state of deep unconsciousness, the hunter, nearly frozen, had what we would call an archetypal vision. That is why everything disappeared suddenly and he found himself numb in the snow; that was the moment when he returned to consciousness and saw animal tracks in the snow beside him — the last "signs" of the "messengers."

59   This story illustrates how a ritual comes into existence. As it was in the case of Black Elk, the defining moment is the archetypal experience of an individual. If the impact is strong enough, there is a need to spread it abroad and not keep it to oneself. On a small scale, I have come across similar things in analysis, when an analysand had an archetypal experience and kept it to him or herself. Keeping it to oneself is the natural reaction to a personal experience that one does not want others to disparage. But then other dreams come that say that the individual should stand up for this inner

vision, tell it to one's wife or husband, saying, "I have had an experience and have to stick to it. This is why I now have to tell you about it, for otherwise you will not understand my behavior. I have to be loyal to my vision and act in accordance with it." In married life, one cannot suddenly begin to behave quite differently without giving any explanation. Or perhaps it must be communicated to a group, as happened to Black Elk.

60 Both stories offer a plausible explanation of how a ritual comes into existence. The basis is an invasion of the archetypal world into the collective time consciousness of a group through the intermediary of an individual. A single person experiences it first and then announces it to the others. Minor invasions of the unconscious or dreams can alter a ritual later. There is a famous thirty-year-old ritual called *Kunapipi* amongst Australian indigenous peoples. A meritorious ethnologist, Ronald M. Berndt, has collected the dreams referring to it.[7] In his book *Kunapipi,* Berndt gives a collection of their dreams, all of which had made some slight alteration or minor additions to the ritual. The dream is told to the tribe; if the alteration is good and fitting, it is added to the ritual. In analyzing Catholics, I have seen that this model still works in some way.[8] I remember a nun who dreamed about the Mass; the whole service was normal until the moment of the Sanctus; after the bell was rung, there was an interruption. In this most holy moment of the Mass, the moment of transubstantiation, the bishop went to the pulpit and gave a short, prosaic, and down-to-earth sermon on the meaning of God becoming man. After his words, Mass was resumed, as if that nun's unconscious desired to point out that some understanding of the mystery had been lost sight of.

61 There is still another type of archetypal story that is worth mentioning. If you read *Fairy Tales of World Literature,* you will see that in certain ethnological groups fairytales are told as animal tales, and even in the Grimm collection there are very many animal tales.

---

[7] Ronald M. Berndt, *Kunapipi: A Study of an Australian Aboriginal Religious Cult* (Melbourne: F. W. Cheshire, 1951).

[8] A person dreams about a ceremony. The unconscious then makes suggestions that tend to add new elements to the ceremony. [Addition by the translator of the French edition].

According to Laurens van der Post's *The Heart of the Hunter*,[9] about eighty percent of the Bushman tales are animal tales. The word "animal" in this connection is not very appropriate because although the characters appear as animals, they are at the same time anthropomorphic beings. Just as in the Eagle Festival story, in which there are eagles that are human beings and two minutes later are again eagles, there is the same idea in Bushman stories. Sometimes, it is said, "The hyena, which naturally was a human being, said to his wife...." Very often, however, this is not said explicitly, but in the story the hyena takes a bow, or makes a boat, and so on. These figures are human beings in the shape of animals, or animals in the form of human beings, but they are not what we nowadays would call animals.

62 Certain anthropologists quarrel about whether these figures are animals disguised as human beings or human beings disguised as animals. But that is idiotic, to my mind. They are just what they are! They are animals *and* human beings. No primitive would puzzle about it; there is no contradiction. From the standpoint of depth psychology, they are symbolic animals, for we make another distinction: The animal is the carrier of the projection of human psychic factors.[10] As long as there is still an archaic identity, and as long as one has not taken the projection back, the animal and what one projects onto it are identical; they are one and the same thing. You see it beautifully in those animal stories that represent archetypal human tendencies. They are human because they do not represent animal instincts but *our* animal instincts, and in that sense they are really anthropomorphic. For instance, if a tiger in a story represents greed, it is not the real greed of the tiger that is represented, but *our own* tiger-like greed. If we are as greedy as tigers, we dream about a tiger. So it is an anthropomorphic tiger. Animal stories are exceedingly frequent, and there are many investigators who assert that they are the most ancient type of

---

[9] Laurens van der Post, *The Heart of the Hunter* (London: Vintage Book, 2010).

[10] Projection: the unperceived and unintentional transmission of unconscious content upon an outer object or subject. One aim of becoming conscious is the gradual withdrawal of projections. [Addition by the translator of the French edition]. See Marie-Louise von Franz, *Reflections of the Soul: Projection and Re-collection in Jungian Psychology* (Chicago: Open Court, 1995); especially 1–9.

mythological story. I am very much tempted to believe that the most ancient and basic form of archetypal tales are stories about anthropoid animal beings, where fox speaks to mouse and hare talks to cat.

63   Because I am known as being interested in fairytales, families repeatedly pull me in to tell their children fairytales. Doing so, I have noticed that, below a certain age, children prefer animal stories. When you start stories about princes and princesses being stolen by the devil, they ask, "What is the devil?" and so on. They need too many explanations. But if you say, "The dog said to the cat...," then they listen most eagerly. So it seems that animal stories are something like the basic material, the deepest and most ancient form of tale.[11]

---

[11] "We have been looking at the relationship between fairytales, legends, animal stories, rituals, myths, and religious fairy tales, and want to leave it at that. I have discussed this question only to the extent that it was necessary, and I have quite deliberately not gone into any debates and hypotheses that are discussed in the literature on the topic." [Addition by the translator of the French edition].

◊

Chapter 3
A Method of Psychological Interpretation

64 The next problem is the method of interpretation of fairytales. Basically, we apply Jungian psychology. How do we approach the meaning of a fairytale? How do we stalk it? It is, indeed, like stalking a very evasive stag. And why do we interpret fairytales at all? Again and again, investigators and specialists on mythology attack Jungians on the grounds that a myth speaks for itself; that you have only to unravel what it says, and you do not need psychological interpretation for this is only reading something into it which is not in it — in other words, it is believed that the myth with all its details and amplifications is quite clear in itself.

65 This seems to me to be only half true. This approach is true in the same way that, as Jung says, a dream is its own best explanation, which means that any interpretation of a dream is never as good as the dream itself. Thus, a dream is the best possible expression of inner facts, and you could just as well say that a fairytale and a myth are the best possible expression of what they want to say. So, in that sense, those who basically reject interpretation and carefully study the myth itself are right. Any interpretation is a darkening of the original light that shines in the myth itself. But if someone excitedly tells you a marvelous dream and you sit back and say, "What a dream you had!" he or she will say, "But I want to know what it means!" You may then answer, "Well, look at the dream! It tells you all it can. It is its own best possible interpretation." That has its merits because then the dreamer goes home and keeps turning the dream around in his mind. It might happen that an interpretation pops into the dreamer's mind, like an illumination. This process of "rubbing one's

churinga stone"[1] — treating the dream as one might a churinga stone or some talisman by "rubbing" it until it gives you some strength — has the merit of not being interrupted by a third person who interposes himself.

66   On the other hand, this method is often not sufficient, for the most amazing and beautiful dream messages are often not understood. Then the dreamer is like somebody who has an enormous bank balance and does not know about it because he has lost the safe key or account number. And what is the use of that? It is certainly true that one should be tactful, hoping and waiting to see whether the dream will not build its own bridge towards the dreamer's consciousness. Perhaps this process can take place by itself, which would certainly be more genuine. People are much more impressed by what they find out about their dreams than if one presents them with an interpretation, even if it is a good one. But most often all those millions remain in the bank unused and people remain impoverished.

67   There is another reason why interpretation should be practiced: People tend to interpret their own dreams and myths within the framework of their own conscious assumptions. A thinking type, for instance, will naturally tend to extract only some kind of philosophical thought which he feels is contained in the dream, but he will overlook the emotional message and the feeling circumstances. I have also known people, men especially, who, when they are caught in their own anima mood, project their mood into the dream and perhaps see only its negative aspects. In this instance, a dream interpreter is useful, for he says, "Yes, look here! The dream begins very badly, but the lysis is very positive! It does, indeed, say that you are still a fool or half-blind, but it also says there is a treasure waiting for you." The interpretation is a bit more objective for the dream or tale is not only pulled into the already existing trend of consciousness. Hence, we practice interpretation in Jungian analysis.

68   As I have already suggested, interpretation is an art or craft that can be learned only through practice and experience. However, there

---

[1] Cf. C.G. Jung, vol. 13, *CW* (Princeton, NJ: Princeton University Press, 1983), § 128.

are some rules to guide one. Just as we do for a dream, we divide an archetypal story into its different aspects. We begin with the exposition (place and time). In fairytales, time and place are always evident because they begin with "once upon a time" or something similar, which means in timelessness and spacelessness — in the nowhere-ness realm of the collective unconscious. For example:

69   "Far beyond the end of the world and even beyond the Seven Dog Mountains there was once a king…."
        "At the end of the world, where the world comes to an end with a wall of boards…."
        "In the time when God still walked about on earth…"

70 There are many poetical ways of expressing this once-upon-a-time, which, in the tradition of Mircea Eliade, most mythologists now call the *illud tempus* — an absence of time, a timeless eternity, a "now and for evermore."

71   Then we turn to the *dramatis personae* (the people involved). I recommend counting the number of people at the beginning and at the end. If a fairytale begins, "The king had three sons," one notices that there are four characters, but the mother is lacking. The story may end with one of the sons, his bride, his brother's bride, and another bride — that is, four characters again, but in a different setup. Having seen that the mother is lacking at the beginning and that there are three women at the end, one would suspect that the whole story is about redeeming the feminine principle, as is the case in one of the stories I shall use later as an illustration.

72   Now we proceed to the *exposition*, to the *naming of the problem*. Perhaps, for example, it is in the form of the old king who is sick, or the king who discovers every night that golden apples are being stolen from his tree. Or it might be that his horse has no foal, or that his wife is ill and somebody says she needs the water of life. Some trouble always comes at the beginning of the story, because otherwise there would be no story. So you define the trouble psychologically as well as you can and try to understand what it is.

73　　Then comes the *peripeteia,* which can be short or long: This involves the ups and downs of the story that can go on for pages because there can be many *peripeteiai;* or perhaps there is only one. Generally, the climax, the decisive point, is reached here, where either the whole thing develops into a tragedy or it comes out right. It is the height of the tension, which is always a turning point. Then, with very few exceptions, there is a lysis, which sometimes depicts a catastrophe. One could also say a positive or negative lysis: an end result that is either that the prince gets his princess and they marry and live happily ever after, or they all fall into the sea and disappear and are never heard of again (the latter being either positive or negative, depending on how one looks at it). In very primitive stories, there is neither a lysis nor a catastrophe: The story just peters out. It suddenly gets stupid and fades away, as if the storyteller were suddenly to lose interest and fall asleep.

74　　A lysis can also have an ending with a double meaning, something you do not find in other kinds of legends or mythic material, namely, a happy ending followed by a negative remark by the storyteller. For instance, "And they married and there was a big feast, and they had beer and wine and a marvelous piece of meat, and I went to the kitchen but when I wanted to take some, the cook gave me a kick in the pants, and I rushed here to tell you the story." Or as Russian fairytales sometimes end, "They married and were very happy. They drank a lot of beer and wine, but mine ran through my beard and I never swallowed any." Or as some gypsies say, "They married and were happy and rich to the end of their lives, but we, poor devils, are standing here shivering and sucking our gums with hunger" — and then they go around with their hat, collecting.

75　　These formulas at the end of a fairytale are called a *rite de sortie,* because a fairytale takes you far away into the childhood dream world of the collective unconscious, where you may not stay. Imagine that you lived in a peasant house and you stayed in the fairytale mood, instead of going to the kitchen. If you do not kick yourself out of the story, you will certainly burn the roast because you will continue to think about the prince or the princess. So the story must be accentuated at the end with, "Yes, that is the fairy tale world, but we find ourselves in this bitter reality. We must return to our everyday work and may not be absent-minded and puzzle about the story." We have to be ousted out of the fairytale world.

76   So much for the general method by which we see the structure and bring some order into our material; above all, we should remember to count the characters and to notice the number symbolism and the part that it plays. There is another way that I sometimes adopt but which cannot be done with all stories. A Russian story, for instance, that tells of a tsar who has three sons, could be presented in the following way:

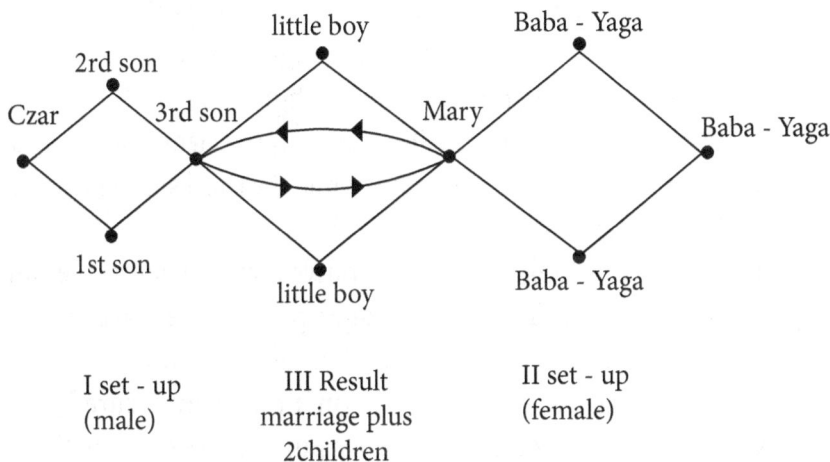

| I set - up (male) | III Result marriage plus 2children | II set - up (female) |

77   At first there is a male quaternity in which the mother is lacking, and the hero, the fourth of the system, goes into the beyond (into the unconscious, we would say), where there are three witches (Baba Yagas) and the Princess Mary, whom the hero wins. At the end, the hero redeems Mary, and they marry and two sons are born. So there is a quaternity that is purely male and one that is purely female, and in the end we have (in the middle) a mixed quaternity of three males and one female. You can also use this sort of diagram when a fairytale lends itself to it. There are a lot of stories structured in this way; if they are not, that is also revealing because a lack of pattern tells you something, too, as does an irregular pattern in science. The

exception is also a part of the phenomenon, but then you have to explain why it is present.

78   Let us continue with the rules of our method. We look at each symbol in the order in which they appear. Let us say, for example, there is an old king who is sick because he needs the water of life, or there is a mother who has a disobedient daughter. We have to amplify this, which means that we must look up all the parallel motifs we can get a hold of. I say *all* because initially you will probably not be able to find that many. You may stop when you reach two thousand! In the Russian tale "The Virgin Tsar," for instance, the story begins with an old tsar and his three sons. The youngest son is the hero of the story, "the innocent one." Elsewhere, I compared the tsar's behavior to that of the main function.[2][3] This hypothesis cannot be convincingly proven on the basis of a single tale because the tsar is not eliminated at the end, nor does he fight his son. But if you draw in all other parallel stories, it becomes quite clear that the tsar represents the outworn main function, while the third son represents the inferior function that brings renewal.

79   Thus, we have to look at the comparative material before we can say anything definite. To get the bigger picture, we have to ask whether a particular motif occurs in other tales and how it appears there. Only then is our interpretation on a relatively secure basis. For example, if in a fairytale a white dove puts a curse on something or someone, you might conclude that it represents a witch or a wizard. This might be true in that story, but if you look up what a white dove usually means, you will be astonished. As a rule, in the Christian tradition the white dove signifies the Holy Ghost, and in fairytales it generally means a loving, Venus-like woman. Therefore, you have to ask why something that is usually a symbol for positive Eros appears to be negative in this particular story. This gives you a different slant on the image than the one you might have if you had not taken the trouble to look up other stories. Suppose you were a

---

[2] Hedwig von Beit, *Symbolik des Märchens: Versuch einer Deutung*, vol. 1 (Bern: Francke, 1992), 417.
[3] Generally speaking, one is oriented towards one's main function. For this reason, it is more conscious and more differentiated than the other functions. Cf. Jung, *Psychological Types*, vol. 6, *CW*, esp. §§ 666 ff.

doctor performing your first autopsy and found the appendix on the left side and did not know, through comparative anatomy, that normally the appendix belongs on the right. It is the same with fairytales: You have to know the average setup — and that is why you need comparative material — to know the "comparative anatomy" of all the symbols in a fairytale. This background will help you to understand the specific much better, and only then can you fully appreciate the exception. *Amplification* means *enlarging through collecting a quantity of parallels*. Once you have a collection of parallels, you can then move on to the next motif, and in this way you move through the whole story.

80 There are two more steps to be taken for next we have to construct the context. Let us say that in the fairytale there is a mouse, and you have amplified it but see that this mouse behaves in an unusual way. Having read, for instance, that mice represent the souls of the dead, or witches, and that they are animals of the devil and an animal of Apollo in his winter aspect. They are the bringers of the plague, and they are also soul-animals because when somebody dies, a mouse comes out of the corpse, or the deceased appears in the form of a mouse, and so on. You look at the mouse in your story and some of the mice in your amplifications fit the mouse in your story, and explain it, while others do not. Now what do you do? In a case like this, I first take the mice that explain my mouse, but I keep the other mice in my pocket, or in a footnote, because sometimes, later in the story, some of the other aspects of the mouse will appear in another hidden constellation. Let us say that in your fairytale it is a positive mouse and there is no witch-mouse around, but later in the story there is something about a witch. Then you say, "Aha! There is a connection between these two images, so it is a good thing that I know that mice can also be witches."

81 Then comes the next essential step, which is the interpretation itself — the task of translating the amplified story into psychological language. At this point there is a danger of remaining half within the mystical mode of expression and talking about "the terrible mother who is overcome by the hero." Such a statement becomes

correct only if we say, "The inertia of unconsciousness is overcome by an impulse toward a higher level of consciousness." That is, we must use strictly psychological language. Only then do we know what the interpretation is.

82   If you are critical-minded, you might say, "All right, but then you are simply replacing one myth with another — by the Jungian myth, you might say." To this, one can only answer, "Yes, we do that, but we do it consciously; we know quite well that if in two hundred years someone were to read our interpretations, they might say, 'Isn't that funny! They translated the fairytale myth into Jungian psychology and thought that was it! But we know that it is...'" And they will bring a new interpretation, and ours will be counted as one of the outgrown interpretations — an illustration of how such material was regarded at that time. We are aware of this possibility and know that our interpretations are relative, that they are not absolutely true.

83   But we interpret for the same reason fairytales and myths are told: It has a vivifying effect and helps one to feel peacefully connected to one's unconscious instinctive substratum, in the same way that the telling of fairytales always did. Psychological interpretation is our way of telling stories: We still have the same need today and crave the renewal that comes from understanding archetypal images. We know quite well that our modern interpretation is just our myth. We explain an X by a Y because Y seems "to click" for us now. One day this will no longer be the case. There will then be the need for Z as an explanation. Therefore, we should never present our interpretation with the undertone of "this is it." We can only say in psychological language what the myth *seems* to represent and then modernize the myth in this psychological form. The only reliable criterion for an interpretation is one's feeling. Is it satisfactory, and does it "click" with me and with other people? And do my own dreams agree? When I write an interpretation, I always watch my dreams to see if they agree. If they do, then I know that the interpretation is as good as I can make it, according to my own nature. But if my psyche says, "You have not answered *this* yet," then I know that I must not go further. There may still be other

revelations in the story, but I have reached my own limits; I cannot go beyond myself. Then I can sit back satisfied, having eaten what I could digest. There is a lot more meat there, but I cannot digest it psychically.[4]

---

[4] If I have not understood a fairytale, or have not understood it sufficiently, I always have dreams about it. Take a fairytale and try to interpret it, and you, too, will see how this happens. I have never seen anyone try to interpret a fairytale with a certain amount of enthusiasm without their being given a reaction from the unconscious. For some reason, the unconscious is very interested in fairytale interpretation. One could say that interpreting fairytales generally has a vivifying effect upon the unconscious, and if you stray far from the path, you will be given peculiar reactions from the unconscious. I depend upon them. I know no better system. As we have no criteria of proof, the best thing to do is to say that I am happy with my interpretation and it makes me feel well, and if my unconscious has no more to say about it, then I have done all that I can. But of course, it is never the last word on the subject.

◊

Chapter 4

A Tale Interpreted: "The Three Feathers"

⁸⁴ We can now proceed to the more practical problems of interpretation. For didactic reasons I have taken for interpretation a very simple Grimms' fairytale, not with the idea of making it fascinating or interesting, but simply to show you the method of interpretation. I will try to show you how to proceed to get at the meaning of a story.

⁸⁵ *The Three Feathers*

There was once a king who had three sons. Two were intelligent, but the third did not talk much and was stupid and was called "Dummling." As the king grew old and weak and thought about his death, he did not know which of his sons should inherit his kingdom. So he said to them, "Go out into the world, and the one who brings me the most beautiful carpet shall be king when I die." To prevent any quarreling, he went outside the castle, blew three feathers into the air, and said, "As they fly, so you must go." One feather went towards the east, the other to the west, and the third just a little way straight ahead, where it fell to the ground. So one brother went to the right, the other to the left, and they laughed at Dummling, who had to stay where the third feather had fallen to the ground.

⁸⁶ Dummling sat down and was sad. Suddenly he noticed that there was a trapdoor beside the feather. He lifted it up, found steps descending, and went down into the earth. There he

came to another door upon which he knocked, and from inside he heard,

87 "Virgin, green and small,
Shrivel leg,
Shrivel leg's dog,
Shrivel back and forth.
Let's see who is outside."

88 The door opened and Dummling saw an enormous fat toad sitting there, surrounded by a circle of little toads. The fat toad asked him what he wanted. He answered, "I would like to have the finest and most beautiful carpet." The toad called a young toad, saying,

89 "Virgin, green and small,
Shrivel leg,
Shrivel leg's dog,
Shrivel back and forth.
Bring me the big box."

90 The young toad fetched the big box which the big toad opened, and from it she gave Dummling a beautiful carpet, a carpet so beautiful and so delicate that it could never have been woven on earth. He thanked her for it and climbed up again.

91 The two other brothers thought their youngest brother too silly ever to be able to find anything. "Why should we make a big effort looking," they said and brought home to the king some coarse linen stuff that the first shepherd woman they met had been wearing around her body. At the same time Dummling came home with his beautiful carpet, and when the king saw it, he said, "By rights the kingdom should go to the youngest." But the other two gave their father no peace, saying that it was impossible to make Dummling the king because he was so stupid, and they asked for another competition. So the king said, "Whoever brings home the most beautiful ring shall have my kingdom," and he led the

three brothers outside and blew three feathers into the air and ordered them to follow them. Again the two eldest went to the east and to the west, and for Dummling the feather went straight ahead and fell down by the door in the ground. Again he went down to the fat toad and told her that he needed the most beautiful ring. She again had the big box fetched and from it gave him a ring that gleamed with precious stones and was so beautiful that no goldsmith on earth could have made it. The other two again laughed about Dummling, who wanted to search for a gold ring, and they went to no trouble but knocked the nails out of an old cartwheel and brought that to the king. When Dummling showed his golden ring, the king again said, "The kingdom is yours." But the two elder brothers tormented the king until he set a third competition and said that the one who brought home the most beautiful wife should have the kingdom. He blew the three feathers again, and they fell as before.

92 Dummling went straight to the fat toad and said, "I need to bring home the most beautiful woman." "Oh," said the toad, "The most beautiful woman! She is not at hand just now, but you shall have her." She gave him a hollowed-out carrot to which six mice were harnessed. Dummling said sadly, "What shall I do with that?" The toad replied, "Put one of my little toads into it." So he took one at random out of the circle and put it in the yellow carriage. It had scarcely sat down before it was transformed into a beautiful girl, the carrot into a coach, and the six mice into six horses. He climbed into the carriage, kissed the girl and brought her to the king. His brothers, who had not taken any trouble to look for a beautiful woman, came back with the first two peasant women they had met. When the king saw them, he said, "The kingdom goes to the youngest after my death." But the two brothers deafened the king with their cries. "We cannot allow you to make Dummling the king," and requested that the one whose wife could jump through a ring which hung in the middle of the

room should have been preferred. They thought, "The peasant women will be able to do that because they are strong, but that delicate girl will jump to her death." The old king agreed. The two peasant women jumped through the ring, but they were so awkward that they fell and broke their thick arms and legs. Thereupon the beautiful girl whom Dummling had brought home sprang as lightly as a deer through the ring, and no further objection was possible. So he was given the crown and ruled in wisdom for a long time.[1]

93   You will probably recognize an accumulation of well-known motifs in this simple classical story. Johann Bolte and George Polivka[2] say that this fairytale was found by the Grimms in 1819 in Zwehrn (Germany) and that there is also another German version (from the region of Hesse) which has slight variations: Instead of a carpet, linen should be brought back, and when Dummling goes down into the earth, he does not find toads but a beautiful girl who is weaving linen; it is a beautiful girl who gives him the linen. She only turns into a frog when she comes up to the surface of the earth. So it is not quite the same problem. Under the ground she appears as a beautiful woman, but as soon as she comes to join Dummling on the earth, she is only a frog. When the frog arrives at the king's court in the carriage, it cries out, "Kiss me and *versenk dich*." *Versenken* really intimates meditation, so it would mean that Dummling should sink down into himself in meditation — which seems a very strange expression for a frog in a fairytale. It repeats this three times, so Dummling takes the frog and jumps into the water with it, for he has understood *versenken* to mean that he should submerge himself in the water, which is also a meaning of the word. The moment he kisses it and jumps into the water, it turns back into a beautiful girl. There are other Hessian variations where the three feathers are replaced by three apples that are rolled in different directions, and

---

[1] The Grimm Fairytales.
[2] Bolte and Polivka, *Anmerkungen zu den Kinder- und Hausmärchen*, vol. 2, 30. Parallel to this I recommend volumes 1 to 4½ of the *Enzyklopedie des Märchens, Handwörterbuch zur historischen und vergleichenden Erzählforschung* (Berlin, 1977 ff.).

there is a French variation in which the toad is replaced by a white cat.

94   I will not repeat all the possibilities but will mention only a few of the more frequent ones. In the northern versions and in several Russian parallel stories, it is spheres, balls, or apples that are rolled. Often the motif of the feathers is replaced by arrows that the father shoots in three directions. The bride is either a toad, a frog, or, as in the French version, a white cat; she can be a monkey, a lizard, a puppy, a female rat, a turtle, and sometimes even a stocking, or a nightcap — not even living objects.

95   At the end of all these variations — among which the Russian are the most interesting — there is a short annotation explaining that the motif of blowing a feather to indicate the direction one should take was a general medieval custom in many countries. If people did not know where to go, if they were lost at a crossroads or had no special plan, they would take a feather, blow on it, and walk in whichever direction the wind took it. That was a very common kind of oracle by which you could be guided. There are many medieval stories referring to this and even folklore expressions such as "I shall go where the feather blows."

96   We will begin with the first few sentences. Our exposition runs: There was a king who had three sons. Two were intelligent, the third, however, seldom spoke and was simple-minded. The king, who was old and weak, did not know to whom he should give his kingdom. This is the opening psychological situation. The last sentence sets the problem, which we could formulate in the question: Which of the three sons should inherit the kingdom?

97   The opening situation of the king and his three sons is exceedingly frequent. The Grimm collection alone, which is merely a fraction of all existing possibilities, has at least fifty or sixty such stories that start off with a king and his three sons. It is not a normal family for there is neither mother nor sister, and the initial setup of people is purely masculine. The female element, which you expect in a complete family, is not represented. The main action is concerned with the finding of the right female, upon which the

inheritance of the kingdom depends, and that the hero does not perform any masculine deeds. He is not a hero in the proper sense of the word. He is helped all the way through by the feminine element, which solves the whole problem for him and performs all the necessary deeds such as weaving the carpet, finding the ring, and jumping through the ring. The story ends with a marriage — a balanced union of the male and female elements. So the general structure seems to point to a problem in which there is a dominating male attitude. It is dealing with a situation that lacks the feminine element, and the story tells us how the missing feminine is brought up and restored.

98   We have first to investigate the symbolism of the king. An expanded study of the king is to be found in *Mysterium Coniunctionis* in the section headed "Rex and Regina."[3] In primitive societies, the king or the chief of the tribe generally has magical qualities; he has mana.[4] Certain chiefs, for instance, are so sacred that they may not touch the earth and are always carried by their people. In other tribes the vessels that the king has used for eating and drinking are thrown away. No one may touch them for they are taboo. Some chiefs and kings are never seen because of a similar taboo; if you were to look at the king's face, you would die. Of certain chiefs it is said that their voices thunder and their eyes emanate lightning.

99   In many primitive societies, the prosperity of the whole country depends on the health and state of mind of the king, and if he becomes impotent or ill, he has to be killed and replaced by another king whose health and potency guarantee the fertility of the women and cattle, as well as the prosperity of the whole tribe. James George Frazer mentions instances in which it is not customary to wait until the king becomes impotent or sick; instead, he is killed at the end of a certain period.[5] Behind this is the idea that after a certain time a king is worn out and must be replaced. In certain tribes the idea

---

[3] Cf. C.G. Jung, "Rex and Regina," in *Mysterium Coniunctionis: An Inquiry into the Separation and Synthesis of Psychic Opposites in Alchemy,* 2nd ed, vol. 14, *CW* (Princeton, NJ: Princeton University Press, 1989), §§ 349–543.
[4] Cf. Jung, *The Dynamic of the Unconscious,* vol. 8, *CW,* § 123.
[5] James George Frazer, *The Golden Bough* (Munich: BookRix, 2019).

prevails that the killing of the king, who embodies a kind of protective or ancestral spirit for the tribe, does not imply really killing him, but rather represents a further development: The old house is pulled down so that the spirit can move into a new one and continue to reign in that. It is believed to be always the same sacred, totemistic spirit that rules. By being killed, he is, so to speak, being provided with a better physical vessel.

100   We can say, therefore, that the king or chief incorporates a divine principle on which the entire welfare — psychic and physical — of his people depends. He represents the divine principle in its visible form; he is the incarnation or embodiment of the divine — its dwelling place. In his body lives the totem spirit of the tribe. He therefore has many characteristics that would incline us to look at him as a symbol of the Self, because the Self, according to our definition, is the center of the self-regulating system of the psyche, upon which the welfare of the individual depends. In Christian iconography kings were often depicted holding a globe of the earth with a cross upon it in their right hand. They carried a number of other symbols that we know from various mythological associations represent the Self.

101   In many primitive tribes there is a split between medicine man and king or chief — that is, between spiritual and worldly power. The same thing happened in our civilization in the terrible fight between *sacerdotium* and *imperium* (church and state) in the Middle Ages. Both powers claimed to be visible, incarnate symbols of the divine principle for their subjects — or, one could say, they claimed to be symbols of the unobservable archetype of the Self.

102   In all cultures and in alchemical symbolism, which you can read about in Jung's book, you see this dominating idea that the aging king is unsatisfactory in some way. In early cultures, when the ruler was impotent, whispers circulated throughout the harem and the tribe silently decided to kill him. Or he may have been unsatisfactory in other ways: He may have been too old to perform certain tasks any longer, or his time was over — he had reigned his ten or fifteen years. Then came the inevitable idea of the king's sacrificial death.

In more advanced civilizations, as, for instance, in the Old Kingdom of Egypt, the practice was replaced by a ritual of renewal, a symbolic death and resurrection of the king, as was performed in the Sed festival. In other countries there was a so-called carnival king. Some criminal who had been condemned to death was allowed to live for three days as a king. He was taken out of prison and clothed as a king, and as he had all the insignia, he could order whatever he liked. He could have all the women he wanted, all the good dinners he liked, and everything else, and after three days he was executed. Other races have a ritual in which the process of killing is carried out on a puppet, on a small dog or some other animal in place of the king.[6] Behind all of these different traditions we see the same motif — the need for renewal through death and rebirth.

103   If we apply this to our hypothesis of the king being a symbol of the Self, we have to ask: Why does a symbol of the Self age? Do we know any psychological factors that correspond to this fact? If you study the comparative history of religions, you will note the tendency for any religious ritual or dogma that has become conscious to wear out after a time, to lose its original emotional impact, and to become a dead formula. Although it also acquires the positive qualities of consciousness — such as continuity — it loses the irrational contact with the flow of life and tends to become automatic or mechanical. This is true not only of religious doctrines and political systems but for everything else as well, because when something has long been conscious, it becomes a dead world. If our conscious life is to avoid becoming petrified, there is a need for constant renewal through contact with the flow of psychic events in the unconscious, and the king, being the most central symbol in the contents of the collective unconscious, is naturally subject to this need to an even greater extent.

104   You can therefore say that the symbol of the Self is especially exposed to this general difficulty of needing the constant renewal of understanding and contact. It is also especially threatened by the possibility of becoming a dead formula. In this sense, the aging king

---

[6] Abraham sacrifices a ram instead of his son Genesis 22:1–19.

represents a dominant content of collective consciousness and underlies all the political and religious doctrines of a social group. In the East, for many layers of the population, this content appeared as the Buddha, and with us, until now, it was Christ, who, indeed, has the title "King of Kings."

105   In our story the king apparently has no wife, or, if he has one, she does not appear. What would the queen represent? If we take the king as representing a central and dominant symbolic content of collective consciousness, then the queen would be its accompanying feminine element — the embodiment of the feelings and irrational impulses that are attached to this dominant content. It can be said that in every civilization there is a *Weltanschauung* with a central God-image that dominates it. This includes a certain habit or style of life, a feeling style, and this Eros style of a society influences how people relate to one another. The feeling tone of this collectivity would be the queen who accompanies the king; for instance, in the Middle Ages, the Gothic idea of Christ would be incarnate in the king of that time, while the representations of Eros — to be found in the poems of the Troubadours — would be manifested in the Virgin Mary, who is the Queen of Heaven related to the king — to Christ. She set the pattern for feminine behavior, both for the man's anima as well as for women. In Catholic countries, women tend to adapt naturally to this pattern, while the men try to educate their anima to fit into this style of erotic behavior and style of relationship.

106   Thus, we see the close connection between the king and the queen, the Logos principle dominating a certain civilization and collective attitude, and the Eros style accompanying it in a specific form. That the queen is lacking means that the latter aspect has been lost and therefore the king is sterile. Without the queen he can have no more children. We must assume, therefore, that the story has to do with the problem of a dominant collective attitude in which the principle of Eros — of relatedness to the unconscious, to the irrational, to the feminine — has been lost. This must refer to a

situation in which collective consciousness has become petrified and has stiffened into doctrines and formulas.

107   Now this king has three sons, so there is the problem of four males, three of whom are adapted in the way they should be, while the fourth is "below the mark." Naturally, people who know Jungian psychology will jump to the conclusion that these four are obviously the four functions of consciousness: the king being the dominant or main function and the two elder sons being the auxiliary functions, while Dummling would be, of course, the fourth, inferior function.[7] This is right, but only with some reservation — *cum grano salis* — because Jung's theory of the four functions refers to an individual. In fairytales we do not have the inner story of one individual and therefore cannot look at it from this angle. We have, rather, to amplify the motif of the male *quaternio*, and there, for example, we find motifs such as the four sons of Horus, the four Evangelists, and other quaternio that surround a main symbol of the Self.

108   These quaternio that one finds in the comparative history of religion and in mythology cannot, to my mind, be interpreted as the four functions as they appear in an individual. They represent a more basic pattern of consciousness from which the four-functional pattern of consciousness is derived. If we know how to diagnose a type and have a number of people before us, we can say that this man is a thinking type and his inferior feeling probably makes such and such trouble. Thus, certain aspects of his behavior appear to be typical, while others are more individual. So it can be said that the problem of the four functions always appears in an individual in a certain setup, but that there are general basic trends underneath. One might wonder why on earth human consciousness always tends to develop four functions in each person? One can reply that it seems to be an inborn disposition of the human being to build up a four-functional conscious system. If you do not influence a child, he or she will automatically develop one conscious function, and if you analyze that person at the age of thirty or forty, you will find this four-functional structure. The underlying general disposition is

---

[7] Cf. Jung, *Psychological Types*, vol. 6, *CW*, 330–407.

mirrored in the main quaternarian symbols in mythology, as well as in the four winds, the four directions of the compass, and also these four royal figures of our fairytale.

109   To be accurate, you would need to say that the king does not represent the main function but is rather the archetypal basis of that function, i.e., he represents the psychological factor that builds up the main functions in all people. You might say that I am contradicting myself, for earlier I said that the old king was the dominant of collective consciousness and now I am saying that he symbolizes the disposition that builds up main functions. How does that link up? Is that a contradiction? If you reflect on how a main function builds up, then you will see that it builds up in the first half of human life and generally serves collective adaptation. If a child is good at playing with practical things, his father will say that he should later become an engineer. The child is encouraged, and at school, he will be very good in those fields and very bad in others; so he will be proud of what he can do well and will do that most often because there is a natural tendency to always do what one can do well and to neglect the other side. This one-sidedness slowly builds up the main function, which is the function one uses to adapt to collective requirements. Hence, the dominant of collective consciousness also constellates the main function in the individual.

110   Let us look again at medieval man for whom the dominant of the Self is the figure of Christ. If he is a thinking type, he will meditate upon the essence of Christ; if he is a feeling type, he will be moved by the prayers he hears, rather than thinking about the symbol of Christ and he will relate to Christ through his main function — through his feeling. In this way, the king, who represents the dominating symbolic content of a collective conscious situation, is connected with the main function in all people.

111   Logically, the other sons would have to be interpreted along the same lines: The two sons who are intelligent and clever would represent the typical basis for building up the two auxiliary functions in a human being, while Dummling would represent the basis of building up the inferior function. But Dummling is not only this;

he is also the hero, and the whole story is concerned with what happens to him. We must therefore briefly discuss what the hero means in a mythological story because, if you read many psychological interpretations of myths, you will soon see that there is a constant shift between interpreting the hero as a symbol of the Self and as a symbol of the ego. Sometimes interpreters contradict themselves even within the same text. They begin as if the hero were an ego, then shift to his being the Self.

112 Before we discuss this problem, we have to be clear as to what we mean by ego. The ego is the central complex of our field of consciousness. Naturally, everyone has an ego. So, if we speak of *the* ego, which is already an abstraction, we mean the "I" of all the people we know. If we say, "The ego resists the unconscious," we are making a general observation, something that applies to the average ego, stripped of any subjective and unique qualities. We now have to look at the symbol of the hero in myths. What does the hero usually do? He is very often a savior: He saves his country and his people from dragons, witches, and evil spells. In many stories, he is the finder of the hidden treasure. He frees his tribe and leads them out of all sorts of danger. He reconnects his people with the gods and with life, or he renews the life principle. It is he who goes on the night-sea journey, and when he comes out of the belly of the whale, all those who were swallowed before him generally come with him. Sometimes he tends to be overly self-confident and, in certain myths, he is even destructive. Then the gods, or some enemy powers, decide to destroy him. In many hero myths he is the innocent victim of evil powers, or the hero is a trickster who plays both good and bad tricks, who not only frees his people but also gets them into difficulties; he helps certain people and destroys others by mistake or through thoughtlessness. So he is half a devil and half a savior, and, at the end, he is either destroyed, or reformed and transformed. Thus, there is a great variety of hero types: the Dummling, the trickster, the "strong man," the innocent, the beautiful youth and the sorcerer who performs his deeds by magic, while others do so with power and courage.

113   We know from the investigations of child psychology that the main tendency of the unconscious in the first twenty years of life goes into building up a strong ego complex. Most difficulties in youth result from disturbances in this process by negative parental influence, or through some traumatic or other hindrance. The child psychologist Michael Fordham has described cases in which the ego complex is not able to build itself up. There are natural processes in the psyche of a child that we can watch for they are mirrored in dreams. One can see in them how the ego is created. They show how the ideal of the hero is a model for this development. Papa often fills this role, as do tram conductors, policemen, elder brothers, or big boys in the class above (at school), who receive the child's transference. In secret daydreams, the child imagines that that is what he would like to become. The fantasies of many little boys are of wearing a red cap and waving the trains on and off, or of being the chief, the big boss, the king, and the chief-of-police. These model figures are projections produced by the unconscious; they appear either in the dreams of young people, or are projected onto outer figures. They catch the fantasy of the child and influence the growth of his ego. Every mother knows that. For instance, if you take a little boy to the dentist and say perhaps, "Well, you are an Indian chief, so you can't cry when a tooth is pulled out," this strengthens his ego so that he will force back his tears. It is a method that is constantly used in education; it is a trick. If a boy admires Albert in the next class and behaves badly, and you say, "Albert wouldn't do that," the boy at once pulls up his socks.

114   Those are typical psychological processes showing how the ego complex, the center of the field of consciousness, is slowly formed in a young person. If you look more closely at these processes, you will see from dreams that *they stem from the Self* and that *it is the Self that builds up the ego.* A graphic representation would show first the unknown psychic totality of a human being — thought of as a sphere, not a circle. In the upper part of the sphere is the field of consciousness. Everything within this field is conscious. Its center is the ego complex. Anything that is not connected through some

thread of association to my ego complex I am not conscious of. Before this field of consciousness exists, the self-regulating center (the Self is regarded as both the totality and the regulating center of the whole personality, and it seems to be present from the very beginning of life) builds up the ego complex through certain emotional and other processes.

115   If you study the symbolism of the ego complex and of the Self, you will see that the ego has the same structures and is to a great extent a mirror image of this center. We know the representations of the Self in, for instance, mandala construction.[8] The ego has the same fourfold subdivision. The center of the Self slowly builds up the ego complex, which then mirrors its original center and which, as we all know, often succumbs to the illusion of being that center. Most people who have not been in a Jungian analysis naturally believe — because of their emotional conviction that "I am I" — that my "I" is the whole thing. This illusion comes from the ego having been formed from the center of totality. In childhood there is the tragedy of separation: The child is thrown out of its ego-Self oneness. The typical example of this is the feeling of being thrown out of Paradise. One experiences the first shock of being incomplete and discovers that something perfect has been lost forever. Such tragedies mirror the moment when the ego begins to become an entity apart from the Self. From then on, the ego is established as a self-existing factor; its connection with the center is partly lost.

116   Now the ego, as far as we can see, functions properly only when it achieves a certain adaptation to the whole psyche. This means that it functions best if a certain plasticity is kept — in other words, if the ego is not petrified and can still be influenced by the Self through dreams, moods, and so on, so that it can adapt to the whole psychological system. It looks to us as though nature did not intend the ego to be the ruler of the whole psychological setup, but rather to be an instrument that functions best if it still obeys the basic instinctual urges of the totality and does not resist them.

---

[8] Cf. Jung, "On Mandala Symbolism," in *Archetypes and the Collective Unconscious*, vol. 9/I, *CW*, §§ 627–28.

117   Imagine, for instance, that your instinct tells you to run away in a dangerous situation. You do not require a very conscious ego to tell you that. If a bull chases you, you do not need to consult your ego; you had better consult your legs, which know what to do. But if the ego functions *with* your legs, so that while running away from the bull you also look for a good hiding place or a fence to jump over, then the situation is perfect: Your instincts and your ego function in accord with each other. If, on the other hand, you are a philosopher whose legs want to run away but who thinks, "Stop! I must first find out whether it is right to run away from a bull," then the ego blocks the instinctual urge; it has become autonomous and anti-instinctive and has a destructive effect. This is how we can recognize a neurotic person. A neurosis could be defined as an ego formation that is no longer in harmony with the whole personality. When, on the other hand, one's ego functions in accordance with the larger totality, it reinforces itself and improves the innate cleverness of the basic instinctive arrangement.

118   Naturally, there are times when the ego would also be useful in resisting instinct. Imagine, for instance, the North Arctic lemmings that get an instinctual urge to migrate into another country where they will find a new food supply. Driven by an instinctual urge, they come together and march ahead. If, by some bad luck, they come to a sea or a river, they go into it and drown by the thousands. I am sure you know this story, which has always puzzled zoologists, for it shows the silly lack of adaptation of some natural instincts. Konrad Lorenz once gave a lecture at the Jung Institute with many such examples. I recall the story of a bird which, to please its mate in the mating season, produces an enormous red sack on his chest with which to enforce his mating song. This red sack is so heavy that he cannot fly, so his enemies gather and butcher the bird. So that is not a very good invention. A beautiful red tail or a red behind like a baboon's to please his wife would be much better and would not prevent him from flying away.

119   So you see, instinctual patterns are not only positive. Imagine if a lemming were able to ask itself what it was doing and to reflect

that it did not want to drown. Given that it had the chance to go back, it would save its own life. Perhaps this is why nature has invented the ego as a new instrument for us. We are a new experiment of nature, for we have an additional instrument for regulating our instinctual urges. We do not live according to our patterns of behavior only, but have this strange addition known as "the ego."

120   The ideal situation, as far as we can see, is when the ego has a certain plasticity to obey the central regulation of the psyche. But when it hardens and becomes autonomous, acting according to its own reasons, there is often a neurotic constellation. This happens not only to individuals, but also collectively, which is why we speak of collective neuroses and psychoses. Whole groups of mankind can drift into a split situation and deviate from their basic instinctual patterns. Disaster is then close at hand. This is why, in hero stories, there is nearly always an exposition of a terrible situation: The land is drying up because toads are blocking the water of life, or some dark enemy has come from the north and is stealing all the women and there is no fertility in the land. Whatever the terrible story is, the hero has the task of putting it right. The dragon may be demanding all the king's maidens to be sacrificed. Everyone in the country is already wearing black, and now the last princess has to be given to the dragon. This is the moment the hero arrives.

121   The hero is the one who restores a healthy, conscious situation. When all the egos of a tribe or nation are deviating from their instinctive, basic totality pattern, he is the one ego that restores them all to health and normal functioning. It can therefore be said that the hero *is an archetypal figure that presents a model of an ego functioning in accord with the Self.* Produced by the unconscious psyche, it is a *model* to be looked at. It is a model that demonstrates a "correctly functioning" ego, an ego that operates in accordance with the requirements of the Self. This is why, to a certain extent, the hero also seems to be identical with the Self: He serves as its instrument and completely expresses what the Self wants to have happen. In a certain sense, the hero *is* also the Self, for he expresses

its healing tendencies, or embodies them. So the hero has this strange double character. From the feeling standpoint, this is easy to understand. If you hear a hero myth, you identify with the hero and get infected by his mood. Let us say, for instance, that an Inuit tribe is starving. Hunting has been poor, and it is known that natural man gives up very readily. They die from discouragement before it would have been physically or psychologically necessary for them to do so. Into this situation comes a storyteller who tells about a fellow who made contact with ghosts and thereby saved his starving tribe, and so on. This puts them on their feet again, purely emotionally. The ego adopts a heroic, courageous, and hopeful attitude that saves the collective situation. This is why a hero story is a vital necessity in difficult life conditions.[9] If you can once again embrace your hero myth, you can live. You feel instinctively encouraged by it.

122   When you tell fairytales to children, they at once and naively identify and get all the feeling of the story. If you tell them about the ugly duckling, all the children who have inferiority complexes hope that in the end they, too, will become a princess.[10] This functions exactly as it should; it provides a model for living — an encouraging, vivifying model that reminds one unconsciously of all of life's positive possibilities. There is a beautiful custom among indigenous peoples of Australasia: When the rice does not grow well, the women go into the rice field and squat among the rice and tell it the myth of the origin of rice. Then the rice knows again why it is there and grows like anything. This is probably a projection of our own situation — it is certainly true for us. When we hear our myths, we believe we know again what we are living for. This changes our whole mood about our lives and can even sometimes change our physiological condition.

123   If you interpret the hero in this way, then you see why Dummling would be the hero in our story. Since the king is the dominant of the

---

[9] For the same reason, an "evil hero," a tyrant, can also succeed. Cf. C.G. Jung, "Wotan," in *Civilization in Transition*, 2nd ed., vol. 10, *CW* (Princeton, NJ: Princeton University Press, 1978), 203–18.
[10] Hans Christian Andersen, "The Ugly Duckling," in *Complete Fairy Tales and Stories*, trans. Erik Christian Haugaard (Palatine: First Anchor Books, 1983), 216–24.

collective conscious attitude that has lost contact with the flow of life, especially with the feminine — with the Eros principle — Dummling represents the new attitude that is capable of becoming conscious and contacting the feminine. He is the one who brings up the toad-princess. Characteristically, he is the one who is called "stupid" and is seemingly unlucky. But if you look at his behavior more closely, you see that he is simply spontaneous and naïve; he takes things as they are. The other two brothers, for instance, cannot accept facts. Each time Dummling wins, they want another competition, saying that that one was not right. But Dummling always simply does the next thing, even when he has to marry a frog or toad. He just goes along with it. It is perhaps not very pleasant, but that is just how it is. Obviously, it is this quality of acceptance that is emphasized in our story.

124   We should always look at these stories as we do at the dreams of individuals and ask what conscious situation is compensated by such a myth. Then it is clear that such a story compensates the conscious attitude of a society in which patriarchal schemes with all their "oughts" and "shoulds" dominate. Because it is ruled by rigid principles, irrational, spontaneous adaptation to events is lost. It is typical that Dummling stories statistically occur more frequently in Western society than in others, and it is obvious why that is so. We are the people who, by an overdevelopment of consciousness, have lost the flexibility of taking life as it is. This is why Dummling stories are especially valuable for us. We also have an overwhelming number of stories where the hero excels through just plain laziness; he simply sits on a stove and scratches himself, and everything simply falls into his lap. These stories compensate a collective attitude that puts too much emphasis upon efficiency; then these lazy hero stories are told with great delight. There is something healing about them.

125   The king does not know to whom he should leave the kingdom. He deviates from his probable former behavior for he leaves it up to fate to settle the matter. In other stories, the old king is given a dream, a prophecy, or some other sign about who is to be the next

king, whereupon he channels all his passion, strength, and skill into destroying his possible successor. There are thousands of examples, for example, Grimms' "The Devil with the Three Golden Hairs." Sometimes the king gives a possible successor a chance, but if he does not fit in with his plans, he begins to resist.[11]

126   There are neurotic people whose ego attitude has drifted away from their whole psychological nature, and yet they come into analysis without great resistances for they just want to know what comes next. When their dreams produce some new life, they take it and go on their way, with practically no resistance. With them, the "succession of the king" — replacing one ego attitude with another — is relatively easy. But there are others who are quite different. They describe their symptoms, and you look at their dreams, but if you even mildly suggest what the trouble might be, they jump down your throat and argue. It may be anything else, but it is certainly not *that*. *That* they *know* is all right. These people fight back forever. This type of ego formation has already stiffened to such an extent that it absolutely blocks the possibility of a renewal. I often say to such people that they have the attitude of a person who goes to a doctor and asks the doctor to please cure them — but not to examine their urine because that is something private. A lot of people do this. They go into analysis but keep the main formation in their pockets because it is nobody's business to know about that. In such patterns of behavior you recognize the old king (which, in an individual, means one's center of consciousness) who resists renewal.

127   Naturally, this pattern is to be found in the collective situation as well. A whole society may at first be violently antagonistic towards some religious reform, and afterwards suddenly acknowledges it. To mention a classical example, twelve sentences written by Saint Thomas of Aquinas, the great pillar of the Catholic Church, were originally condemned by a Concilium (in 1320). Here one can see that through a collective prejudice of the time, something that is later recognized as not being inimical to the dominating attitude is at first resisted. Examples of this extend into political and religious

---

[11] 1 Sam. 18 (The expulsion of David).

persecution, or being slurred by the media; all of this is going on now and always will in social setups around the world. Clearly, there is a kind of phobia that anything new is in itself terrifying. This is all typical behavior of the "old king" that can ramp up and petrify into mistrust, hate, and real tragedy. In our fairytale, the opportunity for renewal does not lead to crisis or tragedy. It is a rather mild story, which is why it is not particularly interesting, but it has many of the classical features we need for our interpretation.

128   We come next to the ritual of the three feathers. This traditional custom is not very different from throwing a coin. Whenever consciousness cannot decide rationally, one can have recourse to such a chance event and take that as an indication.[12] That the coin falls this way or the wind blows that way is a "just-so" story taken as a meaningful hint. That this ritual brings success is important because it is the first move towards giving up ego determination, one's own conscious reasoning. One could say that this old king proves to be not too bad because, though he will soon be dead and therefore has to be replaced by a successor, he is quite willing to leave it up to the gods to decide who shall come next. This again fits the whole setup of the story, which is not dramatic and which has not stiffened into a conflict.

129   If one goes deeper into the symbolism of the feather, one sees that in mythology, feathers generally represent something very similar to the bearer of the feathers — the bird. According to the principle of *pars pro toto* (a part stands for the whole), a magical form of thinking, the feather signifies the bird, and birds in general represent psychic entities of an intuitive and spiritual character. For instance, the soul of the dead leaves the dying body in the form of a bird. There are medieval representations of this. Even now, in the parents' bedroom in every house in certain villages of Upper Wallis, there is a little window called the "soul window." It is opened only when someone is dying, so that the soul can leave through it. The idea is that the soul, a fluttering being, flies out, like a bird escaping

---

[12] One of the most famous methods of oracle techniques is Richard Wilhelm, *I Ching: The Book of Changes* (New York: Dover Publications, 2012); cf. also Marie-Louise von Franz, *Number and Time* (Asheville: Chiron Publications, 2022).

from its cage. In *The Odyssey*, Hermes gathers the souls of Ulysses' enemies; they chatter like birds (the Greek word is *thrizein*) and follow him with wings like bats. Also, in the underworld where Enkidu, the friend of Gilgamesh, goes, the dead sit around in feather garments of birds. Birds stand for an almost bodiless entity, an inhabitant of the air, of the sphere of winds. The bird has always been associated with breath and therefore with the human psyche. Birds are often to be found in the stories of North and South American Indians, who had the custom of gluing feathers to an object — an indication that it is psychically real. In the same way, a South American tribe uses the word for feather as a suffix to describe something that only exists psychologically. You can speak of a fox-feather, an arrow-feather, or a tree-feather, the word "feather" indicating that the fox or the arrow or the tree is not contained in physical reality but exists only in psychic reality. When North American Indians and certain Inuit tribes send messengers inviting others to a religious festival, the messengers carry sticks with feathers on them, the feathers making the bearer sacrosanct. Because they carry a spiritual message, such messengers may not be killed. By attaching feathers to himself, the primitive marks himself as a psychic and spiritual being.

130   Since the feather is very light, every breath of wind carries it. It is very sensitive to what one could call invisible and imperceptible psychological, spiritual currents. In most religious and mythological connections, wind represents the spirit, which is why we use the word "inspiration." In the miracle of the Pentecost, the Holy Ghost filled the house like a tremendous wind (Gen. 1:2). When ghosts appear, movements of air or currents of cold wind accompany them. The word *spiritus* is connected with *spirare* (to breathe). In Genesis, the *Ruach Elohim* (the Spirit of God) broods over the waters. Therefore, you can say that an imperceptible wind whose direction you can only discover by blowing a feather would be a slight, barely noticeable, almost inconceivable psychic tendency — a hidden basic tendency in the momentary flow of life.

131   That is what happens when someone comes into analysis and tells you all his troubles and you say, "Well, I am no more intelligent than you. I do not see through this, but let us look at what the dreams say." We try to see where the current in the dreams seems to point. According to our Jungian point of view, dreams are not only causal but also have a final aspect. We therefore look to see where the energy tends to go. We "throw a feather in the air" and look to see the direction it takes. Then we say, "Let's go that way because there is a slight tendency in that direction."

132   This is just what the king does. He makes himself completely flexible and consults the supernatural powers. One feather goes to the east, the other to the west, and Dummling's feather settles on the ground right away. According to some more witty variations, it settles on a brown stone just in front of him, and then Dummling says, "Well, that means I can go nowhere." He finds his way into the depths, which is in beautiful accord with his character. Very often we look God-knows-where for the solution of our problem and do not see that it is right in front of our noses. We are not humble enough to look downward but stick our noses up in the air. Jung often told the beautiful story of a Jewish rabbi who was asked by his pupils why in the Bible there were so many instances of the apparition of God, whereas nowadays such things did not happen, and the rabbi replied, "Because nowadays nobody is humble enough to bend down low enough."[13]

133   Visions of God in dreams or in waking life are not rare, but nowadays people do not dare talk about them, except for when they visit their analyst, usually thinking that they are little crazy. But because Dummling is naïve and unsophisticated, he has a naïve and unsophisticated attitude towards life. He is led naturally to what is on the ground and right in front of his nose — and there it is. We know from the first sentence of the story that it is the feminine that is lacking. It is found in the earth and nowhere else. That belongs to the inner logic of the whole story.

---

[13] Cf. Jung, *Memories, Dreams, Reflections*, 355.

◊

Chapter 5
"The Three Feathers" Continued

¹³⁴ After having amplified the three-feathers motif, we must now take the second step of expressing its psychological meaning in a nutshell.

¹³⁵ Feathers represent thoughts or fantasies. They replace, *pars pro toto*, birds. The wind is a well-known symbol for the inspiring spiritual quality of the unconscious. So this motif would mean that one lets one's imagination or thoughts wander, thereby following the inspirations that well up from the unconscious. You might perform this ritual if you are at a crossroads and do not know which direction to take. Instead of deciding out of ego considerations, you wait for a hunch from the unconscious and let it have a say in the matter. We could understand this as a compensation for the dominant collective situation that seems to have lost contact with the irrational, feminine element. If a single man, or if a whole civilization, loses contact with the feminine element, it usually implies a too rational, too ordered, too organized attitude. Feelings, irrationality, and fantasies are connected to the feminine. Instead of telling his sons where to go, this old king makes a gesture towards possible renewal by allowing the wind to tell them. Dummling's feather falls onto the ground in front of him where he discovers a trapdoor with steps beneath it leading into the depths of Mother Earth. In the Hessian parallel, the frog princess tells him that he should *sich versenken* — he should go into the depths. This means that the downward movement is emphasized.

¹³⁶ A trapdoor with steps leading into the earth indicates that what he enters is not a natural cavity. Human beings have left their traces; perhaps there was once a building here, or it is the cellar of a castle of which the upper part has long ago disappeared, or it was once a

hiding place in a former civilization. When figures go down into the earth or into the water in a dream, people often interpret that superficially as a *descensus ad inferos*, as a descent into the underworld, into the depths of the unconscious. But one should see whether it is a descent into unconscious virginal nature or whether there are layers and traces of former civilizations. The latter would indicate that there are elements which had once been conscious but which have sunk back into the unconscious, just as a castle may fall into ruins. The cellars, however, remain, leaving traces of a former way of life.

137   Interpreted psychologically, this would mean that the unconscious not only contains our instinctive animal nature but also traditions of the past, by which it is partially formed. This is why, in analysis, elements of an earlier civilized past frequently reappear. A Jew may not care in the least about his cultural past, but cabbalistic motifs appear in his dreams. I once saw the dreams of a Hindu who had been educated in America and who had not the slightest conscious interest in his cultural past, but his dreams were full of Hindu godheads still alive in his unconscious. It has often been believed that Jung had a tendency to force people back into their cultural background and suggested, for instance, that he encouraged Jews to dig up Orthodox symbolism, or Hindus should again pray to Shiva. This is not at all the case. There is absolutely no "should" or "ought to" about it; it is simply a question as to whether or not such elements come up and want to be recognized in a person's unconscious.

138   How can it be that in our story the feminine element was at one time more conscious and has now sunk back into the unconscious? The original pagan Germanic and Celtic religions had many cults of Mother Earth and other nature goddesses, but the one-sided patriarchal superstructure of the Christian civilization slowly repressed this element. If it is a question of bringing up the feminine element and integrating it again, we shall — at least in Europe — find traces of a past civilization in which the feminine was much more conscious. With its cult of the Virgin Mary and the

Troubadours, recognition of the anima was much more alive in the Middle Ages than it was from the 16th century onwards, a time which, in our part of the world, is characterized by an increasing repression of the feminine element and of Eros culture. We do not know the date of this fairytale, but the opening situation shows a condition in which the feminine element is not recognized, though obviously it had been at one time. There is, therefore, a relatively good chance of getting back to it. Dummling goes down into the earth step by step and does not fall headlong into it or get lost in the dark. In the Hessian parallel, the steps have a round cover, like a manhole, with a ring in it. The ring suggests that this is not only the way to the anima, but that it is also the way to the Self.

139   When Dummling goes down, he finds a door and knocks at it. He hears this strange little poem.

140   Virgin, green and small,
       Shrivel leg,
       Shrivel leg's dog,
       Shrivel back and forth.
       Let's see who is outside.

141   It is a kind of childish ditty with only a partly understandable, dreamlike combination of words. When the door opens, Dummling sees an enormous toad surrounded by a circle of little toads, and when he says he wants a beautiful carpet, the toad pulls it out of the box.

142   We must first amplify the poem. In many other variations of this fairytale, a frog replaces the toad, so we have to look at the frog as well. In general, the frog in mythology represents a masculine element, whereas the toad is feminine. In Europe, there is the frog prince[1], and, in African and Malayan stories, the frog is also a male being, while in practically all other civilizations the toad is feminine. In China, a three-legged toad lives in the moon where, together with

---

[1] Cf. Grimm and Grimm, "The Frog King, or Iron Heinrich," in *Complete Fairy Tales*, trans. Jack Zipes (London: Vintage Books, 2007), 2–6.

a hare, she produces the elixir of life. According to a Taoist tradition, she has been fished up from the "well of truth" and, as a kind of protective spirit, she works with the hare to make the elixir pills that heal and prolong life.[2] In our civilization, the toad has most often been associated with the Earth Mother, especially in her function of helping at childbirth. She was, and still is, regarded as being a representation of the uterus. In Catholic countries, there is the custom of asking it for a leg, a hand, or some other part of the body to be cured. A wax image is made of the injured part and suspended as an *ex voto* (a token of the fulfilment of one's vow) in the church where healing was requested. If a woman had a disease of the uterus, she suspended a wax toad in the church, for the toad represents the uterus. In many churches and chapels in Bavaria, toads made out of wax surround the statue of the Virgin Mary. There, the Virgin Mary has taken over the function of the Greek goddess Artemis Eileithyia, the helper in birth, the positive mother who helps the woman carry the child and give birth to it without harm. This analogy of toad and uterus shows how much in this connection the toad actually represents the maternal womb, the mother — precisely what is lacking in the royal family in our fairytale. The big toad in the middle could be looked upon as the mother of all the little toads sitting around her. Our Dummling does not marry the big toad; he is told to take one of the little ones out of the ring. She turns into the beautiful princess, which shows that the big toad is the mother figure from whose circle he gets his anima. As we know, the anima is a derivative of the mother image in a man's psychology. This is why the Mother Earth goddess in her animal form is at the center of the image.

143 We shall now try to illuminate the function of the rhyme that allows Dummling to enter the underground room. The image of *shrivel* is rather more difficult to understand than the toad. Certainly in German the word *hutzel*, the original word, is always associated

---

[2] Cf. M. Maier, *Atalanta Fugiens*, 5, Emblem. [Addition by the French translator: "The text mentions interesting legends about toads, in particular about her relationship to stone and to alchemical gold." Facsimile-Druck der Oppenheimer Original-Ausgabe of 1618 with 52 engravings by Matthäus Merian de. Ae., ed., Of Lucas Heinrich Wüthrich, Kassel and Basel 1964].

with old age, ancientness, a process that has lasted for a long time. In this context, it could allude to the fact that the Mother Goddess has been excluded from the realm of consciousness and neglected. Down in the cellar, she has become all shriveled up, like an old apple. Now we come to the leg (*Bein*), which I am inclined to interpret rather as a bone (also *Bein* in German) than as a leg because of a widespread ritual for a love charm in German, Swiss, and Austrian countries. According to this ritual, one has to take a living toad or frog and throw it into an ant heap; then one must run away and not listen because toads or frogs can scream: This would mean he has been cursed by it. The ants will then eat the toad or frog until only the bones are left. If one secretly touches a woman's back with it without her noticing, she will fall hopelessly in love with one.

144   Toads and frogs are very much used in witchcraft and magic for love charms and aphrodisiac potions. The poisonous nature of the toad is very much emphasized in folklore. If touched, a toad does indeed exude a liquid that, although not dangerous to humans, can cause eczema, a slight inflammation of the skin; smaller animals can be killed by this exudation. In folklore this fact is much exaggerated, and the toad is looked upon as a witch's animal. Its pulverized skin and its legs are the basic ingredients of practically all witch potions.[3] To sum up, the toad is an earth goddess who has power over life and death: It can poison or give life, and it has to do with the love principle. It is brown-green, the color of vegetation and nature.

145   The third line in the verse speaks of *Hutzelbeins Hündchen* — of a paw or dried bone and a little dog. This strange connection becomes clearer if you look up Bolte-Polivka's collection where you will find that in many French parallels, the redeemed princess does not appear as a toad but as a little dog. The foot of a frog brings to mind the paw of a dog. Obviously, there is a shifting or intermingling of motifs for sometimes the princess also appears as a cat or mouse. As a dog, she is much closer to the human realm than as a frog; so this would mean she had been neglected and had regressed to an

---

[3] In Morocco, for example, one finds small, dried animals (lizards, chameleons) hanging in the stalls of the herbalists of magic potions. [Added by translator of the French edition].

unconscious level, but not as low or as far away as a regression to the level of an amphibian would mean. So Dummling finds the lacking feminine element in a nonhuman form, as a cold-blooded animal, or as a warm-blooded mammal. The central position of this large toad, that is surrounded by a ring of smaller toads, shows that along with the feminine, the symbol of totality is constellated.

146   We must now go into the symbolism of the carpet. In European civilization the carpet became known only after we came into contact with the East. For the nomadic Arab tribes, who are still famous for their carpet weaving, the carpets they use in their tents represent the continuity of earth. They serve the feeling of having earth under one's feet. Wherever they go, they first spread out one of their beautiful carpets, usually with a sacred pattern, over which they put their tent. The carpet is the basis upon which they stand, as we do on our earth. It also protects them from the evil influences of foreign soil.

147   All the higher warm-blooded animals, including mankind, have a strong attachment to their own territories.[4] Most animals have an instinct to defend their territory against invaders. Mice have been taken and let loose miles from their homes, but they walk back through all the dangers and difficulties. Only when the chance of survival is nil does a mouse not return, but tries to get a new territory by fighting and driving out another mouse. In its own territory an animal has a kind of quick, intimate knowledge of the whole situation so that it can hide at once. If it sees the shadow of a hawk in a strange territory, it has to look around to find a place to hide and may lose just those seconds required for its escape. Heinrich Hediger, a professor of zoology at Zurich University, has tried to establish the fact that the territorial instinct in animals is derived from mother attachment. Accordingly, an animal's original territory is its mother's body; the young animal grows in and lives on the mother's body, the clearest example being the kangaroo. Instead of remaining in their home territory, many young animals

---

[4] Konrad Lorenz, *On Aggression*, trans. Marjorie Kerr Wilson (London: Routledge, 2002); and Robert Ardrey, *The Territorial Imperative: A Personal Inquiry into the Animal Origins of Property and Nations* (Königstein: Athenäum, 1997).

are carried around by their mothers — on their mother's back, or, like the monkeys, clinging to the fur of their mother's underbelly. These animals leave their mother only by degrees and keep returning to her until they can feed and defend themselves. According to Hediger, this instinct is later transferred from its mother's body to its territory. We know that when animals are caught and transported, they make a home territory of their transport cage. If it is destroyed and they are put into a new "home" right away, they may die. An animal's transport box must always remain available in the new place so that the animal can slowly acclimatize itself to its new home. Again, it is the feeling of the mother's womb — a habitat with a maternal quality — that is transferred onto the new territory.

148   We are just the same. If you cut off elderly people from their roots, or make them move their homes, they often die. Many cling in an absolutely amazing way to their territory. If you have ever watched your own dreams during a move, you will know that psychological upsets happen in your own psyche. Women, especially, suffer tremendously when they lose their territory, which is why Jung once said that he felt sorry for American women (and how many women are in this situation today) because of how they have to move from one place to another. Men can stand it much better for they have a greater tendency to roam, but for a woman, it is really difficult. In our culture, too, territory is secretly connected to the mother, and for some North African nomadic tribes the carpet is precisely this: the continuity of the maternal soil. As they possess very little and live practically every night on a different bit of sand, they carry their symbolic territory with them.

149   Islamic, and also Jewish, people may not make an image of their Godhead. Thus, with the exception of verses from the Koran, the elements in their carpets are mostly abstract designs that have a symbolic meaning. Most often used are motifs of the gazelle, the camel, the tree of life of Paradise, the sacred lamp, and so on, that have been transformed into geometrical designs. Carpet specialists can read these patterns and are able to say that this is a lamp and that is really a gazelle. Most of the elements in Oriental carpets refer

to religious ideas: The lamp refers to illumination through Allah's wisdom, and the gazelle represents the human soul seeking the Godhead. So, for these people, the carpet represents not only Mother Earth but also the inner basis of their whole life. Carpets very often appear in this way in the dreams of modern people. Think, for example, of the quotation from Faust, spoken by the spirit who visits Faust at the beginning of Part One:

150

> So schaff ich am sausenden Webstuhl der Zeit
> Und wirke der Gottheit lebendiges Kleid.
> (Thus at Time's whirling loom I ply
> And weave the vesture of God.)

151 I think Goethe got this motif from Pherekydes's creation myth that speaks of the earth as an enormous sort of cloak with woven patterns in it, spread over a world oak.[5] From these amplifications, you see that the woven cloak or carpet with its designs is often used as a symbol for the complex symbolic patterns of life and the secret designs of fate. The woven textile represents the greater pattern of our life, which we do not know while we are living it. We constantly build our lives upon our ego decisions, and it is only in old age when we look back that we see a continuous pattern woven into it. Some people who are more introspective know it a bit before the end of their lives and are secretly convinced that things have a pattern, that they are led, and that there is a kind of secret design behind the ephemeral actions and decisions of a human being. Actually, we turn towards dreams and the unconscious because we want to find out more about our life pattern in order to make fewer mistakes and to not cut into our own inner carpet with our knives, but to fulfill our destiny instead of resisting it.

152   This purposiveness of an individual life pattern, that gives one a feeling of meaningfulness, is very often symbolized in the carpet. Generally, carpets, especially Oriental ones, have complicated meandering patterns, like those you might follow when in a dreamy

---

[5] Cf. Jung, *Archetypes and the Collective Unconscious*, vol. 9/I, *CW*; and Eliade, *Shamanism*.

mood, when you feel that life goes up and down, moving forward and then veering off again. Only if you look from afar, from a certain objective distance, do you realize that there is a pattern of wholeness to it. Therefore, it is not off the point that at the palace where the feminine principle has been forgotten, there are no precious carpets. They need a new carpet for they urgently need to once again find the pattern of life.

153   The fairytale tells us that the inventions of the unconscious and the secret pattern that is woven into a person's life are infinitely more intelligent and subtle than human consciousness: They are more subtle and superior to anything man could invent. One is again and again overwhelmed by the genius of that unknown mysterious something in our psyche that is the inventor of our dreams. It picks elements from our impressions throughout the day, from something the dreamer has read the evening before in the paper, or from a childhood memory, and makes a nice kind of "potpourri" out of it. Only when you have interpreted its meaning do you see the subtlety and the genius of each dream composition. Every night we have that carpet weaver at work within us, who makes those fantastically subtle patterns, so subtle that, unfortunately often after an hour's attempt to interpret them, we are unable to find out the meaning. We are just too clumsy and stupid to follow the genius of that unknown spirit of the unconscious that invents dreams. But we can understand that this carpet is more subtly woven than any human could ever achieve.

154   Naturally, the king and the two elder brothers do not accept this first test, and so the second time they have to find the most beautiful ring. Once again, the ritual of the three feathers follows, and the elder brothers bring an ordinary iron cartwheel with its nails pulled out, being too lazy to look for anything better, while Dummling goes down to the toad and gets a beautiful golden ring, sparkling with diamonds and precious stones. The ring, as a circular object, is one of the many symbols of the Self. But in fairytales there are so many symbols of the Self that we have to find out what specific function of the Self is emphasized in this particular symbol. We know that

the Self, being the central regulating factor of the unconscious psyche, has an enormous number of different functional aspects. It preserves the balance or, as we saw before with the hero symbol, it builds up an ego attitude that is in the right balance with the Self. The symbol of a ball, for instance, would represent more the capacity to effect movement out of itself. To the primitive mind, a ball was an object with an amazing propensity for moving according to its own volition. As the ball becomes the thing that can move without any outside impetus, natural man suppresses the small detail of an initial push being needed. The ball moves according to its own inner life-impulse and keeps moving through all the vicissitudes and frictions and difficulties of the material world. Therefore, it stands for this unique factor in the unconscious psyche that Jung discovered: its capacity for creating movement born out of itself. This means that the unconscious psyche is not a system that reacts only to already existing outer factors; rather, it can produce something new out of itself without any traceable causal impulse. It has a capacity for spontaneous movement that, in many philosophies and religions, is otherwise only attributed to the Divinity, to the Divine Creator of the world. The psyche has something of this divine power in itself. Thus, for instance, we can analyze someone for a long time and the dreams seem to discuss certain obvious life problems and the person feels all right, but suddenly he has a dream out of the blue that starts something completely new. A new creative idea that one could not expect or explain causally has arisen, as if the psyche had decided to bring up something new. These are the great, meaningful, and healing psychological events in one's life. This power is symbolized by a sphere or ball. This is why in fairytales the hero so often follows a rolling apple or a rolling sphere to some mysterious goal. He simply follows a spontaneous Self-impulse of his own psyche. I have amplified the symbol of the ball in order to clarify its difference to the ring and to show that the description "a symbol of the Self" is not specific enough. One always has to go into the particular function of each symbol of the Self.

155   Besides its quality of roundness that makes it an image of the Self, a ring generally has two further functions: It symbolizes either a connection or a fetter. The marriage ring, for instance, can mean connectedness to one's partner, but it can also mean a fetter — which is why some people take it off and put it in their pocket when they go traveling. So whether it is a fetter or a meaningful connection depends upon your own feeling towards it. If a man gives a ring to a woman (whether he knows it or not), he expresses the wish to be connected to her in a supra-personal way, not just in the manner of an ephemeral love affair. He wants to say, "This is forever. It is eternal." A ring means a connection via the Self, not only via wavering ego-moods. Thus, in the Catholic world, marriage is a sacrament. The connection is not only that of two egos making up their minds to have, as Jung expressed it, "A little financial society for the bringing up of children." If a marriage is more than that, it means the recognition that something supra-personal — or in religious language, divine — enters into it. A connection like this has quite a different meaning to that of being in love or of expressing the coming together of two people to pursue their common interests. The ring expresses an eternal connection through the Self.

156   Whenever an analyst has to cope with marriage troubles, or has to accompany a human being through the last terrifying steps to the guillotine of his wedding day, very interesting dreams often point in the direction of the marriage being necessary for the sake of individuation. This interest on the part of the unconscious gives the person in question a profoundly different basic attitude towards the everyday troubles that may arise in the marriage. One then knows that, for better or worse, it is one's fate asking one to work through to a higher level of consciousness, and that one cannot just throw one's marriage over the first time something upsets one. This is secretly expressed by the wedding ring, which symbolizes a connection through the Self.

157   In general, a ring means any kind of connectedness. Within this spectrum, it sometimes has quite different aspects. Before performing many religious rituals, people must take off their rings.

No Roman or Greek priest was allowed to perform any sacramental act without first removing all of his rings. He had to connect with the Godhead and therefore had to put aside all other connections, i.e., he had to strip himself of all other obligations so that he could be open to only divine influence. In this sense, the image of the ring stands — very often negatively in mythology — for being tied to something to which one should not be tied, for being enslaved by some negative factor, for instance, a demon.[6] In psychological language, being bound in this way would symbolize a state of being fascinated by some emotional unconscious complex and becoming a slave to it.

158   In amplifying the symbolism of the ring, we could include not only rings for the finger but also all other rings, for example, a witch's ring, a magical circle one enters into, or a hoop that one carries. In a broader sense, a ring has the meaning of what Jung describes as a *temenos*, a sacred space set apart either by circumambulation or by establishing a circle upon the ground. A circle like this can be drawn upon the ground. Jung writes about this in detail in *Psychology and Alchemy*. In Greece, a temenos was simply a small sacred place in a wood or on a hill into which one was not allowed to enter without taking certain precautions. It was a place within which it was forbidden to kill. If someone who was being persecuted took refuge within a temenos, he could be neither captured nor killed while there. A temenos is an asylum within which one is *asulos* (inviolable). As a place of the cult of some god, it signifies the territory that belongs to that godhead. Witches' rings have a similar meaning. The magic circle is a piece of marked off earth, a round place reserved for a numinous, archetypal purpose. Such a place has a double function: It protects what is within it and excludes what is outside of it, thereby concentrating upon what is within. This is what these circular forms generally mean. The word *temenos* comes from *temno*, to cut. It indicates that one is being cut or removed from the

---

[6] See, for instance, John Ronald R. Tolkien, *The Lord of the Rings*, 3 vols. (London: Harper Collins, 1993). [Added by the translator of the French edition: "In this story, the ring symbolizes psychic power. The entire epic describes in great detail the obligations that anyone who is in possession of the ring must face."]

meaningless, profane layer of life — that a part of life is being cut out and isolated for a special purpose.

159 The ring in our story is golden. In the planetary system, gold, as a most precious metal, has always been ascribed to the sun and is generally associated with incorruptibility and immortality. It is everlasting and in former times was the only known metal which did not decay or become black or green and resisted all corrosive elements. Gold treasures can be buried in the earth and dug up unharmed after a thousand years, unlike copper or silver or iron. So gold is the immortal, transcendental element. It is the eternal, the divine, and most precious thing. This is why a wedding ring is made of gold: It is meant to last forever and should not be corrupted by any negative earthly influence. Precious stones emphasize this even more. Generally, they symbolize indestructible psychological values.

160 The two elder brothers do not want to accept the fact that the youngest son has also won the second test, so a third one is set. This time the kingdom will belong to the one who brings home the most beautiful wife. Dummling goes down to his toad, but this time the toad is not quite so ready to help. She says, "Well, well, the most beautiful wife! That is not at hand just now, but you shall nevertheless have her!" So it seems to be a little bit more difficult this time. She gives Dummling a yellow scraped-out carrot drawn by six mice. On her orders, he takes one of the toads and puts it into this carrot vehicle. As soon as she sits down and they set off, she turns into a beautiful princess sitting in a beautiful coach. Thus, in order to get this most beautiful woman, he cannot just seize her, as he does the carpet and the ring; he needs to have a special vehicle for her. It becomes clear that the lady toad can only be transformed when she sits in that carrot vehicle, and it begins to move, carrying her toward the king's palace.

161 In other versions, the beautiful girl exists from the very beginning. If you remember, in the Hessian version, Dummling finds a beautiful girl working at a spinning wheel down in the earth; it is only when she comes up that she is a frog. That is a very strange thing, for sometimes she is a toad or a frog in the earth and changes

when she moves upwards, towards the human world. In other versions, she is a beautiful human being while down in the earth, but when she is above, in the ordinary world, she is a frog. When Dummling jumps into a pond with her, she turns into a human being again. This is a relatively frequent variation. We therefore have to go into this symbolism more closely. From the steps that led down into the earth, we concluded that the cult of the mother, or the relationship to the mother principle, must previously have been integrated into the realm of human awareness, but that it later regressed into the unconscious. Our story is concerned with once again bringing up something that previously had been consciously realized in the human realm. The many parallels that tell us of a beautiful woman who is sitting down in the earth waiting for her redemption confirm this hypothesis.

162   The anima — which means for a man the realm of fantasy and the way he relates to the unconscious — was once integrated in the field of consciousness and had reached a human level. Because of unfavorable cultural circumstances, it has nevertheless been shut off and repressed into the unconscious. This explains why this beautiful princess is down in the earth, waiting for somebody to bring her up. It also explains why she is looked upon, and appears, as a frog. On the earth, at the king's court, a conscious attitude rules that scorns the irrational and sees the anima only as a frog. This means that in the conscious realm an attitude prevails which has a contemptuous "it is nothing but…" outlook upon the phenomenon of Eros. In these circumstances, the anima appears to be a frog in the eyes of the men at the king's court. A modern example of this can be found in Freudian theory in which the phenomenon of Eros is reduced to our biological sex functions. Whatever comes up, it is explained in the "nothing but" terminology of rational theory. From the Freudian standpoint, a Gothic cathedral is only a morbid surrogate for unlived sex, as is proven by its phallic towers![7] This viewpoint denies the world of the anima, an approach that is typical not only of the

---

[7] This statement is derived from a seminar that was held at the C.G. Jung Institute. This theory was further developed. See C.G. Jung, "Symbols and the Interpretation of Dreams," in *The Symbolic Life*, vol. 18, *CW* (Princeton, NJ: Princeton University Press, 1989), chap. 2.

Freudian school. A moral prejudice against Eros, or a repression of the Eros principle for political or other reasons, may also reduce the anima to a frog or a louse or whatever other form and level she may be repressed into. This means that a man's anima becomes as undeveloped as the Eros function of a frog. A frog, however, is not completely unrelated. It is possible to tame frogs, and you can make them take their food from you; they have a certain capacity for relatedness. Men who have a frog anima would behave in much the same way. So we understand why, in the Hessian version, something must be done in order to restore the human nature of the anima. But in our fairytale, the anima firstly appears as a toad that needs a carrot vehicle to bring her up, enabling her to once again become a human being.

163   In the Russian version of the Frog-Princess, Dummling has to introduce his frog-bride to the tsar's court. The hero is horrified to imagine what will happen when she turns up, hopping along in the form of a frog. She begs him to trust her and says that when he hears thunder, he will know that she is putting on her wedding dress. When he sees lightning, he will know that she has finished dressing. The rain will signify her arrival.[8] Shivering with horror, Dummling waits in the thunderstorm for his frog-bride to appear. Then she arrives as a beautiful woman in a golden coach drawn by six horses.

164   So this Russian Dummling has "only" to trust her and be ready to stand by her, even if she appears in a ridiculous and inhuman shape. In other versions, the frog-princess, like the famous frog-prince, asks to be accepted. She asks to eat from Dummling's plate and be taken into his bed, meaning she wants to be fully accepted as a human being in private life, in all her uniqueness and despite the possible loathing this may engender. That is the price. Only then does she transform herself into a human being. So we can say that in all the different variations, the frog-princess is redeemed through trust, acceptance, and love.

---

[8] Toads are connected to the moon and to rain. In China, they eat the demons of drought. (Added by the translator of the French edition.)

165   But in our story, it is not of primary importance for the frog-princess to be trusted; rather, she needs to be given a vehicle: the carrot. In the *Handwörterbuch des Deutschen Aberglaubens* (Dictionary of German Superstitions), one can read about the sexual significance of the carrot.[9] It is said that when you sow carrot seed in Baden, you say, "I sow carrots, boys and girls, but if anyone steals some of them, may God grant that we have so many that we do not notice it." Sowing carrot seed is like sowing girls and sowing boys. In other parts of the country they say, "Now I sow carrot seed *for* the boys and girls...." There are a lot of other amusing allusions about carrot sowing which all hinge on the fact that carrots seem to be the food of very poor people, so one must always be very generous and say, "I sow these carrots, not only for myself, but for my neighbors as well"; then one harvests a lot. Once, however, a man felt stingy, and he said, "I sow these carrots for myself and my wife!" He got only two when he dug them up. From all of this you can see that the carrot, like most vegetables, has an erotic, and especially a sexual, meaning. You can say that the vehicle that brings up the anima is sex. The carrot vehicle symbolizes the manner in which Eros generally enters a man's consciousness: in the form of sexual fantasies.

166   In some ways, mice have a similar meaning. In Greece, they, and the rat, belong to the sun god Apollo, to the boreal or winter phase of Apollo, to the dark side of the sun principle. In Switzerland, mice are connected to the devil, and Goethe's *Faust* mentions them in this role — as "Der Herr der Ratten und der Mäuse" (lord of rats and mice). In the *Handwörterbuch des Deutschen Aberglaubens*, mice are looked upon as being soul animals. In psychological terms, this would mean that small rodents represent the unconscious personality of a human being. As mentioned above, the soul can leave the body in the form of a bird, but sometimes also as a mouse. In certain verses or rituals, it is said that you should not hurt or insult mice because poor souls might dwell in them. A famous Chinese

---

[9] Cf. Mackensen, *Handwörterbuch des Deutschen Aberglaubens*.

poet describes, to my mind beautifully, what these rodents also mean:

167

Rat in my brain,
I cannot sleep; day and night
You gnaw out of me my life.
I am slowing fading away,
Oh, rat in my brain,
Oh, my bad conscience.
Will you never give me peace again?

168 While the rat and the mouse do not necessarily stand for a bad conscience because of their inherent nature, in this little poem they stand for any worrying thought that unsettles one, that constantly secretly and autonomously gnaws at one's attitude and systematically undermines it. You probably know those sleepless nights when you worry, and every little thing becomes a mountain of difficulty. You cannot sleep, and your worries go around in your head like a mill. It is really very similar to being disturbed by mice. Those damned creatures gnaw and nibble all night; you bang on the wall, and for a moment there is peace, and then they start again. If you have ever gone through that, you will recognize the analogy of the mouse and the worrying thought — a complex that gives you no peace. The mouse represents an obsessive nocturnal thought or fantasy that bites you whenever you want to sleep. It very often also has an erotic quality, which you see in those cartoons in which women stand on tables with their skirts pulled up when a mouse runs about. In this sense, Freudians often interpret mice as sexual fantasies. This can be true when the obsessive gnawing thought is a sexual fantasy, but actually it can mean any kind of obsession that constantly gnaws at one's conscious mind. The carrot, that points towards sex, and the mice, meaning nocturnal worries and autonomous fantasies, carry the anima figure up into the light and can be understood as being the substructure of the anima.

169   As soon as Dummling brings together the young toad and the vehicle, the toad turns into a beautiful woman. In practical terms, this would mean that a man can bring his entire anima up into the light if he has the patience and the courage to accept his nocturnal sex fantasies and to look at what is hidden within them. He would have to let them continue and write them down, allowing for further amplification. If, when doodling, he says, "Now what am I doing here?" and develops the sex fantasy he has expressed in his drawing, often the whole anima problem comes up. If he becomes conscious of this problem and attempts to integrate his anima into his life, she gradually becomes more human and less cold-blooded. The repressed feminine world is able to arise and slowly enter consciousness. The initial trigger, however, is very often some kind of sexual fantasy or an obsession of some kind: the necessity to look at women's curves in the tram, or to watch strip tease shows. If he lets such thoughts come up with whatever they bring with them, a man can, in this way, discover his anima, or rediscover her (if he has repressed her for a while). If a man neglects relatedness, the anima immediately regresses. As soon as the anima becomes unconscious, she becomes obsessive — she becomes a mouse again, so to speak — an intruding fantasy.

170   Let's return to our fairytale. Even the third test does not convince the king and the two elder brothers. In this three-step process lies a classic motif: Three steps are often necessary, and then comes a finale. One often reads that the number three plays a big role in fairytales, but when I count the stages, it is generally four: In the Dummling story, there are three tests: the carpet, the ring, and the lady. But then comes the act of jumping through the ring as the finale. Wherever you look, you will see that this is a typical rhythm in fairytales. There is a three-step sequence that leads to a final event. For instance, a girl loses her lover and has to find him again at the end of the world. She goes firstly to the sun, which shows her the way to the moon, which shows her the way to the night wind. Finally, in the fourth step, she finds her lover.

171   Or the hero comes to three hermits or three giants, or he has to overcome three obstacles. The three are always clear units: 1, 2, 3, with a certain similar repetition, which is why the fourth is so often ignored, for the fourth is not just another additional number unit; it is not another thing of the same kind, but something completely different. It is as if one counted, one, two, three — go! The one, two and three lead up to the real solution that is represented in the fourth. While the three steps point towards something that is in movement — something dynamic — the fourth generally points towards something that comes to rest.

172   In number symbolism, three is considered a masculine number — as all odd numbers are.[10] Since the number one does not count as a number — it is the unique thing and therefore not yet a counting unit — the number three is the first masculine odd number. It represents the dynamism of the one. I refer you to the number symbolism in Jung's paper *A Psychological Approach to the Dogma of the Trinity*.[11] To put it very briefly, the three is generally connected with the flow of movement and thus with time, because there is no time without movement. We all know of the three Norns, the ancient goddesses of fate, who represent past, present, and future. Most of the gods of time are triadic. The three has always the symbolism of movement in it because for movement you need two poles and the exchange of energy between them — for instance, the positive and negative electric poles and the current that equalizes the tension.

173   In mythology, one figure is often accompanied by two followers: Mithras with the Dadophores (torch bearers), or Christ between the two thieves. Such triadic mythological formations stand for the oneness and its polarity; they stand for the one thing which unites, and the opposites as the two poles between which the uniting center appears. A certain difference has to be made between three things of the same kind, or a group of three where the one in the middle is really the whole thing and the two opposites are represented as a

---

[10] Cf. Von Franz, *Number and Time*.
[11] Cf. C.G. Jung, *Psychology and Religion: West and East*, 2nd ed., vol. 11, *CW* (Princeton, NJ: Princeton Press, 1989), chap. 2.

kind of illustration of what that wholeness represents. So there is a dualism and a connecting third thing.

174   Basically, you will never go wrong if you bear in mind that the three has to do with movement and time. Mostly what is meant is an inexorable unilateral movement of life. That is why the story, the peripetia, in fairytales is often divided into three phases, and then comes the fourth as a lysis or catastrophe. The fourth phase leads into a new dimension, one that is not comparable to the previous three steps.

Chapter 6
"The Three Feathers" Completed

175   Dummling brings home his bride who has turned into a beautiful princess whilst in her carrot carriage. Upon their arrival at the king's court, the two elder bothers will again not accept the solution and ask for a fourth and final test. A ring is suspended from the ceiling in the hall and all three brides have to jump through it. The peasant women whom the two other brothers have brought jump and fall, breaking their arms and legs. Probably because of her past life as a frog or toad, only the youngest son's bride jumps through the ring with great elegance, so that all protest is abandoned and the youngest son gets the crown and reigns with wisdom for a long time.

176   Earlier in the story we spoke about the ring as a symbol of union. In its positive meaning, it stands for a consciously chosen obligation towards some divine power, that is, towards the Self. In its negative aspect, it expresses the fascination of being caught, for instance, of being caught in one's emotions, or in a complex: One is caught in a vicious circle. Our fairytale presents yet another aspect of a ring's symbolism, namely, jumping through a ring or hoop. This test involves two simultaneous skills: One has to jump high while simultaneously aiming at the center in order to get through it. In folklore, there is mention of old spring festivals in which young men on horseback had to spear the center of a ring — a spring fertility rite and acrobatic test all in one. Aiming at the center of a ring in a contest brings us closer to the meaning of this symbolic act. Though it seems rather remote, a parallel can be drawn to the art of archery in Zen Buddhism.[1] Here, too, the idea is to aim at the center, not in the extraverted way Westerners would do it using their physical skill

---

[1] Eugen Herrigel, *Zen in the Art of Archery* (Eastford: Martino Fine Books, 2020).

and conscious concentration, but by a form of deep meditation by means of which the archer puts himself inwardly into his own center (what we would call the Self), from whence, quite naturally, he can hit the outer target.[2] In this way, Zen Buddhist archers can effortlessly hit the target with their eyes shut and without taking aim. The aim of this exercise is to help one find one's way to one's own inner center without being distracted by one's thoughts, ambition, or ego-impulses.

177   As far as I know, jumping through a burning ring is no longer practiced, except in the circus, where it is one of the most popular tricks. Tigers and other wild animals have to jump through burning rings. The more undomesticated the animal, the more exciting it is to see it jump through a ring, a motif to which I shall return later. Aiming at the center of a ring is not difficult to interpret. Although it occurs in an outer symbolic action, it corresponds to the secret of being able to find the inner center of one's personality. The aim is the same as the aim of Zen Buddhist archery. There is, however, a difficulty. The one who jumps has to leave the earth — leave reality — and reach the center in a movement through midair. So, once airborne, the anima-princess figure must jump to just the right height to get through the center of the ring. It is emphasized that she can do this well, while the peasant girls find it difficult. They are awkward and fall and break their arms and legs, as if the force of gravity was too strong for them.

178   This points to a very subtle problem in connection with the realization of the anima. Men who know nothing about Depth Psychology tend to project the anima onto a real woman, experiencing her entirely on the outside. But if, through psychological introspection, they realize that the attraction exerted upon them by the anima is not only an outer factor but is something that they carry within themselves — an inner image of a feminine being that is the true ideal and the soul's Guide — then often the ego believes itself to be caught in a pseudo-conflict between the inner and outer realms. It says, "I don't know if this is about my inner anima or if it

---

[2] von Franz, "The White Parrot," in *Individuation in Fairy Tales*, 1–70.

concerns the real woman on the outside. Should I follow up an anima fascination in the external world, or should I see it as an inner figure and take her as being purely symbolic?" When men talk like this, there is always this undertone of something being "purely symbolic." With our strong disbelief in the reality of the psyche, there usually comes the question, "Must I realize it only within? May I not have something on the outside as well, something concrete?" Here we see how consciousness, with its extroverted bias, gets caught in a false conflict between concrete outer and symbolic inner realization and, in this way, artificially divides the phenomenon of the anima.

179   This occurs if a man cannot lift his anima away from the earth, if she is unable to jump, as the frog lady can, but rather is like an oafish peasant. If a man finds himself in a conflict like this, it indicates a lack of differentiation in his feelings; it is a typical conflict, raised not by the feeling function but by thinking, that makes an artificial contrast between inside and outside, between ego and object. Actually, the answer is that there is neither the outside nor the inside because it has to do with the reality of the psyche per se, and that is neither outside nor inside. It is both and neither. It is precisely the *anima* that wants to be realized as a reality per se. If the anima comes to one from the outside, she has to be accepted on the outside; if she comes from within, she is to be accepted there. The task is not to make any artificial and clumsy difference between the two realms. The anima is a unique phenomenon, the phenomenon of life. She represents the flow of life in a man's psyche. He has to follow its torturous ways that move precisely between the borders of inside and outside.

180   Another aspect of this pseudo-conflict can be found in the question, "Must I think of my anima with spiritual devotion? For instance, pray to the Virgin Mary, instead of looking at a beautiful woman's legs and loving her sexually?" There is no such difference! The upper and lower are one and, like all contents of the unconscious, have a whole range of what we call spiritual and instinctual manifestations. In their archetypal appearance, both

factors form a oneness, and it is only consciousness that cuts them apart. If a man has really learned to contact his anima, this whole problem collapses for then the anima will manifest immediately. The man will remain concentrated upon her reality and will look away from such a pseudo-conflict. To put it in very plain and simple words, he will constantly try to follow this feeling, his Eros side, without considering any other elements. In this way, he will walk on the razor's edge through seemingly incompatible worlds.

181   Keeping to what Jung calls "the reality of the psyche" is like an acrobatic achievement, because our consciousness has the natural tendency to be pulled into unilateral interpretations, by always formulating a program or a recipe, instead of simply following the flow of life that runs between the opposites. There is only one loyalty or constancy within all that: a loyalty to the inner reality of the anima. This is beautifully expressed in the jumping through the ring: While the anima is in a midair position, she aims accurately at the center and moves through it.

182   Another typical anima conflict the unconscious raises to force a man to differentiate his Eros is the marital triangle. When he gets into this conflict, he is liable to say, "If I cut off the other woman, I am betraying my own feeling for the sake of conventionality. If I run away from my wife and children with the woman on whom my anima projection has fallen, then I am behaving irresponsibly and am following a mood which will collapse fairly soon, as one knows. I cannot do both, but also I cannot prolong an impossible situation forever!" If the anima wants to impose itself upon a man's consciousness, she often brings about such a conflict. His wife's animus will say, "You must make a decision!" And the girlfriend's animus blows up and says, "I cannot just hang on like this!" Everyone and everything push him towards making wrong decisions. Remaining loyal to the reality of the psyche is the only possible solution here. In general, the anima tends to maneuver a man into a situation from which there is no escape.

183   Jung said that being in a situation where there is no way out is the classical beginning of the process of individuation. It is *meant*

for one to be in a situation without a solution: The unconscious wants the hopeless conflict in order to put ego consciousness up against the wall, so that the man's ego realizes that whatever he decides, it will be the wrong decision. Thus, the superiority of the ego, which always acts from the illusion that it has the responsibility of decision-making, will be overcome. It would, of course, be equally wrong to make no decision, to just let everything run its course, and wriggle out of it, for then nothing happens. But if a man is ethical enough to suffer to the very core of his personality, then, generally, the Self manifests because of the insolubility of the conscious situation.

184   In religious terms, one could say that a situation with no solution is meant to force one to rely on an act of God. In psychological language, a situation like this, that the anima arranges with great skill in a man's life, is meant to drive one's ego into a condition in which it is capable of experiencing the Self, insofar as it is able to be inwardly open to an interference by the *tertium quod non datur* (the third, which is not given, that is, the unknown thing). The anima is, as Jung says, the guide towards realization of the Self, sometimes in a very painful manner. When thinking of the anima as a soul guide, we are apt to think of Beatrice leading Dante up to paradise, but we should not forget that Dante's redemption came only after he had gone through hell and Purgatory.[3] Normally, the anima does not take a man by the hand and lead him right up to paradise; she firstly puts him into a hot cauldron where he is nicely roasted for a while.

185   The anima in our story aims at the center, while the peasant women represent an undifferentiated, clumsy attitude that is overly glued to the idea of concrete reality, which is why they do not reach the center: They represent a too "primitive" and undifferentiated feeling attitude. In this connection, I would recommend Jung's talk *The Symbolic Life.*[4] There he points out that we are all caught in rationalism: Our rational outlook on life includes being reasonable,

---

[3] The traveler, Dante, arrives in the depths of hell, in the center of the earth, where he discovers Lucifer's body. He follows this body and discovers that gravity has changed direction, causing him to exit at the antipodes. Then he climbs the Mountain of Purgatory and from there he enters the heavenly realm, into its center: the rose where the divinity resides. [Added by the translator of the French edition].
[4] Cf. Jung, *Symbolic Life*, vol. 18, *CW*, chap. 3.

but this excludes all symbolism. Life for people who are still embedded in the living symbolism of some religious tradition is much richer than our exclusively rational existence is. As Jung himself discovered and demonstrated, one can find one's way back to some living symbolism — not to the traditional symbolism, which is lost to us modern people, but to the still-living function of the soul. The soul is the source that generates symbols. We get to it by attending to the unconscious and to our dreams. By attending to one's dreams and by really taking them into account, the unconscious of modern man can rebuild symbolic life. But this presupposes that you do not interpret your dreams purely intellectually but really incorporate them into your life. Then there will be a restoration of your "symbolic life." It is no longer confined within the framework of a collective religion but can unfold within the individual. One no longer lives merely with the reasonableness of one's ego and its rational decisions; rather, together with one's ego, one lives embedded in the flow of psychic life that expresses itself in symbolic form and requires symbolic action.

186   Essentially, we have to find out what our own psyche proposes as a symbolic life form in which we can live. Here, Jung insists on something that he practiced in his own life: When an archetypal dream symbol comes up in a dominating form, one should take the trouble to reproduce it in a picture, even if one does not know how to draw. One should cut it in stone, even if one is not a sculptor — in other words, one should relate to this unknown content in some "real" manner. One should not leave one's analytical hour forgetting all about it, letting the ego organize the rest of the day: One should stay with the symbols of one's dreams throughout the day and try to see where they want to enter the reality of one's life. This is what Jung means when he speaks of the necessity of living the "symbolic life."

187   The anima is the guide and, simultaneously, the essence of this realization of a symbolic life. A man who has not understood and assimilated his anima problem is not capable of living this inner rhythm; his conscious ego and his mind can tell him nothing about this. In the variation of our fairytale from Hessian, the frog is neither

immediately nor permanently transformed into a beautiful woman; quite the contrary, for in the upper world she appears in the form of a frog, whereas in the lower world she is a beautiful girl. In the upper world there is a final test, for the frog calls out, "umschling mich" (embrace me) and "versenk mich" (immerse yourself). "Versenken" implies lowering something into the water or into the earth. In its reflexive form "sich versenken" — used in mystical language – it means to go into a deep meditation. One sinks down into one's inner water or earth, into one's own abyss, one's inner depths.

188   The frog anima makes this mysterious call, and Dummling understands it. He embraces the frog and jumps with her into the pool; in this moment she transforms herself into a beautiful woman, and they come out together as a human couple. If we take that quite naïvely, we can say that Dummling has to follow her into *her* kingdom, accepting *her* way of life. As amphibians, frogs and toads go through a stage of being larvae in water and, after a meta-morphosis, they live on land. They represent that moment in evolution when an animal leaves its maternal waters in order to find a terrestrial habitat, while remaining related to the element of water without which no amphibian can live or reproduce. Symbolically speaking, a frog represents the moment when human consciousness comes face to face with the unconscious.

189   The princess is a frog who likes to jump constantly into water, where she feels happy and at ease. The prince who jumps into the water with his princess in his arms participates in her life in water. So it can be said that the bridegroom follows the bride into *her* home, instead of the other way around. Because he accepts her as she is, she is transformed into a human being. In psychological terms, acceptance of the frog and the frog's life means jumping into the inner world, sinking-down into one's inner reality. Once again, we reach the same conclusion: It is the anima's intention to convert rational consciousness (embodied in the male ego) to acceptance of the symbolic life. It should trustingly surrender to it without any ifs or buts, without any rational objections, and say, "In God's name, whatever happens, I will jump in and realize it." This needs courage

and naïveté. It means the sacrifice of one's intellectual and rational attitude, which is difficult for women, but much more difficult for a man because it goes against his conscious tendencies, especially those of modern Western man.

190   When the anima becomes human, it is a meeting of the opposites: He goes towards her, and she comes up towards him. If the tension between the conscious situation and the unconscious content is too great, any gesture from the one side generally improves the other as well. Very often, men dream, for instance, of their anima as a prostitute; they suppose that she is too low down and do not want to go as far as that as it is against their ethical principles. If a man overcomes such stiffened prejudices and makes a generous gesture towards the lower part of his personality, there is often a change: His anima comes up onto a higher level. One should not, however, tell people this for it would lessen the merit of the sacrifice that has to be made without any calculation. But if one is courageous and honest, very often a miracle happens, and this so-called low part of the personality, which has only been banished to that state by the haughtiness of the conscious attitude, comes up onto a human level.

191   There is a third, a Russian, version of our fairytale of the Frog Princess. Her redemption in it takes a different form that throws new light upon the "symbolic life." It goes as follows:

192

> There was a tsar who had a wife. They had three sons who were like falcons: beautiful young men. One day, the tsar called them together and said, "My sons, my falcons, the time has come for you to find wives." He told them to take their silver bows and copper arrows and that they should take aim with them in foreign lands, and at whatever door the arrow fell, there each should find his bride. Two arrows fell into other tsars' courts, and those men found relatively nice women. But Ivan Tsarevitch's arrow fell into a nearby swamp, and there he found a frog with his arrow. He said, "Give me back my arrow." The frog replied, "I will return your arrow,

but only on condition that you marry me." So Ivan Tsarevitch returned to the court and cried and related what had happened. The tsar said, "Well, that's your bad luck, but you cannot get out of it: You must marry the frog." So the eldest son married a tsar's daughter, the second son a prince's daughter, and the third son married the green frog from the swamp.

193 Many things are different in this story. There is a feminine influence at the court, so the king is not at all hostile to marriage with a frog; there is not such tension between male and female, or between acceptance and nonacceptance of frog life. But naturally Ivan is very unhappy.

194 One day, the tsar wants to see which of his daughters-in-law can weave the most beautiful towel. Ivan goes home and cries, but the frog hops after him and tells him not to cry, but to lie down and go to sleep and it will be all right. As soon as Ivan is asleep, she throws off her frog skin and goes out into the yard and calls and whistles. Her three maids appear and weave the towels. When Ivan wakes up, they are given to him by his frog-wife, who has again assumed her frog skin. Ivan has never seen such towels in his life, and he takes them to the court, and everybody is deeply impressed. Then there is another test: Whoever makes the best buckwheat cake will win. Once again, this is made in the night while Ivan is asleep. The tsar then tells his sons to come to a dinner party on a certain day together with their wives. Ivan again goes home crying, but the frog-bride says he should not worry but should go on ahead. When he sees rain beginning to fall, he should know that his wife is washing herself. When the lightning comes, he should know that she is putting on her ball gown for the court. When he hears thunder, he should know that she is on her way. The dinner party begins, and the two other wives are there, beautifully dressed. Ivan is very

nervous. A terrific thunderstorm begins. They all mock him and ask where his bride is. When the rain starts, he says, "Now my dear woman is washing herself," and when there is lightning, he says, "Now she is putting on her ball gown." He does not believe it and is in despair, but when it thunders, he says, "Now my little dove is coming." And at that moment a beautiful coach with six fiery horses arrives, and out of it steps a most beautiful girl — so beautiful that everyone falls silent and feels quite shy.

195   At the dinner table, the other two daughters-in-law notice something very strange for the beautiful girl puts a part of her food into her sleeves. The other two brides think this is very odd, but that it may be good manners, and they do the same thing. When the dinner is over, there is music and dancing. The former frog-girl dances with Ivan Tsarevitch, and she is so light and dances so beautifully that she hardly seems to touch the floor. As she dances, she waves her right arm, and out of it falls a little bit of food that is transformed into a garden with a pillar in it. Around this a tomcat circles, then it climbs up it and sings folksongs. When it comes down, it tells fairytales. The girl goes on dancing and makes a gesture with her left hand, and there appears a beautiful park with a little river in it and on the river there are swans. Everybody is astonished at the miracle, as if they were little children. The other sisters begin to dance, but when they throw out their right arm, a bone comes out and hits the tsar on the forehead. When they fling out their left hand, water shoots into his eyes.

196   Ivan looks in amazement at his wife and wonders how such a beautiful girl could emerge out of a green frog. He goes into the room where she slept and sees the frog skin lying there. He picks it up and throws it into the fire. Then he goes back to the court, and they go on amusing themselves till morning, when Ivan goes home with his wife. When they get home, his

wife goes to her room and cannot find her frog skin. At last, she calls out and asks Ivan if he has seen her dress. "I burnt it," says Ivan. "Oh, Ivan," she says, "what have you done? If you had not touched it, I would have been yours forever. But now we must separate — perhaps forever!" She cries and cries, and then says, "Good-bye! Seek me in the thirtieth foreign kingdom, where Baba Yaga, the great witch, and her bones are." Then she claps her hands and changes into a cuckoo and flies out of the window. Ivan grieves bitterly. Then he takes his silver bow and fills a sack with bread, hangs bottles over his shoulder, and goes on his long quest.

197 Ivan walks for many years. He meets an old man who gives him a ball of thread and tells him he should follow it to Baba Yaga. Ivan spares the life of a bear, a fish, and a bird that beg him to have pity on them. He gets into all sorts of difficulties, but the fish and falcon and bear help him. Finally, at the end of the world in the Thirtieth Kingdom, he comes to an island on which there is a forest. In the forest there is a glass palace. Ivan goes into the palace and opens an iron door, but nobody is inside. He opens a silver door, but there is nobody in the room, so he opens a third door made of gold, and behind this door sits his wife, combing flax. She looks so woebegone and worn out from her work that she is dreadful to look at. But when she sees Ivan, she falls on his neck and says, "Oh my beloved, how I have longed for you. You have arrived just in time. Had you come just a little later, you might never have seen me again." And she cries for joy. Although Ivan does not know whether he is in this world or the next, they embrace and kiss. Then she changes herself into a cuckoo, takes Ivan under her wing, and flies back. When they arrive home, she changes again into human form and says, "It was my father who put a curse on me and who gave me to a dragon to serve for three years, but now I have paid the penalty." So they came

home and lived happily together and praised God, who had helped them.[5]

198   In our Russian version, the anima figure performs this fantastic magic not by jumping through a ring, but with the food that she puts into her sleeve. When she moves her right arm, the food is transformed into a garden with a tomcat that sings songs and tells fairytales. When she moves her left hand, she creates paradise. Even more clearly than in the version from Hessian, we see here that it is the anima that creates the symbolic life. She transforms ordinary food into spiritual food, generates art and mythological tales, and she restores paradise, a kind of archetypal world of fantasy. The tomcat represents a nature spirit that is the creator of folk songs and fairytales. It also shows the close connection of the anima (as a muse) with man's capacity for artistic work — the anima is the bridge to the world of creative imagination.

199   The dancing, that creates a kind of *fata morgana* — a fantasy world — is a similar motif to jumping through the ring. Both activities evoke the symbolic life: One follows one's dreams, day fantasies, and impulses that come up from the unconscious. Fantasy gives life a glow and a color that a too-rational outlook destroys. *Fantasy* is not just whimsical ego-nonsense: It comes from the depths of the unconscious. It constellates symbolic situations that give life a deeper meaning. Here again, the other women take this secret too concretely. Just as the peasant women could not jump through the ring and broke their arms and legs, the daughters-in-law also fail for they put food in their sleeves for the wrong reason — for ambition. Finally, a new situation arises: Ivan makes a mistake by burning his wife's frog skin. That the anima first appears in an animal skin, either as a fish or mermaid, or, most frequently, as a bird, before she turns into a human being is a most widespread motif to be found in completely different connections in many other fairytales. Generally, her lover keeps her former animal skin or bird

---

[5] August von Löwis of Menar, *Russian Folktales*, ed. Reinhold Olesch (London: Bell, 1971).

garment. The woman has children, and everything seems to be in order, but unfortunately the husband insults his wife one day by calling her a mermaid, or a goose, or whatever she was before. She rushes to the old garment, puts it on again, and disappears. Her husband must then go on a long quest to find her again, or she disappears forever, and he dies. In such stories, one feels it would have been better if the man had burnt the skin. But in this Russian story, the opposite is the case. Burning the skin is the wrong thing to do. In the Grimms' tale called "Hans and the Hedgehog," in which a son is cursed and is turned into a hedgehog, the bride's servant burns the skin of the hedgehog. This frees the son, who gives thanks for being redeemed. So the burning of the animal skin is not in itself necessarily destructive; it depends on the context.

200 We do not know why the burning of the skin causes the wife to fly away. We can only imagine that she must go into the night and atone for her sins because of her father's curse. Because its fulfilment is interrupted, the punishment becomes more definite. But this is speculation; the story gives no explanation. The motif of burning animal skin belongs to the many rituals of transformation by fire. In most mythological accounts, fire has a purifying and transforming quality. In alchemy fire is used — as some texts say, literally — to "burn away all superfluities," so that only the indestructible nucleus remains. Consequently, the alchemists burn most of the substances first, destroying what can be destroyed. Whatever remained was seen as a symbol of immortality — the solid kernel that survives everything. Fire is the great transformer. In certain Gnostic texts, fire is also called the great judge for it decides what is worthy of survival and what should be destroyed.

201 In its psychological meaning, fire symbolizes the "heat" of emotional reactions and affects. Without the fire of emotion, no development takes place, and no higher consciousness can be reached, which is why God says, "because thou art lukewarm, and neither cold nor hot, I will spew thee out of my mouth."[6] If someone in analysis is dispassionate about it and does not suffer — if there is

---

[6] Cf. The Bible, Revelations, 3:16.

neither the fire of despair nor hatred, rage, annoyance, or anything of that kind — one can be pretty sure that not much will be constellated, and it will be a "blah-blah" kind of analysis forever. Even if it is destructive, fire — conflicts, hatred, jealousy, or any other affect — speeds up the maturing process. In this sense, it is indeed a "judge" and clarifies things. People who have fire get into difficulties easily, but at least they try something. The more fire there is, the more danger there is of there being destructive effects from emotional outbursts, from all sorts of mischief and devilry, but, at the same time, this is what keeps the process going. If the fire dies, everything is lost. This is why the alchemists always said one must never let one's fire go out. The lazy adept who allows his fire to go out is the person who only nibbles at analytical treatment but never goes into it wholeheartedly. He has no "fire," and therefore nothing happens. So fire is indeed the great judge who determines the difference between the corruptible and the incorruptible, between what is essential and what is not essential. Thus, fire has a sacred and transforming quality in all magical and religious rituals.

202   In many myths, however, fire is the great destroyer, for example, when a myth depicts the destruction of the world by fire. As a rule, those dreams in which a whole town is burned down, or your own house is burned to the ground, indicate an already existing affect that has become completely out of control. Whenever an emotion overruns one's self-control, the motif of a destructive fire appears. Have you ever done horrible, irremediable things while in an affect? Have you ever written a letter that you would give anything not to have written? Or said something because of which you could bite out your tongue? Perhaps you have done destructive things through emotion — something you cannot mend, something you have ruined forever, for example, a relationship with another human being. Declarations of war — often made in a state of affect — set in motion a process of destruction that leads to the conflagration of the world. As one knows from mass phenomena, destructive affect is exceedingly infectious. Someone who blows a fuse and gives way to destructive emotion can generally pull many other people into it:

Mass outbursts in which people are lynched or shot occur in such situations, all because of a sudden fire of affect getting loose. There you see, quite literally, the fearful destructiveness of fiery emotion. You find it also in psychotic constellations where, underneath a rigid surface, terrific emotions are piled up. An outburst is often represented as a huge conflagration: an individual gets into a state of excitement and becomes so dangerous to himself and others that he has to be temporarily interned.[7]

203   The burning of the frog skin indicates the destructive effect of fire, but we must also take into consideration the fact that the frog is a cold-blooded animal and a water creature. Water is the opposite of fire, and the princess is a creature that dwells in moisture. This is probably why the application of fire to her skin is so destructive. It destroys the princess's water quality. What does it mean psychologically if a man applies destructive fire to his "moist," creative anima? We have seen that the anima in our fairytale — and also in practical life — represents the gift of poetic fantasy, the ability to create symbolic forms of life. If, therefore, the hero sets her skin on fire, it would mean a too analytical, too impulsive, too passionate use of creative fantasy. Many people grab their own fantasies and pull them too eagerly into the light of consciousness and interpret them at once with too much intensity. This destroys their secret inner life.

204   Creativity sometimes needs the protection of darkness and asks to be temporarily ignored. This is reflected in the natural tendency of many artists and writers to not show their paintings or writings before they are finished. Passionate reactions such as "Oh, this is wonderful!" to an unfinished work, even though they are positive, can destroy the *chiaroscuro*, the mystical hidden weaving of fantasy that the artist needs. Only when the work is finished can an artist expose it to the light of consciousness and to the emotional reaction of others. If you notice an unconscious fantasy coming up within you, it is wise to not interpret it at once. Do not say that you know

---

[7] Fire dreams are relatively frequent. They reveal dangerous situations. If one succeeds in not panicking, the conflict can be gradually integrated. Then a new attitude, a new order, can come about. Cf. Von Franz, *Golden Ass*, 114–18.

what it is and force it into consciousness. Just let it live with you, leaving it in the half-dark; carry it with you and watch where it is going or what it is driving at. Later, you will look back and wonder what you were doing all that time. You will realize you were nursing a strange fantasy that led to an unexpected goal. For instance, if you do some painting and have the idea that you could add this and that, do not think, "I know what that means!" If you do, then push the thought away and, before you jump at its essential meaning, give yourself to it more and more so that the whole web of symbols expands in all its ramifications. When people do active imagination in analysis, I generally only listen. One can analyze them, as one would a dream, only at the special request of the analysand, or if the fantasies are too overflowing and therefore need cutting down, or if they have come to a certain end. It is much better not to analyze them while they are going on, for if you do, they will catch you and you will think you know what they are about.[8]

205   If an unconscious fantasy or some other content is especially fiery and is heavily laden with affect, it will push through to consciousness, no matter what. But there are certain fantasies that are more "froglike": They come up during the day as a kind of playful thought. In an idle moment, you light a cigarette and a strange fantasy comes, but without much energy attached to it. If you jump at such thoughts in a fiery way, you will destroy them. Like the little creatures — dwarves, and so on — you must not look at them; let them just be there, and do not disturb their secret work. Our frog-woman belongs more to this latter category of creatures for her spirit — her tomcat — sings folk songs and recites fairytales. This is an artistic, playful spirit that inspires, and it could be destroyed if approached too directly. This is probably why Ivan made such a big mistake in burning the frog skin. By doing so, he delayed the true redemption of his anima.

206   That the anima can be found again at the end of the world is a typical motif in fairytales. A man meets his destined bride and, by

---

[8] Cf. Marie-Louise von Franz, "Active Imagination in the Psychology of C.G. Jung," in *Psychotherapy* (Boston: Shambhala, 1993), 146–62; and Barbara Hannah, *Encounters with the Soul* (Asheville: Chiron Publications, 2015).

some mistake, loses her again, and then he has to go on an endless journey into the underworld and through the seven heavens to find her again. This double rhythm of finding and losing corresponds to the pattern of the first apparent blossoming at the beginning of analysis. People who have been stuck in a neurotic conscious attitude for a long time and have thereby lost contact with the flow of life, and who have lost hope of ever getting out of their neurotic rut, experience a breakthrough in analysis. When they come into analysis and receive the warm concern of another human being and, through dreams, suddenly come into contact with the unconscious, or a prospective dream shows that, in spite of the apparently hopeless aspect of life in consciousness, there is an irrational, positive possibility in the unconscious, there is often a remarkable blossoming after the first hours of analysis: The symptoms disappear, and the individual experiences a miraculous healing. Never fall for that! In only about five percent of the cases does this last. In all other cases, the whole misery flows in again, and the symptoms return.

207 Such an initial blossoming usually occurs when the faulty conscious neurotic attitude is far away from the unconscious life tendencies, making it impossible to link the two sides. Initially, this link takes place — things seem to now be all right — but then the opposites stiffen again and everything returns to how it was. Healing has really only taken place when there is a constant state of relationship between consciousness and the unconscious, and not when, through a relationship, a spark flies over. There has to be a condition of continual relationship with the other side. Generally, it takes a lot of time to establish a constant connection, and only then can you say that a healing cure is really solidified and safe from any relapse.

208 This first blossoming is an archetypal event. I have often asked myself why the unconscious or nature — or whatever we want to call it — plays such a cruel trick on people. It firstly cures them, and then lets them relapse. Why should one hang a good sausage under a dog's nose and then take it away? That is not nice. But I have realized that there is a deep meaning, and even perhaps a deeper

intention, behind this. If people are not given a brief glimpse of how it is when things are right, they would never persevere with the miseries of the analytical process. Only the memory of this glimpse of paradise makes them continue on their dark journey. This is why the unconscious offers the marvelous possibility of being cured, of living the right kind of life and of happiness, and then takes it away. It is as if it were saying "This is what you will get later, but you first have to realize this and this and this, and much more, before you can get there." I found out about this secret intention when people who had experienced an early blossoming said, "Well, after all, I was without symptoms at such and such a time, so it should be possible, shouldn't it?" Yes, it should be possible. This initial experience gives them the courage to hold on in a desperate situation. In our fairytale, if Ivan had not seen his bride in her beautiful state and had not had the relationship that he had with her, he would certainly not have walked to the Thirtieth Tsar's Kingdom at the end of the world.

209   There is another interesting motif in this story. The frog lady has been cursed by her father for some prior sin she committed. We do not know if it was a real sin: Perhaps it was only a sin in the eyes of her father. Nevertheless, she did something that annoyed him. As a result, she had to live in the form of a frog and be in the hands of a dragon, from whom Ivan had to rescue her. This is a truly complicated situation. In our main story, "The Three Feathers," we had assumed that the anima had the lowly form of a toad because consciousness had no relationship to the feminine side. In the conscious situation, there was only a king and his three sons, and there was no feminine principle, which meant that the whole feminine world was repressed and existed in a degenerate form. In this Russian version, the balance of the story is weighted differently. From the outset, the tsar has a wife; thus, there is a mother principle and, accordingly, we cannot speak simply of the repression of the anima. We have already mentioned a further "difficulty" that resulted from the frog-lady annoying her father, about whom we do not know much, for which he has put her into this low condition of being a frog. The diagram below illustrates these connections:

Tsar ●━━━━━━● Tsar's wife

● ● ● Three sons

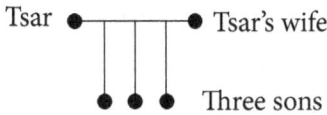

———————————————————————— Threshold of consciousness

Normal process of integration

Frog Princess   Descent into the
                                       unconscious because
Her father   of the curse

210   At the top there are five people instead of four, so it is a completely different setup. You could say that this is a naturally balanced family; there is a little bit more of the male than of the female, but nothing vital is lacking. Below the threshold of consciousness are the frog-lady and her father.

211   So the father, who is only mentioned at the end of our story, puts a curse on his daughter: He removes her into the depths of the unconscious, and takes her away from consciousness. So her father deflects her path and prevents her from coming up and being integrated, which would be the normal process in life. Why the father of the frog-lady is so negative, we do not know, but he certainly seems to not want his daughter to marry on the human level. We can assume that for some reason he is against her becoming conscious. Perhaps he wants to keep her to himself, as fathers often do, but we do not know, and there is no point in speculating about such family troubles in the unconscious. In psychological terms, it means that one unconscious archetypal complex (father) is fighting another archetypal complex (anima) within the unconscious. In my experience, such a conflict is generally the ricochet effect of some disturbance between the two worlds of the conscious and the unconscious sphere. I could give you other examples where it becomes clear that the father below has a conflict-tension with the tsar in the upper world. These two fathers are at loggerheads, but instead of the one attacking the other (the tsar), the lower father removes his daughter from the upper world.

212   Who is this father of the frog-princess — of the anima? In many European stories in which there is a Christian influence, the father of the anima is called the "devil." In European countries with less Christian influence, the father of the anima is characterized as an "older" image of God. For instance, in Germanic countries he appears as an old man with a Wotan-like character; in Jewish legends he is an old desert god or a demon; in Islamic fairytales the fathers of the anima are great jinns, meaning pagan demons of the pre-Islamic time. In general, the father of the anima represents an older image of God that is in contrast to, and repressed by, the ruling God-image. The new ruling dominant of consciousness usually superimposes itself on an older image of the same kind, and often there is still a secret tension between these two factors. This is the situation that makes the anima disappear in this way.

213   This is also the case in practical terms: We often see, for example, that a man's anima is old-fashioned. She is frequently bound to the historical past, and this explains why men who in conscious life are courageous innovators, who are inclined toward change and reform, become sentimentally conservative as soon as they fall into an anima mood: a thoroughly ruthless businessman who thinks nothing of ruining people will sing childhood songs under the Christmas tree, as if he could not hurt a fly. His anima has remained in the traditional world of childhood. You can see the same thing in the area of Eros — for instance, the belief held by some men in institutions. This, too, is an anima effect. Women are known to be more conservative in their conscious lives, which accounts for the folkloric statement that they would still stir the soup with a stick if men had not invented the spoon. The animus of a woman often has an eye to the future, which explains their interest in new movements. In ancient Greece, the Dionysian cult was for the most part firstly picked up by women and carried out by them, just as the early Christian communities were mainly carried by the enthusiasm of women.

214   When the old God-image binds the anima to the past, a rift opens up between the new conscious attitude and the older layer,

where the anima comes from. So there is a grain of truth in the contention of the Grimm Brothers who said that the telling of fairytales belongs to the paganism of the past. In the Russian version, the frog-princess tells the fairytale, and she cannot quite come up to the realm of the ruling tsar as there is a conflict between the father figures. This is a typical situation if there is a conflict in the unconscious: Instead of the repressed content hitting back, it represses some other unconscious content. This is illustrated in the famous story of the lady who scolds the cook: She scolds the cook who shouts at the kitchen maid who kicks the dog who bites the cat — and so on. The conflict is passed on and then surfaces in a completely different realm. You do not know where the real conflict lies, or where it began. This is why, if you are studying fairytales, you must always look at the parallels and at the whole context to find out the deeper connections behind the phenomena. They sometimes lead into unfathomable depths, such as in the Russian version, where, at bottom, it is a question of the image of God.

♦

Chapter 7
A Man's Shadow

215   Though nearly all fairytales ultimately circle around the symbol of the Self, or are given their order by it, in many stories we also find motifs that remind us of Jung's concepts of the shadow, the animus and the anima. In what follows, I shall provide an example of each of these phenomena of the soul. But we may not forget that we are dealing with the objective, impersonal substructure of the human psyche, and not with its personal individual aspects.

216   In itself, the figure of a shadow belongs partly to the personal unconscious and partly to the collective unconscious. In fairytales, only the collective aspect of a shadow figure can occur. It often appears in the form of the hero's shadow. This shadow figure appears to be more primitive and instinctive than the hero, but it is not necessarily morally inferior. In some fairytales, the hero (or heroine) has no shadow companion but displays within himself (or herself) both positive and negative traits, sometimes even daemonic ones. We must therefore ask in what psychological circumstances does the hero-image split into a light figure and a shadow companion. A division of this sort often occurs in dreams. This indicates that an unknown content is approaching consciousness, one whose dark content is only partially acceptable to consciousness. To become conscious of something presupposes a choice on the part of the ego. Generally, only one aspect of an unconscious content can be realized at one time, while the other aspects are rejected. The shadow of the hero therefore embodies that aspect of the archetype that has been rejected by collective consciousness.

217   Although the shadow figure in fairytales is archetypal, we can learn a great deal about the assimilation of the shadow in the

personal realm from its characteristic behavior. In order to illustrate this, I have chosen the Norwegian story, "Prince Ring." Even though we should understand it on a collective level because it is a fairytale, this tale nevertheless provides analogies to the individual problem of integrating the shadow for it shows the typical features of this difficult process.

218 *Prince Ring*

While out hunting one day, Ring, the son of a king, was captivated by the sight of a fleet hind with a golden ring around her horns. Pursuing her wildly, he became separated from his companions and rode into a thick fog in which he lost sight of the hind. He slowly made his way out of the woods and came to a beach where he found a woman hunched over a barrel. Approaching, he saw the golden ring lying in the barrel, and the woman, guessing his desire, suggested that he take the ring. As he reached into the barrel, he found that it had a deceptive bottom, so that the deeper he reached, the farther away the ring appeared to be. When he himself was halfway down, the woman pushed him in, secured its lid, and rolled the barrel into the surf. The outgoing tide bore him away.

219 After a very long time, the barrel was washed ashore, and Ring climbed out onto a strange island. Before he had time to get his bearings, a huge giant picked him up out of curiosity and carried him home to be company for his giant wife. These old giants were very affable and deferred to every wish of the king's son. The giant happily showed the youth his treasures, forbidding him only to enter his kitchen. Prince Ring felt an immense curiosity to know what was in the kitchen and twice was on the verge of entering but stopped himself. The third time he had the courage to look, and a dog called out several times, "Choose me, Prince Ring! Choose me!"

220   After some time, the giants told Ring that they were about to depart this life and offered to give him anything he chose. Recalling the dog's urgent plea, Ring asked for whatever was in the kitchen. The giant was not well pleased but consented nevertheless. The dog, that was called Snati-Snati, leapt wildly with joy at being with Ring, and the prince was a little afraid.

221   They journeyed to a kingdom on the mainland, and Snati-Snati told Ring to ask the king for a small room where he might spend the winter as a guest of the palace. The king welcomed him, but the brow of Rauder, his minister, grew dark with jealousy. Rauder pressed the king to hold a contest wherein he and the new guest would cut down trees to see who could make the biggest clearing in a forest in a single day. Snati-Snati urged Ring to get two axes, and they both set to work. By evening, Snati-Snati had felled half again as many trees as the minister. Then, at Rauder's urging, the king ordered Ring to kill two wild bulls in the forest and to return with their skins and horns. In the encounter Snati-Snati came to the aid of Ring who had been knocked down, and ferociously killed the bulls. He stripped them of their skins and horns, which he brought to the castle, and Ring was greatly lauded for the deed. Next, Ring had to recover three most precious objects, objects now in the possession of a family of giants in a nearby mountain: a golden suit of clothes, a golden chessboard, and shining gold itself. If he could retrieve these objects, he would be allowed to marry the king's daughter and inherit the kingdom.

222   Carrying a big sack of salt, man and dog — with Ring holding on to the tail of the dog — climbed laboriously up the steep mountain and, with difficulty, arrived at the top. They found a cave and, looking through the opening, they discerned four giants sleeping around a fire over which boiled a pot of groats. Swiftly, they poured the salt into the pot. When the giants awoke, they fell greedily on their meal, but, after a few mouthfuls, the giant-mother, who was terrible to look at,

roared with thirst and begged her daughter to fetch water. The daughter agreed only on condition that she should have the shining gold. After a furious scene, the giant-mother relinquished it to her. When her daughter did not return, the old woman sent her son, who first wangled the golden suit from her. Like the daughter before him, Snati-Snati and Prince Ring drowned the son. The ruse also worked with the husband who took the golden chessboard with him, the only difference being that the old man rose again as a ghost and had to be beaten down a second time. The prince and Snati-Snati then faced the terrible witch-giantess, and, as Snati-Snati pointed out, no weapon could penetrate her; she could only be killed with the cooked groats and a red-hot iron. When the witch saw the dog in the entrance to the cave, she croaked, "Oh, it is you and Prince Ring who have killed my family!" There was a desperate struggle, and she was killed. After burning the corpses, Ring and Snati-Snati returned with the treasures, and Prince Ring became engaged to the king's daughter.

223 On the evening before the marriage, the dog begged to exchange places with Ring, so that he slept in Ring's bed and Ring slept on the floor. During the night, Rauder, intent upon murdering Ring, stealthily entered the room with a drawn sword and approached the bed, but as he raised his arm, Snati-Snati leaped up and bit off his right hand. In the morning, Rauder accused Ring in front of the king of having wantonly attacked him. Ring then produced the severed hand still gripping the sword, whereupon the king had his minister hanged.

224 Ring married the Princess, and Snati-Snati was allowed to lie at the foot of the bed on the wedding night. In the night, he regained his true form — that of a king's son also named Ring. His stepmother had changed him into a dog, and he could only be redeemed by sleeping at the foot of the bed of a king's son. The hind with the golden ring, the woman on

the beach and the formidable witch-giantess were, in reality, his stepmother in different guises, who wished to prevent his redemption at any price.[1]

225 This tale opens with the image of a prince hunting. In more than half of all fairytales members of a royal family are the heroes, while in the other half the heroes are ordinary people, such as poor peasants, millers, deserters, and so on. In our story, the main figure represents a future king that, in psychological terms, would represent a still unconscious element that is capable of becoming a new collective dominant in order to bring about a deeper understanding of the Self.

226 The prince chases a deer that has a golden ring between its horns. The mythical parallel to this is the Ceryneian hind with golden antlers, sacred to Artemis. Hercules pursued it for an entire year but was not allowed to kill it.[2] In one version of the myth, he finally finds her in the Hesperides under apple trees that bestow eternal youth. Artemis, the famous huntress, is often transformed into a deer, which indicates the hunter and the hunted secretly sharing the same identity. The hind frequently shows the way or finds the most advantageous point to cross a river. On the other hand, she sometimes lures the hero to disaster or even to death by leading him over a precipice or into the sea or a swamp. Sometimes she adopts and nurtures an orphan or an abandoned child. The mythical stag often carries a ring or a precious cross between its horns, or sometimes he may even have golden horns.

227 In our fairytale the deer is feminine: It embodies an anima motif. A doe with antlers also has masculine traits. So we are dealing with a hermaphroditic being that unites the elements of the anima and the shadow. According to a medieval text, when a stag feels old, it first eats a snake and then swallows enough water to drown it. The snake poisons it from within, and the stag sheds its antlers to rid itself of the poison. Once it is no longer in its body, new horns grow.

---

[1] Adeline Rittershaus, "Snati-Snati" in *Die Neuisländischen Volksmärchen* (Halle: A.S., 1902), 31 ff.
[2] For further parallels, see Carl Pschmadt, *Die Sage von der Verfolgten Hinde,* Dissertation (Greifswald, 1911).

"Therefore," a Father of the Church declares, "the stag knows the secret of self-renewal; he sheds his antlers, and thus should we learn to shed our pride." The shedding of antlers is probably the natural basis of all the mythological attributes of transformation of the deer. In medieval medicine, the bone in the heart of a deer was thought to be beneficial for heart trouble.

228   To sum up: the deer symbolizes an unconscious factor that shows the way to a crucial event. It leads either towards rejuvenation by bringing about a change in the personality (by, for example, leading one to one's beloved), or into the Beyond (to the Hesperides), or to death. It is a bearer of light in the form of a mandala symbol, like the circle or the cross. Like Mercurius or Hermes, the deer makes an appearance as a psychopomp, as a guide into the unconscious, functioning as a bridge to the deeper regions of the psyche. The deer embodies a content of the unconscious that attracts consciousness in order to lead it to new discoveries and new knowledge. It can be equated to an instinct of wisdom that exerts a strong fascination. At bottom, the deer is an image of that unknown psychic factor that endows dreams with meaning. Its death aspect arises when consciousness has a negative attitude towards it; when this happens, the unconscious is forced into a destructive role.

229   In our tale, the deer bears a ring on its horns, and the king's son is called "Ring." Hence, the stag carries an essential component of the prince's own nature — his undomesticated, instinctive side. Together, they are the complimentary sides of that psychic entity of which the prince is the anthropomorphic aspect. At first, he is an aimless hunter who has not yet discovered or realized his individual form. Incomplete as he is, he represents merely the possibility of becoming conscious, and therefore he has to find his own opposite, like the stag in the medieval allegory: He has to swallow and integrate his opposite — "the snake" (in other versions, it is a toad). It is therefore understandable that the deer possesses the secret of the prince's renewal and completion. This is symbolized in the golden ring.

230   The prince goes hunting in the woods — that is, in the unconscious realm — and gets lost in a fog, so that his vision is greatly diminished. Losing his comrades means isolation and loneliness — the typical feeling state that accompanies a journey into the unconscious. The center of interest shifts from the outer world to the inner, which is completely unintelligible to the prince at this stage: The unconscious seems senseless and bewildering to him. The deer leads the prince to a beach where an evil woman sits hunched over a barrel. The object of fascination, the ring, has apparently been cast into the barrel by the hind. The ring is a symbol of the Self, and as a factor that creates relatedness, it represents the task of completing one's inner essential being. The prince is secretly seeking completion. Pursuing the golden ring and led by the attraction of the deer, the prince falls into the hands of a witch who, as we learn later, is Snati-Snati's stepmother. In masculine psychology, the stepmother is a symbol of the unconscious in its destructive role — it stands for its disturbing, devouring character.

231   He plunges into the cask after the ring. The stepmother swiftly shuts the cask and rolls it into the sea, a seeming misfortune that turns out to be fortunate. The prince lands on an island where he finds Snati-Snati, his magical double and helpful companion. Thus the stepmother has an equivocal character: With one hand she destroys while leading one to completion with the other. As the terrible mother, she represents a natural resistance that blocks the development of higher consciousness. But it is precisely this resistance that calls forth the hero's best qualities. In other words, by persecuting him, the stepmother helps him. As the king's second wife, she is, in a way, a false wife, and since she belongs to the old system that the king represents, she must stand for that dull, leaden unconsciousness that accompanies ancestral social institutions. It has the tendency to block a new state of consciousness. This stubborn negative state of remaining unconscious is what rules the shadow of the prince.

232   Before the hero is washed up onto an island's shore, he is afloat in a cask. The cask is the vessel that sustains him upon the waters. It

has a motherly protective character, and it allows the water currents to bear him to the intended place. But it also has a negative aspect for it is the womb into which the hero regresses, and it has the character of a prison that isolates him. This ambiguous image of the cask intensifies the feelings of confusion, of being lost and of being unable to find a way out, feelings already suggested by the motif of the fog. On the plane of psychological reality, the cask can be interpreted as being in a state of possession by an archetype — in this case, being obsessed by the mother. One can say that Prince Ring is now under the spell of a negative mother-image that cuts him off from life and swallows him. The cask corresponds to the whale in the story of Jonah,[3] and the journey of the prince inside of it is a typical night-sea journey; it describes, in other words, a state of transition in which the hero is enclosed in the mother-image as in a vessel. But the cask not only imprisons the hero: It also prevents him from being drowned. This state can be compared to a neurosis that tends to isolate an individual, thereby protecting him. The condition of neurotic loneliness is positive when it protects the growth of a new possibility of life; it is similar to a stage of incubation that aims at the inner completion of a more real and more definitely shaped conscious personality.

233   Like the cask, an island is another symbol of isolation. It is generally a realm inhabited by otherworldly figures; in our fairytale, giants live on it. Islands often harbor projections of the unconscious psychic sphere. Think, for example, of the islands of the dead. The nymph Calypso, "the veiled one," whom Odysseus imprisons, and the sorceress Circe, both live on islands. In a way, both are goddesses of death. In our story, the island is not the hero's goal but is only another station along the way, a further stage of his journey. In the middle of the sea of the unconscious, it represents a split-off part of the conscious psyche (as we know, islands are usually connected with the mainland beneath the surface of the sea). Here it represents an autonomous complex that exists quite apart from the ego, with a

[3] Cf. C.G. Jung, *Psychology and Alchemy,* 2nd ed., vol. 12, *CW* (Princeton, NJ: Princeton University Press, 1993), § 440.

kind of intelligence of its own. A complex is a fragment of consciousness that has a subtle and insidious effect, while it simultaneously fascinates one and remains evasive. Undeveloped people frequently have incongruous and quite separate complexes that almost "jostle" one another. These people hold, for instance, incompatible Christian and pagan beliefs that they do not recognize as being contradictory. The complex builds up its own field of "consciousness" apart from the original field where the old viewpoint still prevails, and it is as if each is an independent island of consciousness with its own harbor and traffic.

234   Giants live on an island like this. Giants are primarily characterized by their size, but they also have a close relation to natural phenomena. In folklore, for example, thunder is thought to be giants bowling, or the resounding blows of storm-giants hammering. Erratic stone formations are thought to be stones tossed by giants at play. Fog appears when the giantesses hang up their washing. There are different families of giants: storm-giants, earth-giants, and so on. In mythology, giants often appear as the "older people" of creation, a race that has died out.[4] In some cosmogonies, they are featured as forerunners of human beings: They did not succeed in raising their level of consciousness. In the *Edda*, Sutr, the giant, is portrayed with a sword that separates the opposite poles of fire and ice. The giant Ymir is created by connecting these opposites. When he is butchered, dwarves emerge as worms from his entrails.[5] We know of the Greek giants as the Titans who rebelled against Zeus and were slain by his lightning. According to the Orphic tradition, men issued forth from the smoke of their burned flesh. Giants became easily drunk with hubris and had therefore to be destroyed by the gods, whereupon men inherited their earth. Giants are a supernatural race that is only half human. In psychological terms, they represent emotional factors of crude force that have not yet emerged into the realm of human consciousness. Giants possess enormous strength and are renowned for their stupidity. They are

---

[4] Cf. Genesis 6:4: "There were giants in the earth in those days."
[5] On the cosmological aspect of the Anthropos, see Von Franz, "The Cosmic Man as Image of the Goal of the Individuation Process and Human Development," in *Archetypal Dimensions*, 133–57.

easy to deceive and are prey to their own affects, which makes them, at bottom, helpless, for all their might. The powerful emotional impulses they stand for are still rooted in archetypal subsoil. If one falls victim to such boundless impulses, one is wild, beside oneself, berserk — and one is as stupid as a giant. One may display gigantic strength, but afterwards one collapses. In happier circumstances, one may be inspired and transported, as in the stories of saints who were helped by giants to build a church in a single night. This would be the positive harnessing of such untamed emotions. A person in a white heat can accomplish a great task.

235   On the island in our fairytale lives a married giant couple. These giants are probably the energetic equivalent, and the archaic form, of the missing parents of the prince who are not mentioned — an unusual lacuna in a fairytale. In a manner of speaking, the giants fill in for the king and queen and take over their role. Their role as substitutes indicates that there is no longer a ruling principle of consciousness, which is why it has regressed into its archaic form. Basically, there is always a dominating force of some sort in life, and if the ruling principle waivers, there is a throwback to earlier ways. In Switzerland, for instance, the ideal of freedom — the ideal of social coherence that brooks no constraint — is as revered as a mystical bride, and whenever there is a threat from without, this ideal is quickened again. In peaceful times it slips from people's grasp, and they revive instead the idea of political associations. If we apply what is happening in the fairytale to the world as we know it, it becomes clear that uncontrolled emotional, collective forces now lord it over the earth. Society is unconsciously being led by primitive and archaic principles.

236   In the kitchen of the giant couple, Ring finds the dog called Snati-Snati, who is the complimentary side of our hero. Historically, the kitchen is the center of the house and is therefore the place of the house cults. The house gods were placed on the kitchen stove, and in prehistoric times the dead were buried under the hearth. As the place where food is chemically transformed, the kitchen is analogous to the stomach. It is the center of emotion in its searing and

consuming aspect and in its illuminating and warming function. This means that the light of wisdom only comes out of the fire of passion. The dog being in the kitchen means that he represents a complex whose activity reveals itself especially in the emotional sphere. Snati-Snati is guarded by the giants both as a sort of secret and as a sort of son. The forbidden room that contains a frightful secret is a widespread fairytale motif. It points towards something uncanny and frightening, something connected to a complex that has been completely repressed and closed off. The dog is equivalent to something incompatible with the attitude of consciousness. Because of this, the prince is reluctant to approach the forbidden room, but at the same time he is fascinated and wants to enter it.

237   Often the figure in the forbidden room is enraged when someone enters. Psychologically, this means that the complex also opposes the opening of the door. The incompatibility sets up a resistance on both sides against being made conscious with the result that they repel each other like two negatively loaded electrical particles. One could say that the repression is an energetic process supported by both sides. The functions of many psychological phenomena are best explained by means of hypothetical analogy to certain functions of natural science. Jung examined these analogies in detail.[6] In our tale, the dog responds at once when he is approached. He is neither a monster nor a god but stands in a good relation to man, except for the fact that he is unnaturally far away from the hero. That the giants do not object to Ring's taking away the dog shows that there is no resistance on the part of the unconscious, and this — the fact that there is no great tension between human consciousness and world of the instincts — gives a rough idea of the date of this tale; it arose soon after the conversion of the Icelandic peoples to Christianity, between the eleventh and fourteenth centuries.

238   The hero and the dog travel to the mainland to the palace of a king, and Snati-Snati says to the prince he should ask for a room in the palace for the winter. The king, his daughter, and the perfidious Ruder (or Raut) live in this palace. It should be noted that this king

---

[6] Cf. Jung, *Structure and Dynamics,* vol. 8, *CW*; and Von Franz, *Number and Time.*

(not the real father of Ring) is the father of the anima, and that the mother is missing. This lack has to do with the fact that both Ring and the dog are under the influence of a negative mother image. Moreover, the king is no longer in possession of his precious treasures: A baneful giant-mother who lives with her family on a mountain is now hoarding them.

239   The minister Rauder (often called "Rot" or "Rothut" — "Red" or "Red Hat" — names that hint at the violence of his emotions) is a frequently found figure in northern fairytales. In "Ferdinand the Faithful and Ferdinand the Unfaithful,"[7] the shadow figure advises the king what the hero, his double, should do. This slanderer at the king's court is a destructive aspect of the hero's shadow — a disturbing function that sows enmity and discord. As Prince Ring is too good and too passive, Rauder stands for his as yet unassimilated dark emotions and impulses — jealousy, hatred and murderous passion. But this evil minister has an essential function for he creates the tasks whereby Ring is able to distinguish himself, and he incites the prince to heroic action. Ultimately, the shadow has a positive value: He has a Lucifer-like, light-bringing quality. Rauder embodies that driving force in the unconscious that is evil only insofar as its function is not understood. As soon as the hero wins the daughter and the kingdom, he disappears. It is a typical ending for the dark shadow to lose its power as soon as the hero triumphs. He would be superfluous if the hero were energetic enough and up to performing his tasks. Like Mephisto, Rauder is unwittingly an instrument of inner growth. This touches upon the problem of evil as seen from the standpoint of nature. As other fairytales also show us, evil incitements provide us with opportunities to increase our consciousness. This seems to be how nature views it and thus creates corresponding opportunities. If we were able to see our own greed, jealousy, spite, hatred, and so on, we could employ these destructive emotions positively for a lot of life

---

[7] Cf. Grimm and Grimm, "Ferdinand the Faithful and Ferdinand the Unfaithful," in *Complete Fairy Tales*, 566–70; cf. also Marie-Louise von Franz, *Shadow and Evil in Fairy Tales* (Asheville: Chiron Publications, 2022).

is bound up in them. If we have this energy at our disposal, it can be used to achieve positive ends.

240   The dominant characteristic of this false and crafty steward is envy. Envy is a misunderstood compulsion to achieve something within oneself that one has neglected. It springs from a vague awareness of a deficiency in one's character, a deficiency that needs to be acknowledged. It points to a lack that needs to be filled. The object of envy embodies what one might oneself have created or achieved. It is therefore a fault that can be remedied. The figure of Rauder shows little that is animal-like or instinctive but rather that which is sinister, cruel, and shrewd — shadow qualities of which the hero could and should be conscious. They are contents that should fuse with and be contained in the archetype of the hero. This leads us to ask the question to what extent such negative factors support the king's position. If the king has these qualities, he imposes impossible tasks on the hero because the new system (personified by the hero) must demonstrate that it is stronger and better than the old one: It should create a better state of collective psychic health and generate a richer cultural life. This is the old king's secret justification: to impose formidable tasks on the one who aspires to inherit the kingdom. This is the challenge behind the struggle between early Christianity and the old pagan gods. The early Christians felt more alive; they had greater vitality and more enthusiasm; they had a hopeful attitude, and they were socially active. The heathens, on the other hand, were disillusioned, and their esprit was worn out. In general, people watch for signs of vitality and join the movement that promises they will be better off, both inwardly and outwardly. This is how a new system "demonstrates" its superiority and wins the anima (the king's daughter) — the souls of men.

241   Service at the court of a foreign king is a recurring motif that arises when the ruling principle of collective consciousness becomes oppressive and the time has come when it should abdicate. The hero who undertakes this is almost always the heir to the throne. If one looks more closely at the tasks of the hero, one finds that they are

generally cultural achievements: the taming or slaying of wild animals, the building of a church in a single night, or some agricultural activity, such as the felling of trees. This implies the clearing of a place where the light of consciousness can fall into the realm of the unconscious and illuminate a part of it. A forest is a region where visibility is limited, where one loses one's way, where wild animals and unexpected dangers may be present. Like the sea, it is therefore a symbol of the unconscious. Early man lived in jungles and forests. Establishing a clearing was a cultural advancement. The unconscious is wild nature: It has the tendency to swallow up every human attempt towards progress. Primitive man had to be eternally vigilant of the forest that constantly tries to return to its original form. It represents vegetative life, an organic form that draws life directly from the earth and transforms the soil while, through plants, inorganic matter becomes living. As plants draw their nourishment in part from the mineral contents of the earth, they signify that form of life that is closely connected with inorganic matter. One can draw a parallel here to the life of the body that is intimately connected with the soul.

242   In order to accomplish the difficult tasks, Prince Ring has to have the help of his other shadow side, the dog, which increasingly takes the initiative. The two become strongly allied. The hero's relationship to his instincts provides him with a sense of reality (that he did not have beforehand), and gives him roots in this world. Ring's second assignment is to vanquish wild bulls. The slaying of the bull was of primary importance in the Mithraic mystery rituals. Vestiges of this still exist in Spain and Mexico. The killing of the bull is a demonstration of the ascendancy of human consciousness over the wild, emotional animal forces. Nowadays the bull is not dominant in the unconscious psyche; on the contrary, our difficulty now is to find our way back to our instinctive animal life. In this story, the hero must assert his self-control and his masculine qualities before the dog can be redeemed.

243   The next section has to do with the giants and the recovery of the stolen treasures. It is important that the action takes place on a

mountain. In the religion of India, the mountain is connected with the mother goddess. Being close to the heavens, it is often the place of revelation, as in the transfiguration of Christ.[8] In many creation myths it signifies the place of orientation, for example, the initial appearance of four mountains at the cardinal points. The apostles and spiritual leaders of the Church were often identified with mountains. Richard de Saint Victor interprets the mountain on which Christ stands as a symbol of self-knowledge for it was the mountain that led the prophets to their inspired wisdom. Often the mountain is the goal of a long quest, or the site of a transition into eternity, and it can sometimes denote the Self. If we sum up the aspects of mountain symbolism in our story, we notice that the mountain has to do with the mother goddess in the person of the giant-mother. The mountain marks the place — the point in life — where the hero, after arduous effort (climbing), becomes oriented and gains steadfastness and self-knowledge, values that are developed through one's efforts to become conscious, to develop oneself. The mother aspect is central to this for, in relation to all that the mother represents, Prince Ring must make a tremendous effort and he must be able to rely upon his instinct. For this reason, Ring allows the dog to lead him.

244   The great value of self-knowledge is symbolized by the precious golden objects that the prince finds on the mountain. It is also symbolized by the salt that Ring tosses into the groats. This induces an agonizing thirst in the giants, so that they emerge from the cave one by one and are all drowned. Salt is a part of the sea and has the inherent bitterness of the sea. Bitterness is also closely associated with tears, sorrow, disappointment, and loss. *Sal,* in Latin, also means "wit" or "joke." In alchemy, salt is called "the salt of wisdom" that endows one with a penetrating spiritual power and it is a mystical world principle similar to sulphur and quicksilver. Salt symbolizes wisdom, a skeptical turn of mind, a piercing intellect and irony. Some alchemists prescribe salt as being the only means of overcoming the devil. On the other hand, salt is praised as the Eros

---

[8] Cf. Matt. 17:1–8; Mark 9:2–9; Luke 9:28–36.

principle and is called "an opener and a unifier." From this we may conclude that salt symbolizes the wisdom of Eros, both its bitterness and its life-giving power — the equivalent of wisdom acquired through feeling-experiences. In our fairytale, the Eros principle leads the hero on his quest, and the salt works to isolate the giants, thereby making it possible to defeat them. Indeed, the hero has a sort of spiritual attitude that is more resourceful than the slow wits of the giants.

245   If we sum up the aspects of the shadow, we see that there are two figures: the dog Snati-Snati and the minister Rauder — an animal double and a malicious human double, one positive and the other negative. The dog is intimately bound up with the hero, whereas Rauder, as the negative shadow of the hero, is a transient figure. The two have played out their respective roles only when the hero is joined with his anima. Psychologically speaking, the dog is an unknown part of man's psyche — like all symbols, it is its own best expression. If we wish to circumscribe its meaning, we recall that in antiquity the dog was regarded as guarantor of eternal life. Think of Cerberus, the watchdog of Hades, or the images of dogs on antique Roman graves. In Egyptian mythology, the jackal-headed god Anubis is a guide into the underworld, and he is said to have gathered together the dismembered body of Osiris. The Egyptian priests who performed the rites of mummification were dressed as an Anubis figure. In Greece, the dog belongs to the God of healing, Asclepius, because he knows how to cure himself by eating grass. Because of its close relationship to man, a dog usually has very positive associations: It is a friend, a guardian, and a guide. But as the carrier of frenzy or madness (hydrophobia), it was also much dreaded in earlier times and was thought to bring disease and pestilence. Of all animals, the dog is the most completely adapted to people and reacts most strongly to moods. Dogs copy man, and they understand what is expected of them. Dogs are the essence of relationship.

246   Snati-Snati, however, is not really a dog, and in the end we learn that he is a prince, also called Ring and also under the spell of the

giant-woman. He could only be freed after sleeping at the foot of the bed of a prince who bore the same name. Snati-Snati represents an instinctive urge which later turns into a human quality. One can also say that this animal drive that needs and wants to be integrated represents a hidden strain of the hero, namely his complementary instinctive side. Its integration brings the hero's realization of himself into real life.

247   Two backbiting brothers of the hero sometimes replace the figure of Rauder as the negative shadow. These brothers generally represent tendencies toward a too one-sided development that is either too "spiritual" or too instinctive. Rauder has a jealous nature with its consequent dangerous tendency to narrow one-sidedness. He symbolizes a passionate, possessive temperament that performs a positive function by imposing impossible tasks on the hero. However, when the anima comes, Rauder must go. He had previously attempted to murder the hero, and was attacked by the dog — by an instinctive reaction that disarms him and defeats his purpose. In his attempt to murder Ring, Rauder shows his hand — and the dog bites it off. To show one's hand means to divulge who one is. Endurance is of great importance when dealing with evil forces. The one who can hold out without losing his temper is the one who wins. In fairytales where there is a wager between the hero and the evil spirit, it is usually the one who is the first to let loose his emotions who forfeits his life. Losing one's temper always means a lowering of consciousness, a lapse into primitive or even animal reactions.

248   Rauder is formidable while pitting his human shrewdness against Ring, but then his animal passion for sheer destructiveness gets the better of him, and that is why the animal overcomes him. Rauder represents an element of evil in the psyche that resists sublimation. It cannot be integrated, which is why it must be thrown out. One alchemist observed that in the *prima materia*, there is a certain intractable amount of *terra damnata* (accursed earth) that defies all efforts at transformation and must be rejected. Not all dark impulses lend themselves to redemption. Some that are soaked in evil cannot

be allowed to break loose and must be severely repressed. What is against nature, against the instincts, has to be stopped by main force and eradicated. The expression "assimilation of the shadow" that we are familiar with is meant to apply to childish, primitive, undeveloped sides of one's nature, depicted in the image of the child or the dog or the stranger. But there are deadly impulses that can destroy a human being. Their presence means that one must be hard from time to time; not everything that comes up from the unconscious may be accepted.

249   Snati-Snati turns out to be a prince, and one wonders why he had been transformed into a dog. This strange metamorphosis has to do with the dual nature of the instinctual, which is an ambiguous phenomenon. Biologists regard it as a meaningful but unreflective mode of behavior of animals — as an inborn pattern of behavior. This pattern consists of two factors: a physical activity and a picture (or image) of the activity that is necessary to energize the activity. The image works as a catalyst for the physical action and represents the meaning of the action. Normally the two factors exist and work together, but they can be separated. If another image is substituted for the original one, the instinctive behavior can attach to the new image. Woodcocks, for instance, that were hatched in a stove directed their mating play towards the wooden clogs of the human attendants, the clogs for them being "imprinted" with the mother-image. These images or pictures are what we call archetypes.

250   Snati-Snati is, therefore, the psychic pattern or image in which the dynamic towards self-realization appears first — as an instinct — but within which there is a human complementary side. The dog form of this drive derives from a collective misconception of individuation. Collective consciousness nourishes this mis-conception, and therein we find the reason for the curse of the stepmother. Every age generates its own convictions on the meaning of the path of individuation. For example, in the Middle Ages, the idea that people should model their entire lives and their inner conduct on the life of Christ is what we would call individuation. Today, there is a current notion that we are healed, fulfilled, and

made complete when our physical instincts, especially the sexual instinct, find expression. According to the Freudians, the root of all evil is sexual repression; if the amatory functions take their natural course, then everything is resolved and in order. Devotees of this belief bend their energy to this purpose but often find that they cannot get rid of their inhibitions in this way. People saddle the instinct with psychological expectations and put a mystical idea of redemption into a biological fact. Thus, something that does not belong to the animal sphere is projected into it. Another example of this sort of mixing can be found in the idea that the full meaning of life is reached when a communist or some other kind of social order enters one's country. The Nazis put the ideal of individuation into their program, but that ideal was spoiled by false (collective) interpretations. The youth of the country gave to it devotion, intensity, and the willingness to sacrifice because they identified it with what we call individuation. Idealism and willingness to sacrifice are admirable in themselves, but they can be steered in a false direction and then become their opposite. When symbolic factors are repressed, they glut the instincts. Therefore, what is symbolic must be separated out so that the genuine instincts can function again. If sexuality is overemphasized, something is put into the animal sphere that does not belong there. A real effort must then be made to integrate the shadow. This allows the instincts to function "normally."

251   If we make a graphic representation of the journey of the prince, we see that his route is circular — like a ring — as the fourth station is secretly identical with the first, for both are ruled by the stepmother.

252   The hero winds up at the place from which he started, but his circuit has netted him the dog (Ring II), the princess, and the kingdom. The whole process is a process of increasing completion, which is ordered like a mandala. This is a typical pattern in fairytales.

253   The course of these four stations leads deeper and deeper into the unconscious. Between stages II and III, the hero leads the way, but between III and IV the dog guides the hero. At the fourth station,

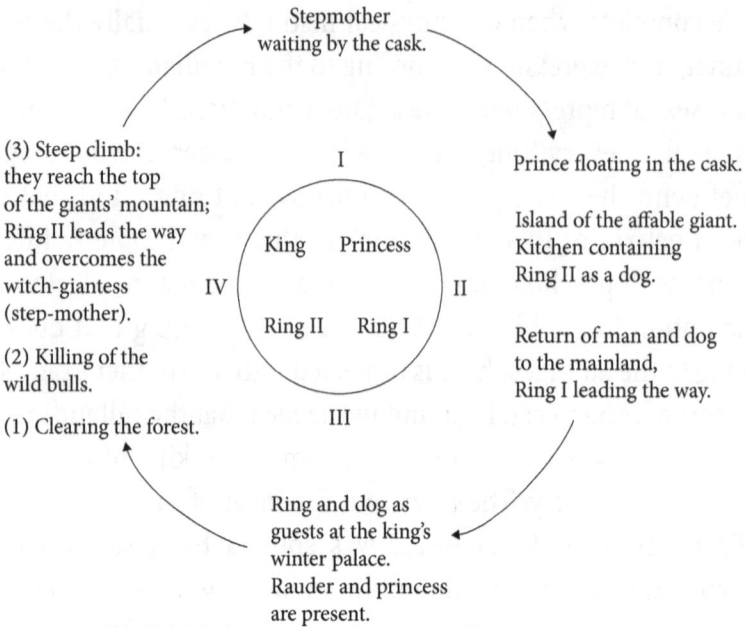

Stepmother waiting by the cask.

(3) Steep climb: they reach the top of the giants' mountain; Ring II leads the way and overcomes the witch-giantess (step-mother).

(2) Killing of the wild bulls.

(1) Clearing the forest.

I

King   Princess

Ring II   Ring I

IV   II

III

Prince floating in the cask.

Island of the affable giant. Kitchen containing Ring II as a dog.

Return of man and dog to the mainland, Ring I leading the way.

Ring and dog as guests at the king's winter palace. Rauder and princess are present.

all evil elements disappear: The giant-couple on the island die of old age, the other giants, including the witch-giantess, are killed, and Rauder is hanged. Stages I and IV have a secret identity because they have to do with the same psychic complex realized on different levels. The hind, the seaside witch, and the giantess are secretly one and the same figure — the one who persecutes Ring I and Ring II. In the fourth stage, what was latent is also fulfilled: marriage with the anima and the emancipation of the second prince from bondage to his dog form. Only with the attainment of the Self are the positive shadow and the anima really won because the situation is now stable. This structure occurs frequently in fairytales that feature royal personages. They generally conclude with a group made up of four people.

254   Taken as a whole, the fairytale "Prince Ring" represents an *energetic process of transformation within the Self*. Potentially, such processes of transformation can also be observed on the material level, for example, the process of transformation within an atom or its nucleus.[9]

---

[9] Cf. Jung, *Aion*, vol. 9/II, *CW*, § 411.

Chapter 8
The Challenge of the Anima

The Bewitched Princess

A man had a son called Peter who no longer wished to remain at home, so he asked for his meager inheritance and departed. On his way he came upon a dead man lying in a field. He had been left unburied because he was poor, and Peter, having a good heart, gave all that he had to provide the man with a decent burial.

Continuing on his way, a stranger joined him, and they decided to travel together. They came to a town where everything was veiled in black as a sign of mourning for the princess, who had been bewitched by an evil mountain spirit. She put three riddles to each one of her suitors, and if he failed to guess every one, she killed him. Although none had been able to redeem her by guessing the riddles and many had lost their lives, Peter decided to try. His companion, who was really the ghost of the buried man, offered to help him. He strapped great wings onto Peter's back, gave him an iron rod, and told him to fly behind the princess that night wherever she might go and to beat her with the rod. Above all, Peter was to take in whatever she said to the mountain spirit whose captive she was, no matter what it was she said.

After nightfall Peter flew to the windowsill of the princess's room, and when she threw open the window and flew away, he followed her, pummeling her with his rod. They came to a high mountain that opened, and both entered a large hall. Peter saw a few scattered stars in the darkness overhead and an altar near the entrance. Then the princess ran into the arms of the mountain spirit who had a snow-white beard and eyes like burning coals. She reported that another suitor would arrive the following day and she wanted to know what riddle to confound him with. The mountain spirit swore that she must kill this man. "The more human blood you drink, the more you are really mine," he said, "and the purer you become in my eyes. Think of your father's white horse and charge the suitor to tell you what you are thinking of." After this, she flew back and went to bed.

257   The next morning Peter presented himself to her and found her sitting on her sofa, quite melancholy, but mild looking and fair. You would scarcely have guessed that she had already sent nine men to their death. She asked, "What am I thinking of?" Without hesitation Peter responded, "Of your father's white horse." She turned pale and bade him return the following day for the next riddle.

258   That night Peter again found the princess, but when he entered the mountain hall, he saw a prickly fish with the moon shining above it on the altar. This time the princess was thinking of her father's sword, and Peter again divined the answer at once.

259   On the third night the spirit-companion equipped Peter with a sword and two iron rods. This time he found that there was a fiery wheel on the altar beside the prickly fish and overhead a sun so bright that he had to hide behind the altar to avoid being seen. He heard the mountain spirit decide that the riddle should concern the mountain spirit's head. "Because no mortal can think of it," he assured the princess. So when she left, Peter resolutely lopped off the head of the mountain spirit, took it with him, and pursued the princess, striking her with both iron rods.

260   The next morning when she asked him to guess the riddle, Peter threw the head of the mountain spirit at her feet, saying,

"That is what you are thinking of." The princess, torn between terror and joy, fainted, and when she recovered, she consented to marry her suitor.

261 On the wedding day, Peter's companion cautioned him to have a large vessel full of water ready when he went to bed that night. "And when the bride gets up, toss her into it," the companion said. "Then she will turn into a raven. Put this raven back in the water, and she will become a dove. Plunge the dove under water, and she will come out in her true form, as gentle as an angel." The companion then disappeared. Peter acted on this advice, redeemed the princess, and later became king.[1]

262 In a parallel tale, the following substitutions and variations occur: The man whose burial the hero pays for is a wine merchant who was wont to dilute his wine with water before selling it. The mountain spirit is a troll to whom the princess rides every night on a male goat. Instead of guessing, the hero must produce the objects she is thinking of, which are a pair of scissors, a golden spool, and the troll's head. Before they reach the domain of the princess, the hero and his companion have to overcome three witches, and then they have a river to cross. The ghost companion makes the crossing possible by throwing the golden spool to the opposite side of the river. It returns by itself, and in this way golden threads unwind back and forth until a bridge is spun, sturdy enough to walk across. After winning the princess, the hero must bathe her in milk and beat her until she loses her troll skin; otherwise, she would have slain him. In return for his companion's help, the hero had agreed to surrender one half of all that he gained. After five years the companion turns up to exact payment, and he asks the hero to divide his child in two. But when the companion sees that the hero is willing to perform the sacrifice, he releases him from his obligation and confides that he

---

[1] Friedrich von der Leyen, Jacob Grimm, and Wilhelm Grimm, "Die verwünschte Prinzessin," in *Das Deutsche Märchen und die Brüder Grimm*, vol. 2 (Jena: Diederichs, 1922 and 1923), 237 ff.

himself may now return to heaven, having cleared his own debt to the hero.[2]

263   The corpse that the hero finds is usually that of some poor wretch who died in debt or the corpse of a criminal or a suicide. The shadow is either human or a spirit. He does not appear in animal form as in the story of Prince Ring, but is a morally inferior person, a cheat who has diluted the wine. In the main version, the shadow lacks life energy — money is energy — and is therefore impoverished. He represents an unlived part of the life within the hero, potential qualities that have not yet been integrated into his character or into the deeds of his ego. Autonomous complexes often thrive behind the scene, without the ego suspecting that they exist. Sooner or later they will be constellated and will appear, usually in an unpleasant form at first.

264   If one were Peter in the story, one might easily assume that one was not responsible for the corpse, but when it is one's own shadow, one is responsible. Only a conscious and responsible attitude transforms the shadow into a friend. Giving one's money for the burial of the corpse means that one has concern for the shadow and devotes energy to it. To those who refuse to do this, the shadow becomes deceptive — he begins to cheat by mixing water with the wine. The nature of this shadow is dishonest: By substituting ordinary water for the more valuable, effort-costing wine, he seeks to get more for less. His crime lies in shirking work. The Greeks considered the act of drinking pure wine to be an act of hubris. The drinking of pure wine was only permitted in the Dionysian mysteries, where it had a religious meaning — wine was the holy means to reach spiritual exaltation, and its use was ceremonial and exceptional and did not apply to everyday consumption. In the Christian symbolism of the Mass, wine represents Christ's blood and signifies Christ's divine nature, while the water represents his common human nature, and the bread, his body. Historically, wine was regarded as being spiritual and water as being common.

---

[2] Clara Stroebe, *The Norwegian Fairy Book*, vol. 2 (Whitefish: Kessinger Publishing, 2008).

265   The guilt of this water-with-wine-mixing shadow is that he blurs the divine and the human in everyday life: He mixes what should be differentiated. The act of mixing could be forgiven, but the dishonesty lies in his palming it off as genuine. People who are led by the shadow cheat themselves by thinking their motives are highly moral. In fact they are crude drives for power. The shadow mixes things in an unclean way, mixing facts with opinions, for instance. People fool themselves that sexual fantasies are mystical experiences. One should call a thing what it is and not pretend a physical thing is spiritual. If one unites wine and water, it should be done consciously and not in an underhanded way. When one is unaware of the shadow, it falsifies the personality.

266   To profit from something without paying a price also has its psychological implications. Imagine a person choosing not to follow his path of individuation because it is difficult. Men, for example, like to suit themselves by making their own arrangements when it comes to some shady corner of their psyche. Women who are in love or are jealous know how to make a scene in order to get their own way. Such behavior is a common human failing; the shadow is a convenient fellow. If he can get returns without effort, he will not feel any obligation to work. To choose what is more difficult is a sign of self-discipline and inner maturity. A lack of psychical energy, as there is in the initial situation in our tale, makes people greedy and dishonest. Anyone who is really committed to their inner life has no energy or time for deliberate conniving or fraudulent maneuvers. But as long as the anima is unredeemed, life does not flow; the energy gets invested in "bad" behavior.

267   The shadow is often the spurned part of the psyche that is not understood. In one version of our story the hero kills himself. This example shows that if one goes too far in repressing one's shadow, if one deals with it too severely over too long a time, an unlived complex can die. This is the aim of the ascetic. When the hero drops the corpse onto the floor, the shadow vanishes as a corpse and reappears as a ghost. It still exists as a shadow problem but on a higher level. The nature of the hero also reveals the nature of the

shadow. Peter is not a king's son but an ordinary lad, the anonymous common man. Often this kind of hero does not even have a name. He represents the average man who is also an aspect of the Self — the Anthropos — the eternal human being in common form.[3] Christ was often referred to as "servant" or "slave." The shadow figure has a compensatory function and is the completion of the hero. The path of this Everyman, Peter, leads from the common form to the special royal form, whose meaning was discussed above. The realization of the Self can be experienced through such widely different classes of heroes as prince or common stable boy. We see, for instance, that young people often identify themselves with an "inner prince" or a supernatural creature. Many others want above all to be ordinary and like everyone else. Each level yearns secretly for the other, and both types are really two sides of the Anthropos, the cosmic Man. The unconscious insists on both sides because, paradoxically, individuation means to become more individual and, at the same time, more generally human.

268   The hero often appears in the role of the deserter. He has left the collective order and finds himself thrown into a special destiny. In our tale the shadow is transformed into a spirit who is not of this world. He becomes the servant-companion of the hero whose skill and knowledge round out the boyish naiveté of the hero. Because the hero is too low, the shadow is spiritual. Ring, being a prince, was high up, so his shadow was animal-instinctive. Peter gives his whole inheritance for the burial. This is far beyond what is customary and even beyond the means of the hero himself — a typical hero attitude. The shadow is disposed of by burial so that it ceases to make any further claims upon human life. After this, it does not come back into life but is transformed into a spirit in the realm where it is at rest.

269   Providing for the burial of the shadow has a double aspect: The hero gives money (i.e., energy) and frees himself of the shadow disturbance. To recognize the shadow is to be willing to make a certain amount of space for it in one's life, but to keep it in its place.

---

[3] On the Anthropos, see Von Franz, "Cosmic Man," 133–57.

In this tale the shadow is allowed to carry out its own purposes — this leads to its spiritualization. When the shadow is only half-conscious, it is most disturbing and indeterminate — it is neither fish nor fowl. The spiritualization occurs because the newly acquired shadow-companion is instrumental in accomplishing the tasks and becomes an arranger of fate, which is the role of Mephistopheles in *Faust*. Only if one throws a shadow is one real. The shadow plunges man into the immediacy of situations here and now and thus creates the real biography of the human being, who is always inclined to assume that he is only what he thinks he is. But it is the biography created by the shadow that counts. Only later, when the shadow has been somewhat assimilated, can the ego partially rule its own fate. Then, however, another content of the unconscious, the Self, takes over most of this fate-arranging function, and that is why the shadow-companion in our story disappears.

270   At first Peter drifts along, without any commitments at home and no specific destination abroad. This is a good precondition for the heroic deed, a point that is stressed in the tale. He gets bored at home, which is why he takes his inheritance and sallies forth. This constellation indicates that energy has already left consciousness and has reinforced the unconscious. One can only discover the mystery of the unconscious as a reality when one is naively curious, not when one wants to harness its power for the furtherance of some conscious design.

271   As soon as the first step is taken in relation to the shadow problem, the anima is activated. In the Norwegian parallel, she has a troll skin because, perhaps, in Nordic fairytales she is more uncanny and troll-like. An anima like this represents a challenge to the traditional Christian life that is moral and safe. In order to amplify this pagan aspect of the anima, let us digress from our story and consider a couple of Scandinavian tales. "The Secret Church" tells the story of a man who refuses to have anything to do with his pagan anima and cripples himself as a result.

272 *The Secret Church*

The schoolmaster of Etnedal loved to spend his holidays by himself in a hut in the mountains. Once, he heard church bells, and since there was no church nearby, he looked about him, astonished, and saw a group of people in Sunday clothes trooping along in front of his hut on a path that had not been there before. He followed them and came to a little wooden church that was also new to him. He was very impressed by the old pastor's sermon, but he noticed that the name of Jesus Christ was never mentioned and there was no blessing at the end.

273 After the service, the schoolmaster was invited to the pastor's house, and over a cup of tea the daughter told him that her father was quite old and asked if the schoolmaster would be willing to be his successor when he died. He begged to be allowed to think the matter over for a time. The daughter said that she would give him a whole year. As soon as she said this, he found himself back in the woods among familiar surroundings. He felt puzzled for a few days and then the matter slipped his mind.

274 The following year he was again in his mountain hut and, noticing that the roof was weathering away, he climbed up with his axe to do some repair work. Suddenly he became aware of someone coming down the path in front of the hut. It was the pastor's daughter. Seeing him, she asked if he was willing to accept the role of pastor. He replied, "I cannot justify it before God and my conscience, so I must refuse." At that moment the girl disappeared and he inadvertently brought the axe down upon his own knee, with the result that he was a cripple for the rest of his days.[4]

---

[4] Cf. Klara Stroebe, *Nordische Volksmärchen: Norwegische Volksmärchen*, vol 2. (Jena: Diederichs, 1940), 22.

275　This tale shows that repressing the anima for conventional reasons results in psychic self-mutilation. If one gets too high up (on the roof), one loses one's natural contact with the earth (the leg). On the other hand, this anima figure is a heathen demon. Here is another example that illustrates the unfortunate consequences that result from an inappropriate way of coping with the problem of the anima.

276　*The Wood Woman*

A woodcutter once saw a beautiful woman sewing in the woods, and her spool of thread rolled to his feet. She bade him return it to her and he did, although he knew that this meant he was submitting to her charm. On the following night, though he was careful to sleep in the midst of his comrades, she came and fetched him. They went into the mountains where everything was quiet and beautiful.

277　There he became infected with madness. One day when the troll-woman brought him something to eat, he saw that she had a cow's tail, and he made it fast in a split tree trunk; then he wrote the name of Christ on it. She fled and her tail was left in the trunk, and he saw that his meal was only cow dung. Many years later he came to a hut in the woods and saw a woman and child, both with a cow's tail. The woman said to the child, "Go and bring your father a drink of beer." The man fled in horror. Later he returned safely to his village. He remained, however, a bit queer for the rest of his days.[5]

278　This tale shows the dangerous spell that the anima casts on a man whose willpower is frail. Yielding to her means losing human contact and going completely wild. To repress the anima means a loss of spirit and of energy. The same type of "dangerous anima figure" appears in a story of the South American Cherente Indians.

---

[5] Ibid., 183–85.

279 *The Star*

A young man who was living in the bachelors' hut looked with longing each night at a brilliant star in the heavens and thought, "What a pity I cannot carry you about in my bottle all day and admire you." One night when he awoke from a deep dream about the star, he saw a girl by his bed with beautiful, deeply shining eyes. She told him that she was the very star that attracted him and that she had the ability to make herself small enough to dwell in the bottle and thus they might always be together.

280 They lived together by night, but during the day he pocketed her in his bottle where her eyes blazed like a wildcat's. The young man soon became very unhappy, and his fears were realized one day when she told him that she was leaving. She touched a tree with a magic rod so that it towered up into the skies and she ascended to heaven. Against his will the young man followed her, although she begged him not to, and high up in the tree he discovered a festival in full swing. He was alarmed to see skeletons dancing in a circle, and he fled in terror. The girl appeared again and told him to take a bath of purification, but it was to no avail. When he touched earth again, he had a splitting headache and soon died.[6]

281 This story portrays the alluring danger of archetypal images of the collective unconscious. It speaks of their power to take one away from reality. The listener realizes that there is no bliss in heaven even if the stars seem to promise it.

282 The anima is portrayed as a miraculous spirit and at the same time as a ferocious animal. When she appears as deathly and dreadful (which is often the case in very simple fairytales), it is important to keep consciousness away from the unconscious. The hero must guard himself against exposure to the dangerous contents. He may not give himself up to anything that fascinates him, neither

---

[6] Theodor Koch-Grünberg, *Südamerikanische Indianermärchen* (Jena: Diederichs, 1921), 206.

to fantasies from within nor to any dangerous and fascinating pursuits from without. So sometimes the anima has to be corked up, her powers reduced and confined. This is especially the case when cultures are young, and it corresponds to the intentional thrusting aside and devaluation of a complex. The anima then appears as a malicious animal with blazing eyes. Her reaction is evoked by the hero's conscious attitude, but at night she resumes her divine form.

283   The Christian religion uses a bottle, as it were, to imprison the anima in order to restrict and repress explosive forces. The cult of the Virgin Mary is just such a vessel for the mother and anima images of man. While this conscious restraint of the power of the anima is often necessary, there is the danger of prolonging it beyond its season. It is a question of feeling and of timing to adopt the right attitude before the unconscious gets too cut off and dams up too much explosive power.

284   In "The Bewitched Princess," the hero must overcome certain problems before he reaches the anima. In other versions, three witches pursue him — initial anima manifestations: Witches often resemble the mother-image, like the figure of the stepmother. And now we come to the image of the spool of thread. We heard that Peter's companion hurls a spool of golden thread across the river to form a bridge. After the two have run across, they dismantle it in time to forestall the witches' crossing behind them. The golden thread symbolizes a secret link to the deeper meaning that is within the unconscious. It is the invisible tie that threads things together, the thread of destiny that is woven by our unconscious projections. The thread is in the hands of the companion who functions as a supra-personal guide to destiny: He is the one who throws the spool of thread. The spool itself holds the balance at a perilous stage between the uncertain present and the immediate future until the bridge to what is to come is built. In these situations in which one oscillates between the opposites, one throws projections onto the outside; one spins threads. At some point, stability is achieved, and one is able to cross over, i.e., to change one's inner attitude.

285 The hero arrives in a city that is in mourning for a captive princess and learns that several princes have perished trying to save her. The anima in our story is under a spell and is trapped because a process in the unconscious has not been understood: Hence her riddles that must first be answered. These riddles of the anima mean that she does not understand herself and is not yet in her right place within the total psychic system. Moreover, she cannot solve this problem by herself but needs the help of consciousness. The hero is in the same fix because he, too, has not yet found his place and he, too, does not know himself. Thus, the riddle is something between both of them, something they have to solve together. It is the riddle of right relationship and reminds one of the riddle of the Sphinx, also half-animal, like the girl dressed in a troll skin in the Norwegian version. The classical question of the Sphinx in the Oedipus myth concerns the *being* of man, which is *the* great mystery we cannot yet understand.

286 When the anima problem is not understood, the anima, like the princess who is a creature of moods, either sulks and becomes silent and sullen, or becomes angry and hysterical. The anima poses a moral problem, although she herself is amoral. She can be counted on to engender the most confused and intricate problems, but if the hero lives up to his name, she can be freed. Then she guides him to higher consciousness. The shadow companion equips the hero with wings so that he can fly in the world of the anima. This means a new conscious attitude, a certain element of spiritualization, because wings belong to a fantasy being rather than to an earthly being. The ability to enter the realm of fantasy is essential to finding the anima; one must be freed from profane reality, at least to the extent of trying to fantasize. Detachment is also needed, objective observation with open eyes, a willingness to observe without interfering and judging. The companion also equips the hero with a rod, a means of criticism to soften the powerful effect of the anima. The rod signifies being resolute and earnest, which is necessary in order to punish the anima for her murderous and demonic behavior. The hero must follow her, stay with her, and yet criticize her negative side. Though he beats

her with the rod, it must not be hard enough to kill her. The princess, like the unconscious, is a piece of nature and therefore undiscriminating. Consciousness surpasses her in its ability to adapt to a situation because consciousness is normally more cool and resourceful; it has patience and appreciates distinctions. But as a piece of nature, the unconscious is unconfined, turbulent, and elemental and powerful.

287   The high mountain that Peter and his companion fly to signifies self-knowledge, which explains the effort that the hero must make in order to enter the large hall — the place where he will discover the anima's secret. The mountain spirit belongs to the archetype of the wise old man, who frequently has a pseudo-daughter in thrall in a sort of incestuous relationship. That he has an altar suggests secret religious ceremonies. This "father" of the anima may be regarded as a kind of priest who simultaneously has something chthonic and of the underworld about him. Analogous to the dragon in the Russian parallel story "The Three Feathers," he is a dark, pagan god. Often, he assigns insurmountable tasks to the hero who wishes to win his "daughter." In our fairytale, the anima presents riddles that he has devised. The mountain spirit behind the anima represents a secret, meaningful plan or intention governing her. This means that behind the anima is the possibility of a further inner development of the hero. The "father" of the anima is the greater wisdom that is indicated by the altar and by the fish being worshipped. The mountain spirit represents a supra-personal force, a spirit that has been neglected in the development of civilization. In the Norwegian version, the mountain spirit is personified by a troll who is the lover of the princess and whose companion is a he-goat — a theriomorphic form of the devil.

288   The idea of a spirit is closely allied to the original idea of the soul lingering on after death and moves between the poles of a subjective and objective phenomenon. Primitives experience spirit as a purely objective occurrence, whereas we tend to believe that a spiritual experience is subjective. But spirit originally was — and still is to a great extent — an autonomous archetypal factor. This is expressed

in the figure of the "old man," a personification of spirit. In fairytales, the old man is usually a helpful figure who appears when the hero is in difficulty and needs counsel and guidance. He represents the concentration of mental power and purposeful reflection, i.e., for genuine objective thought. Symbols of spirit are generally of neutral value, neither positive nor negative. But if they are only positive or only negative, they represent only half of the nature of the archetype that always has a double aspect as, for example, in the figure Merlin.[7] In our fairytale, the old man and mountain spirit is the animus of the anima: He represents the objective spirit behind the anima. Such figures of old men in a mountain are a folklore motif, for instance, the Kyffhäuser legend of the Emperor Barbarossa[8] or Mercurius in alchemy, who is now a boy, now an old man.[9] His character, sometimes destructive, sometimes inspiring, depends upon the attitude of the alchemist. In alchemical tales, the student of alchemy often seeks the truth in the bowels of the mountains where he meets an old man, a Hermes-Mercurial figure. This spirit is both the goal and the inspiration that leads to the goal. He is called "the friend of God" for he has the key or the book that preserves all secrets. The alchemists who asked themselves how this Hermes-Mercurial figure was related to the Christian God, found that he was a chthonic and dark reflection of the God-image.

289   The temple in the middle of the mountain is a frequently occurring motif in European fairytales. A man-made edifice in a mountain means a structured form in the unconscious. It represents a cultural development that was suddenly dropped without having undergone a transition into the mainstream of culture. Such a hidden temple is something like a broken-off cultural shoot, an interruption of cultural development, like the sudden cutting-off of alchemy and of the qualitative view of nature in favor of an exclusively quantitative approach in the 17th century. This leaves the former development intact but merely as a piece of tradition whose

---

[7] Cf. Marie-Louise von Franz, *C.G. Jung: His Myth in Our Time* (Asheville: Chiron Publications, 2022), chap. 14.
[8] Cf. Mackensen, *Handwörterbuch des deutschen Aberglaubens*; see the entry „Mountain".
[9] Cf. Jung, "The Spirit of Mercury," in *Alchemical Studies*, vol. 13, *CW*, 211 ff.

effectiveness has been lost. The anima is bound to the mountain spirit because he has the secret that allows her to live. By contrast, our modern consciousness has not given the soul enough room or enough life and even attempts to exclude it. Therefore, the anima clings to the mountain spirit because she feels that he holds the secret of her life. That he holds the secret has to do with his being pagan and the fact that the pagan way of looking at the world gives the anima a more abundant chance to live.

290   The non-Christian figure of the mountain spirit is a hint at when the fairytale arose. As fairytales, like archetypal dreams, mirror the transformational process in the collective unconscious that progresses very slowly, it takes a long time for the meaning of such images to take root and penetrate consciousness. One can therefore only date them within a margin of about three hundred years. Our tale probably belongs to the Age of Enlightenment, an era in which the application of Christian principles to earthly things was commonplace. Johannes Kepler, for instance, assigned the image of the Trinity to the universe and its three dimensions of space. The Godhead itself he thought of as a sphere of which the Father is the center, the Son the superficies or outer side, and the Holy Ghost the radii. According to Kepler, all creatures long to be spheres, that is, to emulate God. The entire so-called Age of Enlightenment can be described as being based upon a trinitarian form of thinking. The Trinity, however, represents an incomplete standpoint that excludes the problem of evil and the irrational elements in nature. Because of its estrangement from the irrational and from the soul, this enlightened thinking was as one-sided as the mythical thinking that preceded it. In order to counterbalance the new tendency, the inheritors of the traditional way asserted its tenets more loudly with the result that the two sides set up separate camps, and neither was able to complement the other's distortions.

291   The first object that the mountain spirit proposes to the princess to think of in order to baffle the hero is her father's white horse.[10]

---

[10] Riddles are a common theme in myths and fairytales, like the riddle of the sphinx. [Added by the translator of the French edition].

With the father, a new figure — a king, and the real father of the anima — is indirectly introduced. As I suggested earlier, the figure of the old king often symbolizes a moribund system of spiritual and worldly order. The father of the anima, as the representative for a worn-out Christian *Weltanschauung*, stands in contrast to the renegade mountain spirit, who plays a parallel role as the pagan father. The mountain spirit symbolizes an exuberant upwelling of libido that stirs in the unconscious. This means he represents a living archetype, one that, because it was repressed for too long, has become threatening. The hero must be on his guard against the opposites denoted by these two kingly figures, which, like all extreme opposites, are mysteriously one. The king's white horse is a symbol of the unconscious powers that are at the disposal of consciousness.[11]

292   The second object that the princess must think of is a sword. It stands for justice, authority, decisiveness (consider Alexander's slicing of the Gordian knot), and discrimination, both in one's understanding and in one's intention. The motif of the sword plays a great role in alchemy.[12] When, for example, the dragon is cut up by the sword, this signifies the attempt to discriminate the instincts so that undefined unconscious contents are made more definite. One must cut the *prima materia* "with its own sword" — in other words, a conscious decision is necessary in order to free the libido offered by the unconscious. To put it differently, it is the conscious personality that must decide which course of action to take, and this is an essential precondition for the unconscious to go ahead. "Take the sword! Cleave the dragon!" — then something will develop. In the ceremony of the Mass, the sword symbolizes the Logos, and in the Apocalypse, it is the Logos functioning as God's decisive Word that judges the world.[13] The flaming sword placed in front of the Garden of Eden is explained in alchemy as the wrath of the God of

---

[11] Cf. Jung, *Symbols of Transformation*, vol. 5, CW, § 421.

[12] Cf. Jung, "Symbols of Transformation in Mass," in *Psychology and Religion*, vol. 11, CW, § 357.

[13] *The Holy Bible*, The Gospel according to John 1:16: "And he had in his right hand seven stars: and out of his mouth proceeded a sharp two-edged sword: and his countenance was as the sun shineth in his strength." The meaning of this symbolic language becomes clear in the Letter to the Hebrews. Hebr. 4:12: "For the word of God is living, and active, and sharper than any two-edged sword, and piercing even to the dividing of the soul and spirit, of both joints and marrow, and quick to discern the thoughts and intents of the heart."

the Old Testament. In the Gnostic system of Simon Magus, the flaming sword was interpreted as the passion that separates earth from Paradise. The sword can also have a negative meaning, for instance, when it cuts off life opportunities. Like the horse, the sword signifies libido from the unconscious, a portion of psychic power that is available to consciousness. The sword, however, is an instrument made by man, whereas the horse represents instinctive libido.

293   The third object is the head of the mountain spirit, a thing of which no mortal being can conceive. The Greek alchemists declared that the great secret of humankind lies in the brain. In *Timaeus*, Plato also pointed out that the head repeats the ball-form of the universe, or of God; it carries, as it were, man's divine secrets. This is probably one of the reasons why primitives frequently have cults of the head. The Sabians, for instance, steeped a "golden-headed" (blond) man in oil, then cut off his head and used it as an oracle. The alchemists called themselves "children of the golden head," and the alchemist Zosimos taught that the Omega (Ω) is the great secret.[14] In alchemy, the head is also a symbol of the Self. The head was later interpreted as "essence" or "meaning." With the help of the head we have the key to the solution of inner problems. In our story, it is the head that propounds the riddles and is therefore at the bottom of all the riddles of the anima. The hero's acquisition of the head symbolizes the solution of his problem: Whoever is in possession of it is able to understand inner psychic processes. The three objects that the princess should think upon — the horse, the sword, and the head — express the fact that the old conscious system has a certain will and energy, although its dynamism and meaning have reverted to the unconscious. There is therefore a split between conscious energy and unconscious meaning, which is a primary problem of our day.

294   Let us now consider the symbols found in the temple of the mountain spirit. On the hero's first trip the hall is dark and the altar bare. The random stars above are latent, indefinitely dispersed germs

---

[14] Cf. Jung, "The Visions of Zosimos," in *Alchemical Studies*, vol. 13, *CW*, chap. 2, § 95, § 101.

of consciousness. On the second trip, the moon is shining, and a prickly fish lies on the altar. The moon, a symbol of the feminine principle, signifies a feminine-receptive attitude towards the inner and the outer worlds, one that demonstrates a receptive registering of what goes on. In some Chinese poems, the moon brings repose and calm after a previous struggle. The Greek philosopher Anaximander suggested that man was descended from a prickly fish. The fish is famous as a Christian symbol. The apostles were called "fishers of men,"[15] and the fish is a symbol of Christ himself (Greek: *ichthys*). Both Christ and the fish are symbols of the Self. Christ draws the projection of the fish symbol out of nature and becomes its symbol Himself — a symbol of the Self.[16] The fish also plays a prominent role in astrology since it is the zodiacal sign that governs the first two thousand years of the Christian era. There are two fish in it, one vertical, the other horizontal. The one symbolizes Christ in the Christian tradition, and the other, the anti-Christ. It seems that the prickly fish in our tale points to the anti-Christ as a central unconscious, but devilish, content. It is unapproachable, a prickly, slippery content of the unconscious which is hard and dangerous to reach.

295   In the Middle Ages, the fish was thought to be a symbol of earthly pleasure "because it is so greedy"; perhaps also because Leviathan was a fish-monster.[17] Jewish tradition asserts that the pious will eat Leviathan as a Eucharistic meal on Doomsday. As Leviathan is food that is pure, this act means partaking in immortality. So we can see a certain ambivalence concerning the meaning of the fish. In India, the fish is connected with the symbol of the savior. The god Manu transformed himself into a fish and saved the holy books from the flood. In alchemy, a "round fish in the middle of the sea" with no bones and a wonderful fatness is frequently mentioned, and later this fish was connected with a glowing fish that causes fever. The alchemists interpreted the nettle — fire in the sea — as a symbol of divine love or hellish fire; all of

---

[15] Cf. *The Holy Bible*, Luke 5:10.
[16] On the symbolism of the fish and the symbolism of the Self, see Jung, *Aion*, vol. 9/II, *CW*.
[17] Cf. *The Holy Bible*, Job 40:20–28; and Ps. 104:26.

these disparate aspects are generally combined in alchemistic symbolism of the fish. While Christianity does not permit any marriage of heaven and hell, alchemy is given to paradoxical thought. Psychologically, the fish is a distant, inaccessible content of the unconscious, a sum of potential energy loaded with possibilities, but with a lack of clarity. It is a libido symbol for a relatively uncharacterized and unspecified amount of psychic energy, the direction and development of which are not yet outlined. The ambivalence of the fish derives from its being a content below the threshold of consciousness.

296   On the hero's third trip, rays of the sun light up the hall. The change of objects seen by the hero suggests a gradual lightening of the unconscious until clear discernment is attained. A midnight sun inside the mountain recalls the midnight sun shining from below that Apuleius saw in the kingdom of the dead.[18] Not only does the ego carry light, but the unconscious itself has a "latent consciousness." This midnight sun is probably the original form of consciousness that is more collective than it is individual. Tribal peoples and children experience this — a knowledge of "what is known" rather than "what I know." The light in the unconscious is first a "noncentered," diffused haze. Creation myths often divide the creation of light into two stages.[19] There is firstly the birth of light in general and then the birth of the sun. In Genesis, for example, God creates light on the first day, but He creates the sun and moon only on the fourth day.

297   On the altar lies a fiery wheel. In India, the wheel is a symbol of power and victory; it is considered to be a guide to power and the way to power.[20] As the wheel of redemption, it moves the right way along the right line and symbolizes the gradual intensification of religious consciousness. In later times the wheel assumed a more sinister aspect as the "wheel of rebirth" — the senseless circular

---

[18] Cf. Apuleius, *The Golden Ass: or the Metamorphoses*, trans. W. Adlington (New York: Barnes & Noble Books, 2004); and Von Franz, *Golden Ass*.

[19] Cf. Marie-Louise von Franz, *Pattern of Creativity Mirrored in Creation Myths* (Dallas: Spring Publications, 1972), 154–69.

[20] Rhys David, „Zur Geschichte des Radsymbols," in *Ostwestliche Symbolik und Seelenführung*, Eranos Jahrbuch 1934 (Zurich: Rhein-Verlag, 1935), 153–78.

repetition of life processes from which one should try to escape. In either case, the wheel symbolizes the self-moving power of the unconscious — the Self. To move in rhythm with the movement of the psyche — the wheel — is the goal of the Indian. His aim is to stay on the course given by the Self. But the Self may become a negative, torturing factor if its intentions are misunderstood. In Babylonian times, the horoscope or astrological wheel of birth marked the appearance of the fatal wheel whereby man is caught in the wheel of his own destiny. Homage was paid to Christ as the only one who could destroy the wheel of birth by giving spiritual rebirth to the faithful. In the Middle Ages, Fortuna had a wheel, a kind of roulette wheel, which expressed the reckless working of blind fate upon men who are simply caught in their own unconsciousness. The alchemists often saw their work as a circular process of continual purification. The circular movement — the *rotatio* — of the alchemical wheel creates a unification of the opposites: Heaven becomes earthly, and earth becomes heavenly. The alchemists called this wheel of work "the rotating world" and viewed it as a positive symbol. The wheel is even a symbol of God. Niklaus von der Flüe, the Swiss mystic and saint, had a terrifying vision of God that he then had painted covered by a wheel. In this way he sought to soften the terrible God he had experienced, to make him more acceptable and comprehensible.[21] In a Caucasian tale in which God kills a berserk hero by sending a fiery wheel against him that smashes and burns him, the wheel expresses the avenging, ominous side of the Divinity. At midsummer festivals throughout the entire Germanic agricultural region, people roll fiery wheels down the mountains. This custom is a relic of a ritual attempt to support and strengthen the sun. It can also be understood as a symbol of the source of consciousness in the unconscious. Similarly, there is a popular belief in Germanic folklore that speaks of unreleased souls spinning like fiery wheels.

298   The wheel of fire generally refers to the spontaneous movement of the psyche that manifests as passion or as an emotional impulse

---

[21] Marie-Louise von Franz, *Niklaus von Flue and Saint Perpetua* (Asheville: Chiron Publications, 2022).

— a spontaneous up-rush from the unconscious that sets one on fire. When this happens, one may say, "That idea kept on turning in my head like a wheel." Similarly, the revolving wheel illustrates the senseless circular motion of a neurotic consciousness. This happens when one has lost one's connection with one's inner life and is cut off from the individual meaning of one's life. In our tale, the wheel in its roundness is analogous to the mountain spirit's head — a symbol of the Self, but in its dark aspect. A South American Indian tale illustrates the thoroughly destructive aspect of the head: A skull begins to roll in an uncanny way, acquires wings and claws, and becomes a demonic, murderous thing that devours everything. This idea has to do with the separation of head from body and the autonomy of the head, and it shows that contact with life has been lost.

299   In fairytales, the king is often lacking the water of life, from which we may conclude that life has lost its charm. But in our case, the anima has lost the meaning (her head) of life, and this is even truer of the desperate mountain spirit. The anima's unbalanced behavior shows consciousness and the unconscious are in a false relationship.[22] By getting the head, the hero integrates its knowledge and its wisdom. He thereby breaks the spell that had been cast on the princess. Although she is released, she is not yet redeemed because the symbolic head has been grasped only in a negative form. The cutting-off of the head means separating this special content from its collective unconscious background by an intuitive recognition of its specific character. In this way the hero integrates a part of the meaning, but he does not get what it is in its entirety or how it is connected with the collective unconscious. While he is able to discriminate the essential disturbing factor behind the anima and thereby put an end to it, he could not completely realize the roots of

---

[22] "Like vampires, the anima and the mountain spirit love the blood of their victims. The vampire motif is worldwide. Vampires are the spirits of the dead in Hades to whom Odysseus must first sacrifice blood. Their lust for blood is the craving or impulse of the unconscious contents to break into consciousness. If they are denied, they begin to drain energy from consciousness, leaving the individual fatigued and listless. This story indicates an attempt on the part of unconscious contents to attract the attention of consciousness, to obtain recognition of their reality and their needs and to impart something to consciousness." [Added by editor of French edition].

it. In the head is the presence of the god of the early Germans: Wotan — a connection that for the moment remains hidden.[23] The positive aspect of the head becomes apparent only after the process of transformation takes place in the anima. This also reveals the deeper meaning of this macabre head.

300   We have seen that our understanding of many European fairytales is greatly increased if we tap into the rich symbolic fund of alchemical texts. They contain very valuable comparative material for all these speculations were, at bottom, an attempt to blend the natural, heathen strain with the Christian strain in collective consciousness. The one-sided spiritualization of Christianity had brought about an estrangement from the instinct. The alchemists tried to counteract this. As Jung observes in *Psychology and Alchemy*, we are Christianized in the higher levels of the psyche, but down below we are still completely pagan. While most fairytales are pagan, some of them (especially those of a later date) contain symbols that one can understand only as being an attempt on the part of the unconscious to reunite the sunken pagan tradition with the Christian field of consciousness. Unlike in fairytales, the alchemists not only produced symbols (by projecting their unconscious into physical materials), but they also "theorized" about their discoveries. Their texts abound not only in symbols but also in many interesting, semipsychological associations linked up with the symbols. This explains why alchemical images provide an excellent link between the symbols in fairytales and our conscious world today.

301   In alchemy, some of the usual stages of refinement — crude *prima materia* into gold — are: the *nigredo,* the Latin word for the blackness of the material when subjected to fire; the *albedo,* the whitening of the substance which, when washed, becomes silver; and the *rubedo,* the red, which, through further heating, turns into gold. Psychologically speaking, the *albedo* signifies the individual's first clear awareness of the unconscious, with the accompanying possibility of attaining an objective attitude. In order to get in touch with unconscious content, a lowering of consciousness is necessary.

---

[23] Cf. Jung, "Wotan," in *Civilization in Transition*, vol. 10, *CW*.

The *albedo* means a cool, detached attitude, a stage where things look remote and vague, as though seen in moonlight. It is therefore said that the *albedo* is ruled by the feminine and the moon for a receptive attitude towards the unconscious prevails. "Cleansing"[24] denotes the torture of becoming conscious of one's shadow, whereas the former stage, the *nigredo*, marks the first terrible facing of the shadow. The alchemists call this "the hard work." With the progress of the *albedo*, the burden that man carries becomes lighter. Simple heating changes the *albedo* into the *rubedo*, which is ruled by the sun and heralds a new state of consciousness. The sun and the moon, the red slave and the white woman, are opposites that "marry," meaning the union of objective consciousness with the anima — of masculine Logos with the feminine inner principle. With this union, more and more energy is poured into consciousness by degrees, bringing a positive connection with the world, and the possibility of love and creative activity.

302   The image of the mountain spirit is a parallel to Saturn. In alchemy, Saturn symbolizes a dark god that must be raised up into consciousness. Saturn is the head, the round thing, (Zosimos calls Saturn the Omega or head) or the "destructive water." This dynamic mountain spirit does not appear to be a god, but only a priest or an acolyte (Greek: companion, follower), devoted to a god. As I pointed out earlier, in northern countries Mercurius was partially identified with Wotan, as can be seen in many fairytales. With the cutting-off of alchemy and the decline of folklore, people severed the connections with the pagan gods within their unconscious. Prior to this, the pagan gods were active; they made their last stand, as it were, in alchemy, folklore, and astrology. It is, perhaps, indicative that in our tale, the mountain spirit is not redeemed: Only the anima is. Thus, the deeper problem remains unsolved: the continuing presence of Wotan waiting to be roused in the psyche.

303   With the beheading of the mountain spirit, the danger is not yet over. On the wedding night, the hero must plunge the princess three times into water until she is restored to her former self. In the

---

[24] Cf. Michael Maier, *Atalanta Fugiens* (Manchester: Old Book Publishing, 2015).

Norwegian version, he has to wash off her troll skin in milk. Milk played a prominent part as nourishment for the freshly initiated — the "newly born" — in the ancient mysteries. In the Dionysian mountain orgies, the Maenads drank milk and honey. Milk and honey were also the food of the reborn in early Christian baptism. In an ode of Solomon, milk is extolled as a symbol of the friendliness and kindness of God. Saint Paul spoke of the new Christians as children drinking the milk of the new doctrine.[25] Milk is a symbol of the beginning of a divine rebirth in man. The gods of ancient Greece brought milk as a sacrificial offering to the old chthonic gods and to the newly dead. In these cases, milk is cathartic. Think of the many German superstitions about obstructive demons bewitching milk and turning it blue, and the many prescribed precautions against them. Washing the anima in milk means the purging of the demonic elements in her, as well as the purging of her link with death.

304   Skins of animals and of trolls are evidence of an unredeemed nature. In the imagination of the alchemists, the anima sometimes wears dirty clothes, or appears as "the dove hidden in the lead." These images mean that psychological contents that were not sufficiently developed during the "cleansing" turn up in an unpleasant or damaging guise — for instance as a negative animus. You can recognize such a disguise, for example, when a man's spiritual aspiration expresses itself in a craving for drink. The positive impulses of unconscious contents do not see the light of day; they remain not only hidden but "pollute" the instincts, or even materialize in ugly impulses. Indeed, many neurotic symptoms are like troll skins covering up important positive contents of the unconscious.

305   In the German version of our tale, the anima emerged from the first dunking as a raven, from the second as a dove, so she evidently has the flighty element in her.[26] Because she represents an

---

[25] Cf. *The Holy Bible*, Peter 2:2–3: "[…] as newborn babes, long for the spiritual milk which is without guile, that ye may grow thereby until salvation; if ye have tasted that the Lord is gracious."
[26] Alchemy is, amongst other things, "the fixation of the flighty," cf. *Atalanta Fugiens*. The 16th emblem depicts a lion without wings, pinning down a lioness with wings.

uncontrollable, capricious, evasive content, she often appears as a bird. In the Christian world, the raven was thought to be a representation of the sinner and also of the devil. In antiquity, on the other hand, the raven belonged to the sun god Apollo, and in alchemy it symbolizes the *nigredo* (blackness) — melancholy thoughts.[27] The old man in the mountain who is surrounded by ravens is a frequent character in fairytales; he embodies Wotan, the pagan god of the past.

306   The dove, on the other hand, is the bird of Venus.[28] In the Gospel according to John, it represents the Holy Ghost, and in alchemy it represents the *albedo*. Two aspects of the anima must be distinguished: her bird nature that belongs to the other world and her feminine side that is related to this world. The hero must free or separate her flighty, elusive bird nature by bathing her — a requirement that reminds one of his being asked to cut his own child in two. The unconscious must be differentiated from consciousness. The bathing is a sort of baptism, a transformation in the medium of the unconscious. In practical terms, the bathing means pushing the anima back into the unconscious, an act that requires a critical attitude toward what is awakened and emerging into consciousness. Such an attitude is necessary because the anima and the reactions she induces in a man, although apparently human, are often deceptive. For this reason a man must always ask of an anima inspiration, "Is this my own real feeling?" for the feeling of a man can be lyrical and soar like a lark in flight, or it can be bloodthirsty and hawk-like, scarcely human — a mood that is unrelated to the human state. The milk bath serves this purpose of purifying and taking the curse out of the anima.

307   The spiritual companion's final concern is with this cleansing process. When the marriage of the hero and the anima is consummated, the comrade vanishes into the Beyond. He is indeed more than a shadow figure: He is an inspiring, creative spirit. But he

---

[27] Cf. Mackensen, *Handwörterbuch des deutschen Aberglaubens*; see also *Atalanta Fugens*: the 43rd emblem. It depicts a vulture and a raven, symbols of the *nigredo* in connection with Saturn.

[28] The dove (*albedo*), that comes after the raven, represents the spirit of life and of love, that emerges from decomposition and death. The oil for the crowning of the queen is carried to heaven in a vial by a dove. [Added by editor of French edition].

can be this effectively only when the anima loses her demonic qualities. With the fulfilment of the marriage of the hero and his anima, the task of the shadow is accomplished, as it was in "Prince Ring." The primary goal of our tale is therefore not dealing with the shadow. It is mostly concerned with finding and recognizing the genuine inner goal so that the fight between good and evil no longer holds center stage.

Chapter 9

The Woman, the Shadow, and the Animus in Fairytales

9.1 *The Shadow*

Not many fairytales tell about the heroine and her shadow. The usual pattern is that of the good and bad sisters, the one loaded with rewards and the other dreadfully punished. Another variation of this basic model is of a heroine who is neglected by her stepmother who often makes the girl do the most menial housework. These heroines lend themselves equally well to interpretation from the masculine standpoint. They correspond to the positive and negative aspects of the anima.

The female shadow appears so rarely in fairytales because women are not so very sharply separated from their shadows. Nature and culture are more closely interwoven in women than in men. If there is a separation, it is usually because of the influence of the animus. The female psyche displays a pendulum-like tendency to swing from ego to shadow, as the moon moves from new to full and back to new again. There is a Scandinavian tale that seems to be a representative example of the feminine shadow problem. Here, as so often in fairytales, the problem of the shadow is intertwined with that of the animus.

Tatterhood[1]

A king and queen who had no children of their own adopted a little girl. One day when she was playing with her golden ball, she caught the attention of a beggar-girl and her mother.

---

[1] Ethel Johnston Phelps, ed., *Tatterhood and Other Tales* (Old Westbury, NY: Feminist Press, 1978).

The king and queen wished to chase them away, but the beggar-child said that her mother knew of a way to make the queen fruitful. After being coaxed with wine, the old beggar-woman told the queen that she must bathe in two vessels before retiring and then throw the water under the bed; then in the morning she would see two flowers in bloom under her bed, one fair and one foul; she was to eat the fair flower only.

311 In the morning when the queen tasted the fair bright flower, it was so delicious that she could not resist eating the black and ugly one as well. When her time came, her little daughter was grey and ugly and came riding to her on a he-goat. In her hand she held a wooden mixing ladle, and she was able to speak from the very first. An exquisitely fair younger daughter followed. The ugly one was called Tatterhood because her head and part of her face were covered with shaggy tufts. She became a close friend to her younger sister.

312 One Christmas Eve, the noise of troll-women holding a festival reached them, and Tatterhood went out with her ladle to chase them away. The fair princess looked out of the door, and a troll-wife snatched her head off and gave her a calf's head instead.

313 Tatterhood took her unlucky sister on a ship to the land of the troll-women, found her head under a window, and made off with it. With the troll-wives after her, she raced back to the ship and changed the heads back again. They landed in a region ruled by a king who was a widower with an only son. This king wished to marry the fair princess, but Tatterhood made it a condition that the prince should marry her; so the king arranged for the double wedding in spite of the prince's protests about having to marry Tatterhood.

314 On the wedding day, Tatterhood told the prince to ask her why she rode such an ungainly buck. When he did so, she replied that it was indeed a beautiful horse, and the buck

thereupon changed into a beautiful horse. In a similar way, the ladle became a silver fan, her shaggy cap became a golden crown, and she herself assumed a beauty even more radiant than her sister's. The wedding ceremony proved a happier event than anyone could ever have expected.

315 The assimilation of the upper and the lower here is the same theme as in "Prince Ring." Again the shadow is redeemed by being made conscious. One might conclude from this that a woman's shadow presents her with the same difficulties as does a man's shadow for men, but the problem goes deeper and touches upon something archetypal.

316 The motif of the childless royal couple is generally a forerunner of the miraculous birth of a very distinguished child. In itself, childlessness indicates that the connection to the creative earth of the psyche has been broken and that a gulf lies between the values and ideas of collective consciousness and the dark, fertile loam of unconscious, archetypal processes of transformation. We may regard the two leading figures, the fair princess and Tatterhood, as parallels to Ring and Snati-Snati. We took Ring to be an impulse in the collective unconscious that was tending to build up a new form of consciousness. Tatterhood, however, may represent an impulse to restore the feeling connection with the depths of the unconscious and with nature — in alignment with a woman's task in life: to renew feeling values.

317 Before the birth of these two children, the queen does her best to remedy the situation by adopting a girl. This very positive decision evokes — like magic by analogy — a fertilizing reaction in the matrix of the unconscious. By means of the golden ball, which may be taken as a symbol of the Self, the adopted child attracts a poor child and her mother. The function of the Self-symbol is to unite the dark and the light aspects of the psyche, and in this case Mother Nature is constellated. In the fairytale, the beggar-woman personifies the instinctive knowledge of nature. She gives clear advice to the queen to throw the water in which she has washed under the bed and to

eat one of the flowers that will grow in it. To keep the dirty water within the bedroom probably means that the queen should not cast out her own dark side but should accept it within her most intimate surroundings, because in this dirty water — her shadow — lies also her own fertility. This seems to be the age-old maternal secret of the old woman.

318   The bright flower and the dark flower anticipate the opposite natures of the two daughters. They signify their as yet unborn souls and they also symbolize feeling. By eating both flowers instead of just one, the queen reveals an urge to integrate the totality, not only the brighter aspect of the unconscious. By so doing, she also commits the sin of disobedience — a *beata culpa* (a fortunate guilt) — that brings forth new trouble, but with it, a higher realization. This is similar to the motif in "Prince Ring" when he opens the door of the forbidden kitchen and finds Snati-Snati.

319   As the shadow of the new form of life, Tatterhood has all the exuberance and initiative. That she grows up so rapidly points to her demonic qualities and spirit-like nature. The he-goat on which she rides is the animal of the Germanic god of thunder, Thor, and suggests the Dionysian, chthonic and pagan world to which Tatterhood essentially belongs. The ladle characterizes her as witchlike, one who has always got something cooking, who stirs up a welter of emotions that she is able to bring to the boil. The fur cap she wears is a sign of her animal traits and a symbol of a certain animus possession.[2] In some tales, when her father persecutes her, the heroine puts on shaggy headgear that indicates a regression into the animal domain because of an animus problem. It looks as if an animal-like unconsciousness clings to Tatterhood, which implies a possession by animal impulses and emotions. This, however, is only an outer appearance, just as it was with Snati-Snati.

320   In northern countries the pagan layer of the unconscious is still very much alive, and therefore the trolls are depicted as having their

---

[2] Being in a state of possession (through the animus and through an archetype) is a psychic situation in which an unconscious content rules consciousness and floods it. It is above all our dreams that help us to become conscious of the archetypal element that is behind it, and to slowly integrate it into life, thereby accessing new energy and enabling the development of one's personality. [Added by editor of French edition].

midsummer festival at Christmas. When the princess is curious and gapes at them from the doorway, they seize her head and replace it with the head of a calf. According to northern folklore, the trolls themselves often have the tails of cows, and we may conclude from the transposition of the heads that the princess is fascinated by the trolls: She literally loses her head and becomes possessed by contents of the collective unconscious. As a cow, she often appears to be completely silly, gauche, and unable to express herself. Her whole feeling life has fallen under the control of dark powers of the unconscious, and events are occurring in her inner world that she cannot express. Tatterhood is able to outwit the trolls and redeem her sister from this state because, to a certain extent, she shares the trolls' nature. Snati-Snati also knew better than Ring how to overcome the giants.

321   After the heroine has redeemed her sister, the story takes an unexpected turn. Instead of sailing home, they continue their journey into a strange kingdom where there are no women, only a widower king and a prince. Since the first court had several women and a barren king, in the second kingdom we find the elements that make up for what was lacking in the first. The two realms are like two compensatory parts of the psyche: Incomplete in themselves, they form a totality only when put together. When the king proposes to marry the princess, Tatterhood demands the hand of the prince. The double marriage constitutes what Jung calls a marriage quaternity, a four-square symbol of the Self.[3] Tatterhood gets redeemed not only by assisting at her sister's wedding (like Snati-Snati again) but also by inducing the prince to ask certain questions. This recalls the Parzival saga in which Parzival at first fails to ask the redeeming question, consciousness being still too juvenile to be aware of what is growing in the unconscious toward the light. Tatterhood, on the other hand, is the strong, dynamic factor in the unconscious that compels consciousness to realize what is striving to be realized. Here we have a beautiful example of unconscious

---

[3] Cf. C.G. Jung, *The Practice of Psychotherapy*, 2nd ed., vol. 16, *CW*, (Princeton, NJ: Princeton University Press, 1985), §§ 425, 430, 437.

nature itself endeavoring to equip man to reach a new, higher level of consciousness. The impulse has its starting point in the source of the shadow and is gradually and fully humanized.

322   The general structure of this fairytale is interesting as it points to a system that is made up of four parts. There are two groups of four persons. We have the king and queen, their adopted child, and her poor friend. Relations within this group are not harmonious. The helpful intervention of the beggar-woman brings about the coming of the second pair of girls, Tatterhood and the fair princess, who take the place of the former children. The disturbing interference of the trolls indicates that this quaternity is still too artificial and too detached from conscious awareness. When the princess and Tatterhood marry the king and the prince, they merge into a new quaternity. This new group seems to be a model of the Self, like the group of four persons at the close of "Prince Ring." The tale of Tatterhood also opens with a symbol of the Self and culminates in a symbol of the Self. Its basic elements represent eternal processes of transformation that take place within the nucleus of the collective psyche.

323   ## 9.2 The Animus of Women

The animus of women is perhaps less well-known in literature than the anima of men. There are, however, many very impressive representations of this archetype in folklore. Fairytales in particular contain much information on how to deal with this inner figure. How a woman deals with her animus is different to how a man deals with his anima — it is not merely a simple reversal. Every step in becoming conscious of the animus is differently characterized. The following tale is a good example of this.

324   *King Thrushbeard*

A king had a daughter who was beautiful beyond all measure, but so proud and haughty withal that no suitor was good enough for her. She sent away one after the other and ridiculed them as well. Once the king made a great feast and invited thereto, from far and near, all the young men likely to marry. They were all marshaled in a row according to their rank and standing. First came the kings, then the grand dukes, then the princes, the earls, the barons, and the gentry. Then the king's daughter was led through the ranks, but to each one she had some objection to make. One was too fat, "wine-barrel," she said. Another was too tall, "long and thin has little in." The third was too short, "short and thick is never quick." The fourth was too pale, "as pale as death." The fifth too red, "a fighting cock." The sixth was not straight enough, "a green log dried behind the stove." So she had something to say against each one, but she made herself especially merry over a good king who stood quite high up in the row and whose chin had grown a little crooked. "Look," she cried and laughed, "he has a chin like a thrush's beak." And from that time he got the name of King Thrushbeard. But the old king, when he saw that his daughter did nothing but mock the people, and despised all the suitors who were gathered there, was very angry and swore that she should have for her husband the very first beggar that came to his doors.

325   A few days afterwards a fiddler came and sang beneath the windows, trying to earn a few pennies. When the king heard him, he said, "Let him come up." So the fiddler came in, in his dirty, ragged clothes, and sang before the king and his daughter, and when he had finished, he asked for a trifling gift. The king said, "Your song has pleased me so well that I will give you my daughter there, to wife." The king's daughter shuddered, but the king said, "I have taken an oath to give you to the very first beggar-man and I will keep it." All she could say was in vain. The priest was brought, and she had to let herself be wedded to the fiddler on the spot. When that was done, the king said, "Now it is not proper for you, a beggar-woman, to stay any longer in my palace. You may just go away with your husband."

326   The beggar-man led her out by the hand, and she was obliged to walk away on foot with him. When they came to a large forest, she asked, "To whom does that beautiful forest belong?" "It belongs to King Thrushbeard. If you had taken him, it would have been yours." "Ah, unhappy girl that I am, if I had but taken King Thrushbeard."

327   Afterwards they came to a meadow, and she asked again, "To whom does this beautiful green meadow belong?" "It belongs to King Thrushbeard. If you had taken him, it would have been yours." "Ah, unhappy girl that I am, if I had but taken King Thrushbeard."

328   Then they came to a large town, and she asked again, "To whom does this fine large town belong?" "It belongs to King Thrushbeard. If you had taken him, it would have been yours."

329   "Ah, unhappy girl that I am, if I had but taken King Thrushbeard."

330   "It does not please me," said the fiddler, "to hear you always wishing for another husband. Am I not good enough for you?"

331   At last they came to a very little hut, and she said, "Oh goodness. What a small house. To whom does this miserable, tiny hovel belong?" The fiddler answered, "That is my house and yours, where we shall live together." She had to stoop in order to go in at the low door. "Where are the servants?" said the king's daughter. "What servants?" answered the beggar-man. "You must yourself do what you wish to have done. Just make a fire at once, and set on water to cook my supper, I am quite tired." But the king's daughter knew nothing about lighting fires or cooking, and the beggar-man had to lend a hand himself to get anything fairly done. When they had finished their scanty meal, they went to bed. But he forced her to get up quite early in the morning in order to look after the house. For a few days they lived in this way as well as

might be and came to the end of all their provisions. Then the man said, "Wife, we cannot go on any longer eating and drinking here and earning nothing. You must make baskets." He went out, cut some willows, and brought them home. Then she began to make baskets, but the tough willows wounded her delicate hands. "I see that this will not do," said the man. "You had better spin; perhaps you can do that better." She sat down and tried to spin, but the hard thread soon cut her soft fingers so that the blood ran down. "See?" said the man. "You are fit for no sort of work. I have made a bad bargain with you. Now I will try to make a business with pots and earthenware. You must sit in the market place and sell the wares." "Alas," thought she, "if any of the people from my father's kingdom come to the market and see me sitting there, selling, how they will mock me!" But it was of no use; she had to yield unless she chose to die of hunger. At first, she succeeded well, for the people were glad to buy the woman's wares because she was good-looking, and they paid her what she asked. Many even gave her the money and left the pots with her as well. So they lived on what she had earned as long as it lasted, then the husband bought a lot of new crockery. With this she sat down at the corner of the market place, and set it out round about her ready for sale. But suddenly there came a drunken hussar galloping along, and he rode right amongst the pots so that they were all broken into a thousand bits. She began to weep and did not know what to do for fear. "Alas, what will happen to me?" cried she. "What will my husband say to this?" She ran home and told him of the misfortune. "Who would seat herself at a corner of the market-place with crockery!" said the man. "Leave off crying, I see very well that you cannot do any ordinary work, so I have been to our king's palace and have asked whether they cannot find a place for a kitchen-maid, and they have promised me to take you. In that way you will get your food for nothing."

332 The king's daughter was now a kitchen maid and had to be at the cook's beck and call, and do the dirtiest work. In both her pockets she fastened a little jar, in which she took home her share of the leavings, and upon this they lived.

333 It happened that the wedding of the king's eldest son was to be celebrated, so the poor woman went up and placed herself by the door of the hall to look on. When all the candles were lit, and people, each more beautiful than the other, entered, and all was full of pomp and splendor, she thought of her lot with a sad heart, and cursed the pride and haughtiness which had humbled her and brought her to such great poverty. The smell of the delicious dishes that were being taken in and out reached her, and now and then the servants threw her a few morsels of them. These she put in her jars to take home. All at once the king's son entered, clothed in velvet and silk, with gold chains about his neck. And when he saw the beautiful woman standing by the door, he seized her by the hand and would have danced with her. But she refused and shrank with fear, for she saw that it was King Thrushbeard, her suitor whom she had driven away with scorn. Her struggles were of no avail; he drew her into the hall. But the string by which her pockets were hung broke, the pots fell down, the soup ran out, and the scraps were scattered all about. And when the people saw it, there arose general laughter and derision, and she was so ashamed that she would rather have been a thousand fathoms below the ground. She sprang to the door and would have run away, but on the stairs a man caught her and brought her back. And when she looked at him, it was King Thrushbeard again. He said to her kindly, "Do not be afraid. I and the fiddler who has been living with you in that wretched hovel are one. For love of you I disguised myself so. And I also was the hussar who rode through your crockery. This was all done to humble your proud spirit, and to punish you for the insolence with which you mocked me." Then she

wept bitterly and said, "I have done great wrong, and am not worthy of being your wife." But he said, "Be comforted; the evil days are past. Now we will celebrate our wedding." Then the maids-in-waiting came and put on her the most splendid clothing, and her father and his whole court came and wished her happiness in her marriage with King Thrushbeard, and the joy now began in earnest. I wish you and I had been there too.[4]

334   The name Thrushbeard has affinities with Bluebeard, but Bluebeard is a murderer and nothing more. He cannot transform his wives or be transformed himself and embodies the deathlike, ferocious aspects of the animus in his most diabolical form; from him only flight is possible. Animi in this guise are often met with in mythology.[5] This predisposition for malevolence throws into bold relief an important difference between the anima and the animus. In his primitive capacity as hunter and warrior, original man is accustomed to kill, and it is as if the animus, as the masculine component of woman, shares this propensity. Woman, on the other hand, serves life, and the anima entangles a man in life. In tales that feature the anima, her completely deadly aspect does not often appear; rather, she represents the archetype of life for the man. The animus in his negative form seems to be the opposite. He draws woman away from life and tends to "murder" life for her. He often has to do with ghost lands and the land of death and can, indeed, appear as the personification of death itself, as in the following French tale.

335   *The Wife of Death*

A woman rejects all her suitors but accepts Death when he appears. While he is out on his job, she lives in his castle. Her brother comes to see the gardens of Death, and they walk about together. Then the brother rescues the girl, taking her

---

[4] Cf. Grimm and Grimm, "King Thrushbeard," in *Complete Fairy Tales*, 232–36.
[5] "Fitcher's Bird," ibid., 204–206; and "The Robber Bridegroom," ibid., 187–90.

back to life, and she discovers that she has been away for five thousand years.[6]

336 A gypsy variation with the same title goes like this:

An unknown traveler arrives at the remote hut of a solitary girl. He receives food and lodging for a few days and falls in love with her. They marry, and she dreams that he is white and cold, that he is the King of the Dead. He is then compelled to leave her and resume his mournful trade. When finally he reveals to her that he is Death, she dies from the shock.[7]

337 This shows the disastrous effect of the negative animus on a woman. It cuts her off from participating in life, making her feel tortured and unable to go on living. In his attempt to sever a woman's connections with the outside world, the animus may take on the aspect of a father. In "Thrushbeard," there is only a king and his daughter. The princess's inaccessibility and refusal of all suitors is evidently related to the fact that she lives alone with her father. Her scornful, mocking, critical attitude toward her suitors is typical of a woman ruled by the animus, and it tears all her relationships to shreds. Ostensibly, it is the arrogance of the daughter that provokes the exasperation of the father, but actually a father frequently binds his daughter to him and puts obstacles in the path of prospective suitors. This ambiguous background attitude creates the typical ambivalence of parents who hold their children back from life while simultaneously having no patience with them for being unable to escape into life. (Mothers often behave in a similar fashion with their sons.) In retaliation, the father complex working in the daughter seeks to wound a powerful father by causing the girl to take on inferior lovers.

338 In another tale, the animus appears first as an old man who later turns into a youth. The old man — the father image — is only a

---

[6] Cf. Ernst Tegethoff, *Französische Volksmärchen*, vol. 2, Die Märchen der Weltliteratur, ed. Friedrich von der Leyen (Jena: Diederichs, 1923).
[7] Cf. Walther Aichele, and Martin Block, *Zigeunermärchen*, Die Märchen der Weltliteratur, ed. Friedrich von der Leyen (Munich: Diederichs, 1926).

temporary aspect of the animus: Behind this mask is a young man. A vivid example of the isolating effect of the animus is to be found in a tale in which the father actually locks his beautiful daughter in a stone chest. A poor youth rescues her, and they escape together. In a tale from Turkestan, "The Magic Horse," the father sells his daughter outright to a Div, an evil spirit, in return for the answer to a riddle. In the Balkan tale "The Girl and the Vampire," a youth who is actually a vampire abducts a girl and puts her into a grave in a cemetery.[8] She flees underground into a wood and prays to God for a box that she can hide in. To protect herself against the animus, the girl has to suffer being sealed in. The threatening action of the animus and the woman's defensive reaction against it always go hand in glove: Animus activity is revealed in its double nature of either laming one or making one very aggressive. Women either become masculine — assertive and bossy — or they tend to be absent-minded. This may seem charmingly feminine, but it is as if they are partly asleep. Such women have marvelous journeys with the animus-lover: They enter into a submerged daydreaming with the animus, of which they are not fully aware.

339   We must return to the above-mentioned variation of the Thrushbeard fairytale. A prince discovers a box with a girl inside, frees her, and marries her. The box and the stone chest are representations of the state of being cut off from life, which is endured by the animus-possessed woman. But if a woman has an aggressive animus and tries to act spontaneously, it is always the animus that is at work. Some women, however, refuse to be aggressive and difficult, and so they cannot let him out. They cannot see how to handle the animus. In order to keep him off, they are stiff and conventionally correct and frozen, imprisoned within themselves. This also is a state of being lamed, but it comes from the woman's reaction towards the animus. In a Norwegian tale, a woman is compelled to wear a wooden skirt. Such a cumbersome covering

---

[8] Cf. August Leskien, ed., *Balkanmärchen: Aus Albanien, Bulgarien, Serbien und Kroatien*, Die Märchen der Weltliteratur, ed. Friedrich von der Leyen (Jena: Diederichs, 1915).

illustrates her stiffness towards the world and the burden such defensive armor becomes.

340   Historically, the animus, like the anima, often has a pre-Christian form: *Drosselbart* (Thrushbeard) is a name for Wotan, as is *Rossbart* (Horsebeard). The initial difficulties in the tale of Thrushbeard are broken up by the father's exasperation; it causes him to give his daughter away to a poor man for her to marry. In parallel tales, she is beguiled by the beggar's beautiful singing and, in a Nordic parallel, by a golden spinning wheel. In all versions, the animus has a fascinating attraction for her. Spinning has to do with wishful thinking. Wotan, who is the lord of wishes, is the typical spirit of such magical thinking. "The wish turns the wheels of thought." Both the spinning wheel and the act of spinning are proper to Wotan, and in our tale, the girl has to spin to support her husband. The animus has thus taken possession of her properly feminine activity. In such a case, the implicit danger is that it leads to a loss of any real thinking on the part of the woman. It brings about a lassitude, so that instead of thinking, she lazily spins daydreams and unwinds wishful fantasies, or else she spins plots and intrigues. The king's daughter in "Thrushbeard" has fallen into such an unconscious activity. Another favored role of the animus is that of the poor servant who can demonstrate his unexpected gallantry, as in this Siberian tale.

341   A woman lives alone except for her servant. Her father has died, and the servant becomes unmanageable. However, he consents to killing a bear to make a coat for her. After he accomplishes that, she bids him perform ever harder tasks, and each time he rises to the occasion. It turns out that although he seems poor, he is really wealthy.[9]

342   Initially, the animus appears to be poor and often does not reveal the great treasures of the unconscious that are at his disposal. In the role of a poor man or a beggar, he induces the woman to believe that

---

[9] Cf. János Gulya and Ruth Futaky, *Sibirische Märchen*, Die Märchen der Weltliteratur, ed. Friedrich von der Leyen (München: Diederichs, 1995).

she herself has nothing. This is the penalty for a prejudice against the unconscious: a lasting poverty in conscious life, resulting in endless criticism and self-criticism.

343   In the Grimm fairytale, after the fiddler marries the princess, he points out to her the wealth of Thrushbeard, whereupon she greatly regrets having refused him. It is typical for an animus-ridden woman to suffer remorse about something she has failed to do. Lamenting over what might have been is a pseudo-feeling of guilt and is completely sterile. One sinks into the despairing feeling of having utterly ruined one's prospects and having missed life altogether. At first the princess is incapable of doing the housework — another symptom of being possessed by the animus. One is listless, inert, and has a glassy, staring expression. This may sometimes look like feminine passivity, but a woman in this trancelike state is not receptive; she is drugged by animus-inertia and imprisoned in a stone chest.

344   Living in a hovel, the princess must do the house chores and make baskets for money, which humiliates her and increases her feeling of inferiority. As a compensation for high-flown ambitions, the animus often forces a woman into a way of life far below her real capacity. If she is unable to adjust to what does not coincide with her lofty ideals, then she does lowly work out of sheer despair. This is thinking in extremes: "If I cannot marry a god, then I'll marry a lousy beggar." At the same time, a boundless pride persists, nourished by a secret fantasy life in which one dreams passionately of immense fame and glory. Humility and arrogance are closely intertwined. This lowly activity is also a kind of compensation to persuade the woman to become feminine again. The effect of animus pressure can lead a woman to deeper femininity, providing she accepts the fact that she is animus-possessed. In addition, she needs to do something to bring her animus into reality. If she gives him a field of action — that is, if she takes up some special study or does some "masculine" work — this can occupy the animus. At the same time her feeling will be vivified, and she will come back to feminine activities. The worst condition comes about when a woman has a

powerful animus and does not even live it. She is then held in a straitjacket of animus opinions, and avoids any sort of work that seems in the least "masculine." She is then much less feminine than if she were to actually do her work.

345   Because the princess bungles all her tasks, her husband sends her out to sell earthen pots in the market. Vessels are feminine symbols, and she is driven to sell her femininity at a low price — too cheaply and too collectively. The more animus-possessed a woman is, the more she feels estranged from men and the more painful are her efforts to make a good feeling contact with them. Although she may take the lead in erotic affairs, there can be no genuine love or passion in them. If she really had a good contact with men, she would have no need to be so assertive. She acts out of the vague realization that something is wrong and makes desperate attempts to make up for what has been lost because of her animus-imposed estrangement from men. This means she will often walk blindly into a new catastrophe. A new animus attack is bound to follow, as described in our story: A drunken hussar breaks all her vessels to pieces. This symbolizes a brutal outburst of emotion. The wild, ungovernable animus smashes everything, showing clearly that such an exhibition of her unconscious nature does not work.

346   The life with the beggar-husband also brings about the final humiliation, and this occurs when the girl "peeps through the door" to glimpse the splendor of the court world and Thrushbeard's wedding party. Peeping through a crack in the door is interpreted in the *I Ching* as having too narrow and too subjective a standpoint. One is unable to see what one really has. The inferiority of a woman who thinks she must admire others and nurses secret jealousy towards them means being unable to assess one's own real worth. From hunger, she accepts scraps of food thrown to her by the servants. To her intense shame, her greed and inferiority are exposed when the food falls to the floor. The heroine wants to get life on any terms and assumes that she cannot get it in her own right. A king's daughter who accepts scraps thrown to her by servants is, in a certain sense, throwing herself away. She feels ashamed and despises

herself, but this humiliation is what is needed, for only in this way does the heroine realize that she is, after all, the daughter of a king and that Thrushbeard is, in fact, her husband.

347   In our tale, the animus has three different roles — not only is he Thrushbeard, but he is also the wild hussar and the beggar-husband. This ability to transform links him to the Germanic god Wotan. Wotan is the man riding a white horse who leads the wild riders of the night, who sometimes carry their heads in their arms. This legend, that still lingers, comes from the early idea of Wotan as the leader of the dead warriors going to Valhalla. As evil ghosts they still hunt in the woods, and it is death to look at them and to be swept into their ranks. Wotan also goes about as a beggar, an unknown wanderer in the night, and always his face is partly concealed for he has only one eye. A stranger enters, says a few words, and leaves — and afterwards one realizes that it was Wotan. He calls himself the owner of the land, and psychologically this is true: The unknown owner of the Germanic land is still the archetype of Wotan.[10] The Wotan parallel in the Thrushbeard tale is evidenced in another important attribute: Sleipnir, Wotan's eight-legged white or black horse that is as swift as the wind, and corresponds to the drunken hussar on his horse. This indicates that the animus, that is mostly a sort of archaic divine spirit, is also connected with our instinctive animal nature. In the unconscious, spirit and instinct are not opposites. On the contrary, new spiritual germs often manifest themselves first in an up-rush of sexual libido, just as instinctive impulses often only later develop their spiritual aspect. This is because spiritual impulses are generated by the spirit of nature, by the meaningfulness inherent in our instinctive pattern. Women whose spirit has not yet become differentiated and retains its archaic emotional and instinctive characteristics often get excited when they do any genuine thinking. The animal aspect of the animus shows up in, for example, "Beauty and the Beast," but this motif is relatively rare in fairytales. A less well-known example is this fairy tale from Turkestan:

---

[10] Cf. Jung, "Wotan," in *Civilization in Transition*, vol. 10, *CW*.

348 *The Magic Horse*

A girl takes a magic horse and flees from her captor, a Div, a desert-demon. She escapes temporarily but is overtaken by the demon. Finally, the horse plunges with the Div into the sea, and the Div is overcome. The horse then commands the girl to kill him. When she does so, he changes into a heavenly palace, and his four legs become the pillars of the four corners. Finally, the heroine is reunited with her real lover, a young prince.[11]

349 Here the animus is an evil spirit (a Div) on the one hand, and a helpful animal on the other. When the animus takes the form of a destructive and diabolical spirit, the instincts must come to the rescue. One way of dealing with the animus problem is for the woman simply to suffer it through to the bitter end. Indeed, there is no solution that does not include suffering — it seems to be a part of being a woman. In cases where a woman has to escape a state of possession by some ghost or vampire, much can be gained by an extreme passivity toward the animus, and often the wisest counsel is that she should simply do nothing. There are times when one can only wait and try to fortify oneself by keeping the positive aspects of the animus in mind. To overcome possession by an unconscious content by slipping out of its grasp is as meritorious as a heroic victory. The motif of the "magic flight" symbolizes a situation where it is better to flee from the unconscious than to seek to overcome it; by doing so, one avoids being devoured.

350 The motif of the magic flight is prominent in the Siberian tale "The Girl and the Evil Spirit."[12] The heroine, who knew no man and could not say who her parents were, is a herdswoman of reindeer who wanders about, caring for her reindeer by singing magical songs to them. As in "Prince Ring," here, too, we come across the motif of loneliness as a harbinger of a special individual development of the

---

[11] Gustav Jungbauer, *Märchen aus Turkestan und Tibet*, Die Märchen der Weltliteratur (Jena: Diederichs, 1923). Marie-Louise von Franz has interpreted this fairytale in her book *Shadow and Evil in Fairytales*, 305–10.

[12] Gulya and Futaky, *Sibirische Märchen*.

personality. It is a situation in which a flood of inner images can rise up from the unconscious and bring about unexpected reactions. The girl is not destitute or hungry; she can cook and care for herself, and she can keep her reindeer with her by the magic charm of her singing. In other words, she is resourceful, more gifted, and more normal than the girl in the tale of "King Thrushbeard." Her magic gifts signify that she has the ability to express the contents of the unconscious. In analysis, one sometimes sees that a situation is dangerous because the patient's way of conceiving and expressing the turbulent and threatening contents of the unconscious is too feeble and too narrow. This might be caused by a poverty of heart and a failure to give love. It might also be because of a barrenness of mind and spirit. Old bottles are generally unable to contain new wine.[13] The songs on the lips of the girl probably come from her traditional past that may indicate that she has inherited a fortunate constellation of temperament from her ancestors. Nevertheless, she is without any human connections and is cut off from society, which is a great danger for a woman because, without human contact, she easily becomes unconscious and surrenders to the grip of the negative animus.

351   The tale goes on to relate that suddenly a tremendous pair of jaws comes down from heaven, and an abyss opens up, stretching from heaven to earth. This gaping, devouring mouth is the abyss of complete unconsciousness. The girl hurls her staff onto the ground behind her. The staff is a sign of power and of judgment, two royal prerogatives symbolized by the king's scepter. Psychologically speaking, the staff represents a direction-giving principle in the unconscious. The bishop's staff, for instance, was interpreted by the clergy as being a symbol of "the authority of the doctrine": As a staff, it shows the way and makes decisions. In antiquity, the golden staff or magic rod belonged to Mercurius and represents his ability to marshal intractable elements within the unconscious. If one has a staff, one is not wholly passive: One has a direction. At bottom, the staff is a form of the animus.

---

[13] *The Holy Bible*, Matt. 9:17: "Neither do men put new wine into old wine-skins [...]."

352   The girl runs away from the demon, throwing her magic comb and her red handkerchief behind her. Bestrewing one's trail with objects is characteristic of the magical flight. This act of throwing away things of value is a sacrifice; one throws things over one's shoulder to the dead, to spirits, or to the devil, to propitiate those whom we dare not face. It may seem panicky to abandon valuable possessions when one is escaping, but an assailant who is stronger than one is oneself can easily cut one down if one stiffens into a defensive attitude; stripping oneself of certain things gives one mobility and freedom. There are situations in which one has to give up wanting anything at all, and in this way one slips out from underneath the problem; one is not there any longer, so nothing more can go wrong. When one is confronted by a hopelessly wrong situation, one must make a drastic leap to the bottom of open-minded simplicity. From there, one can live through it. What is more, the objects that have been sacrificed generally transform themselves into obstacles for the pursuer. The comb at once turns into a forest — becomes the hair of Mother Earth. Its transformation into a natural object suggests that originally it was an integral part of nature. Actually, there is no thought or instrument that has not originated from nature; that is, from the unconscious psyche. One sacrifices to the unconscious what was once wrested from it. The comb is used to arrange and confine the hair. Hair is a source of magical power, or mana. Ringlets of hair, preserved as keepsakes, are believed to connect one individual with another over a distance. Cutting hair and sacrificing it often means submission to a new collective state — a giving-up and a rebirth. One's hairstyle is frequently an expression of a cultural worldview. Primitive folk tales speak of demons wanting to be deloused and combed when they are caught, which means that the confusion in the unconscious has to be straightened out and made conscious. Hair in wild disarray is often dreamed of at the start of analysis. The comb, therefore, represents a capacity for making one's thoughts ordered, clear, and conscious.

353   The red handkerchief that is thrown away becomes a flame soaring from earth to heaven. To abandon the staff and comb means

that the heroine forgoes both making a plan and marshaling herself. The soaring flame indicates that she puts an inner distance between herself and her emotions — it means stepping back from what one wants. Gaping jaws devour the forest and spit water on the flame, i.e., water and fire battle in the unconscious. As the girl is identified neither with the fire nor with the water, she is able to escape the opposites. She then goes through four animal transformations, each succeeding animal being fleeter of foot than the preceding one. This progression seems to suggest that all higher activities must be relinquished and there must be a burrowing down into the instinctive level. In such situations one can only rely upon one's own inner animal side. There are moments of imminent danger in life when one must not think or even feel or try to escape by struggling — one's only option is to inhabit a kind of animal simplicity, making it possible to go down into oneself. This decisive Oriental attitude of "doing nothing"[14] succeeds where strong resistance would incur failure — the ego escapes and vanishes. This is all a human being can do at certain times; one is best off allowing the persecuting demon to eat up the forest and combat the flames alone.

354   The girl changes into a bear with copper bells in its ears. Bells and similar sounding instruments are used to drive away evil spirits. (Church bells originally had this purpose.) They also announce a decisive moment — think, for example, of the roll of a drum or of thunder — and they induce a psychic resonance in the emotions of the hearer so that he feels that the decisive event is about to happen — for example, the triple bell in the Mass. Bells in the girl's animal ears exclude all other sounds, sounds that she must not listen to because their effect is poisonous — words that the negative animus whispers to her. The damage — the poisoning — occurs when one accepts them and adopts convictions that do not suit one. The instrument that conveys this poisonous influence is the ear, and bells are a defense against noxious animus effects.

---

[14] "Doing nothing" or "not doing anything," known as Wu-wei in ancient Chinese wisdom, is linked to the Tao that has an effect when one's attitude is in accordance with the cosmic rhythm. In other words, one's deeds spring from the Self. Cf. Wilhelm and Baynes, *I Ching*; and Jung, *Alchemical Studies*, vol. 13, *CW*, § 20.

355 The tale ends with the girl falling to earth in a dead faint before a white tent, and suddenly the evil spirit stands before her as a beautiful man. In a sense, she has fled from him to him. Her perseverance in staying true to the one instinctively right course has brought about the enantiodromia, with the result that the menacing demon has transformed itself into a gracious young man. In fact, from the beginning, his secret intention had been to bring her here to his white tent. Together with his three younger brothers, the young man is one of four, and from the four the heroine may choose whom she will have for her husband. This quaternio is an expression of her inner balance and wholeness. The girl chooses the eldest because she recognizes that the realization of her fate lies in accepting the spirit who persecuted her.

356 A further example of a magical flight, one that ends tragically, is the Siberian tale that follows:

357 *The Woman Who Became a Spider*

A woman who can no longer bear living with her father leaves the house. She finds a human head and takes it home with her in order to talk to it. Her father hears her talking and hopes she is together with a real man. When he discovers what is going on, he throws the head onto a dunghill. From there, it rolls into the sea and leaves a trail of blood behind it. The woman follows the trail and comes to a house in which there lives a family of heads. The demon-head, who had been wounded by the humiliation that the father had inflicted upon him, scorns her. Desperate, she runs the wrong way around the house and ends up in the Beyond (in heaven) where a man in a copper boat undresses her with his magical songs. Naked, she follows him to his house and when he leaves, she seeks refuge in the forbidden house of the spider woman next door. A little old woman lives there who spins and tells her that the man in the copper boat intends to murder her; he is the moon spirit to whom all the people on earth pray. The woman opens a door in the floor of the moon spirit's house and stares down at all of mankind's secrets and acts of sacrifice. The spider woman then gives her a rope with which she can lower herself to earth, but when she arrives, she absolutely must open her eyes. She fails to do so in time and she is turned into a spider.[15]

358 This fairytale reminds one of a dream of a real woman — its content seems to mirror real psychic events. This is often the case with early down-to-earth tales like this one for the story has not yet been embellished into a fairytale and is closer to an individual's report of an archetypal experience.

359 The heroine has a negative father complex, which is why it is laid upon her to develop her animus to an even greater degree which, however, the negative complex prevents her from doing. And thus her first attempt at finding a friend brings her together with a skull that lives in the sea, but is, in fact, a spirit that appears on earth as a skull. Amongst indigenous peoples the belief that skulls survive death and are identical to the spirit of the deceased is widespread. Psychologically speaking, an attempt to be friends with a skull indicates that the woman's spiritual nature has not "incarnated" — it is not "real." She is not connected to her instincts and emotions and can therefore not express them. Her manner of thinking is dry, intellectual, and, quite literally, dead. Nevertheless, it is a step forward that she wants to have a relationship to this inner factor. But every step forward is accompanied by an attack from aggressive negative animus tendencies. Her father gets involved and wounds the head, which means that the woman's potential spiritual development is wounded by traditional, conventional opinions (so-called sensible reasoning), and it is repressed. This is why the head spirit that perhaps might have become conscious rolls back into the sea of the collective unconscious.

360 The young woman runs in the wrong direction (anticlockwise) around the house. Instead of trying to become conscious of any

---

[15] Cf. Knud Rasmussen, *Die Gabe des Adlers: Eskimoische Märchen aus Alaska* (Frankfurt: Societäts-Verlag, 1937); cf. Von Franz, *Feminine in Fairy Tales*.

possible meaning behind this loss, she instead falls even deeper into the unconscious.[16] In her desperation, she burrows ever deeper and finally reaches heaven. She has transcended the earthly sphere and flees to a purely archetypal realm that lies beyond the collective unconscious represented by the sea. This at least still contains animal life, but in heaven there are only archetypal figures.

361   The magician in the copper boat is another form of the animus: Larger, less human, and more possessive than the skull, he is more like a magical beloved or a spirit lover. Later the heroine learns that it is the moon spirit to whom her people pray. The animus often adopts the form of a moon spirit who draws women away from life. Because feminine consciousness is so weak in this tale, the moon spirit seems all the more dangerous. A person with a more developed consciousness senses that there is meaningful life stored in the animus. Such a person does not flee or try to assess its value intellectually. One should use the energy that the animus provides. This happens, for example, if one engages the spirit and undertakes some intellectually creative task. If one avoids doing so, as a rule such a spirit takes over. Being in a state of possession can also be one's fate challenging one to commit to one's individuation process. If one is able to acknowledge that one's father or mother complex is stronger than one's own ego, it can be accepted as being a part of one's own individuality.

362   The encounter with the moon spirit bestows the intuitive strength to understand the religious ceremonies and ritual sacrificial offerings that are made on earth. At the side of the moon spirit, the woman becomes a seer and is in danger of becoming a clairvoyant with a trace of madness. Presumably, this is why her feminine instinct — the spider woman — awakens in her the wish to return to earth. A well-known figure in North American myths, the spider woman is ambiguous. Analogous to the dark woman in the box in the tale that follows, she is a figure of the Self. She is the one who gives the heroine a rope with which she can descend to earth. Many women have the tendency to ponder upon their life from time to

---

[16] On the motif of circling to the left see Jung, *Psychology and Alchemy*, vol. 12, *CW*, §§ 286–87.

time, and to lose themselves in a nebulous vortex of speculations. If they are able to touch concrete reality, a standpoint beyond fantasy becomes possible — if one expresses one's thoughts, for example, by writing them down, one is no longer identical with them. A confrontation of black on white helps to differentiate between just having an opinion and something that is valid, which has the effect of an inner strengthening. The woman is instructed to open her eyes as soon as she reaches earth — she must make an effort to become conscious of her actual situation. Tragically, she fails to do so. She is transformed into a spider, into a *spinster*, who is incapable of making her religious experience meaningful for both herself and her people.

363   A further martyrdom of the animus-possessed woman is presented in the following tale:

364   *The Woman Who Married the Moon and the Kele*

A woman, abandoned by her husband, was so faint with hunger that she could only crawl on all fours. Twice she went to the house of the Moon-man and ate the food that she found on a plate. The third time he grabbed her as she was eating, and when he learned that she had no husband, he married her.

365   Each day their food appeared by magic upon the empty plate. When the Moon-man went out, he forbade his wife to open a certain chest and look inside. But the lure proved irresistible, and in the chest she discovered a strange woman whose face was half red and half black. It was she who had been secretly supplying them with food, but she now dies when exposed to the air. When the Moon-man discovered that his wife had disobeyed him, he was very angry. He restored the dead woman to life and took his wife back to her father, saying that he could not control her and that her former husband must have had good reason to abandon her.

366   Angered by the daughter's return, the father invoked an evil spirit to marry her. This demon, the Kele, ate men, even the

woman's own brother, whose corpse he brought her to eat. Acting upon the advice of a little fox, however, she made shoes for the Kele. When she threw them in front of him, a spider-thread descended from above upon which she could climb up to the house of the spider woman. Pursued by the Kele, she continued to climb until she reached the immovable one, the North Star, which is the creator and the highest god. The Kele, who also had arrived there, was imprisoned in a chest by the protective Polar Star. He almost died and was released only on condition that he would no longer persecute the woman.

367 She returned to earth and made her father sacrifice reindeer to the god. Suddenly, the father and then the daughter died.[17]

368 The protagonist was abandoned by her first husband and marries the Moon-man. He soon understands why she had been left. Her sensitivities — her loneliness, poverty and hunger — are typical states that result from animus possession. A woman's attitude largely conditions the events that befall her in the world. Whereas the anima thrusts men headlong into relationships and the confusion that accompanies them, the animus fosters loneliness in women. The hunger is also typical for a woman needs life, relationships with people, and participation in meaningful activity. Part of her hunger comes from an awareness of hidden, unused aptitudes. The animus contributes to her unrest so that she is never satisfied; one must always do more for her. Not realizing that the problem is an inner one, such women assume that if only they could get about more, spend more money and surround themselves with more friends, their life-hunger would be assuaged.

369 The moon god often appears as the mysterious, invisible lover of a married woman in fairytales. The moon is sometimes represented in mythology and in dreams as a man, sometimes as a woman, and at other times as a hermaphroditic being. The moon is closely related

---

[17] Cf. Gulya and Futaky, *Sibirische Märchen*, in: Märchen der Weltliteratur.

to the sun; it is a lesser light that owes its light to the sun. The sun is really a divinity — the source of consciousness within the unconscious — and represents an active psychic factor that can create greater awareness. The moon, however, symbolizes a softer, more diffused consciousness — a dim awareness, as it were. When the sun is feminine — as it is in the German language — it means that the source of consciousness is still in the unconscious, within a welter of details that are not clearly distinguished. How such an instinctive consciousness functions can be seen in the Balinese building tradition: Craftsmen set to work constructing those elements that they are skilled at making; they do not follow any plan or any architect but are guided from within, exactly as if they had a blueprint to follow. When the various parts of the building are assembled, they fit perfectly, even though each element was made in isolation. In this way a temple of an extraordinarily harmonious design is created. Like the sun lighting up the unconscious, an unconscious principle of order apparently operates within these Balinese craftsman.

370   The moon shares the same principle as the sun, but it is more feminine, less concentrated, and not as intense; its light is also a light of consciousness but a milder one. The principle of consciousness operating within the woman in the story is very indefinite, and this is coherent with her state of animus-possession. It is characteristic of the animus to be indefinite in his overall and long-term purposes, although he is sharply insistent when it comes to details. In mythology, the moon is associated with snakes, nocturnal animals, spirits of the dead, and gods of the underworld. And it was not by chance that the alchemists called it "the child of Saturn." To Paracelsus, the moon was a source of poison, like the eyes of women when the moon is troubling their blood. He believed that the moon is a spirit that can renew itself and become a child again, and for this reason it is susceptible to a woman's evil eye: The sidereal spirit is poisoned and then casts its baneful spell upon men who gaze at it. We may psychologically interpret Paracelsus as saying that poisonous opinions (emanating from the animus) can go directly

into the unconscious of others — as if they have been poisoned by an undefined source. Such opinions that one breathes in infect the air and blight the surroundings. Animus convictions sink more deeply into the soul than a merely wrong opinion; they are consequently far more difficult to spot and throw off.

371   The moon divinity in our tale is ambiguous — she hides, for example, a woman in a chest, a dark feminine side of nature. This other woman is undeveloped, secret, buried, but also important for not only does she live, but she is even a provider of nourishment; one could think of her as a preform, or a precursor, of the Self. She is a supporting figure that operates behind the animus (the Moon-man). The mountain spirit in "The Bewitched Princess" was also a hidden vessel of energy that stood behind the princess-anima. While the mountain spirit was a malevolent figure, the woman in the box is a rather dim fertility goddess. By disobeying the Moon-man and opening the chest, the heroine unwittingly kills the dark woman. The transgression for which an innocent victim pays with his life is a variation of the theme of premature enlightenment, a motif that occurs in the antique tales of Eros and Psyche[18] and of Orpheus and Eurydice,[19] well as in the Grimms' tale "The Singing, Soaring Lion's Lark." The point of this is that for everything there is a season. Possession in a woman often produces systematic tactlessness. Where there are any signs of life, she cannot resist poking around. All that should remain in the dim background of consciousness — all that needs darkness in which to grow — is hauled up into the light and lost. Mothers of this disposition tend to drag out all their children's secrets; in this way, their child's spontaneity and its chance to grow are blighted. Such an interfering attitude has an unwholesome effect upon the entire environment.

372   Having lost her feminine feeling, the abandoned woman is driven by curiosity to delve into the background of the Moon-man's secrets. Wild curiosity is an expression of a sort of primitive masculinity in a woman. This hounding, inquisitive spirit makes her

---

[18] Cf. Von Franz, "Amor und Psyche," in *Golden Ass*, 77–121.
[19] Michael Grant and John Hazel, *Who's Who in Classical Mythology* (London: Routledge, 2002).

do the wrong thing and is always at fault. The Moon-man sends her back to her father. Although it is not expressly said, we may suppose that he has sown the seeds of her unhappiness. That both father and daughter die simultaneously at the end shows how close their relationship is. He has put a curse on her and condemned her to live with the evil spirit, Kele. According to primitive belief, an expressed wish can shape unborn events and bring them forth out of the womb of time. This curse clearly indicates that the father fosters the animus's domination of his daughter.

373   The evil spirit Kele is a body eater, a typical practice of the negative animus. Just as vampires drink blood, spirits consume bodies in order to become visible. They seize and feast upon a corpse to gain material reality in the dead person's form. Thus, corpses are bewitched into becoming spirits. A vampire's drive to drink the blood of humans comes from its desperation at being banished from the world of the living. An animus-possessed woman "latches onto" the lives of those in her surroundings because her own sources of feeling and of Eros are withheld from her. Viewed psychologically, spirits are contents of the unconscious. The devouring of corpses is an image of a desperate attempt on the part of the unconscious to enter consciousness in the form of complexes and other contents in order to find realization. The ravenous hunger of a spirit for a body is an unrecognized, unredeemed wish on the part of the unconscious for the fullness of life.

374   In this sense, the red and black woman in the hidden chest bestows magical food and is life-giving. Yet the other woman cannot accept her because she cannot make the connection between the dark woman and the Moon-god. She can deal with neither the undeveloped figure of the Self, nor can she give expression to her own femininity. There is a similar breach between the protecting Polar Star and the evil, body-devouring Kele. Both are divine principles that have been eternally engaged in warfare.

375   Like the girl in "The Magic Horse," the Moon-man's woman is able to escape from the evil spirit with the help of an animal. The animus can draw a woman into a split situation when he creates an

intolerable opposition between spirit and nature. When this happens, a woman has to trust her instinct that, in this instance, is represented by a fox. In China and Japan, the fox is a witch-animal insofar as witches are wont to appear in the form of foxes. An instance of a hysterical and epileptic woman is explained as bewitchment by a fox. In Asian cultural circles, the fox is as much a feminine animal as the cat is in our western world and, like the cat, it represents the primitive, instinctive feminine nature of woman. The fox counsels the woman to throw her shoes at the Kele to hold him back; this allows her to climb up the spider's thread to heaven.[20] The shoe is a symbol of power, which is why we speak of being "under someone's heel" or "following in father's shoes." Clothing may represent our persona,[21] our outer attitude, or an inner attitude; the changing of clothes in the mysteries stood for transformation into an enlightened understanding. Shoes are the lowest part of our clothing and represent our standpoint in relation to reality. They show the measure of our power — how solidly our feet are planted on the ground and how solidly the earth supports us.

376   Throwing the shoe at the Kele is a gesture of propitiation that hinders the spirit in his pursuit. So it is necessary to sacrifice something in order to escape from his grasp. In this case, it is the sacrifice of the old standpoint that is required. When in the clutches of the animus, no woman is able to give up whatever power she may have, or her conviction that it is right and necessary and valuable. The convictions an animus woman has lived by spring from inferior masculine thinking; the less she herself is able to evaluate it, the more passionately she clings to a conviction. This is one reason for the persistence of an animus possession. Unfortunately, such a woman never thinks that anything could be wrong with her and is convinced that the fault lies with the others. The fox is really saying to her, "Don't become stiff. Give up a part of your standpoint and

---

[20] Paul Sartori, "Der Schuh im Volksglauben," *Zeitschrift des Vereins für Volkskunde* (1894), 41, 148, 282.
[21] Cf. C.G. Jung, "The Persona as a Segment of the Collective Psyche," in *Two Essays on Analytical Psychology*, 2nd ed., vol. 7, *CW* (Princeton, NJ: Princeton University Press, 1967).

see what happens." Then at once, a thread from heaven gives her the means of reaching the Pole Star — the animus refined to the highest form, an image of God. Its feminine parallel is Sophia — the highest, most spiritual form of the anima. If one goes deeply into what the animus is, one finds that he is a divinity and that through a woman's relation to him in this form, she enters into genuine religious experience. In our story, the discovery of the Pole Star is identical to the woman's personal experience of God. When the Kele pursues her and storms the summit, a conflict on a cosmic scale rages between him and the Pole Star. The woman is placed between the two overwhelming world principles of good and evil — God and the Devil. When the Pole Star opens his box, light pours out, and when he closes it, snow falls on the earth. The evil spirit is flung into this box and tortured by cruel rays of light. The animus must sometimes be handled severely by a higher power.

377   By going to heaven, the woman removes herself from human reality, which is not a real solution. Anyone in this condition would be very near to borderline psychosis, swinging back and forth between exaggerated negative and positive animus possession. This tale apparently reveals the case of a weak consciousness, which is to be expected in a primitive culture. It therefore makes sense that the Pole Star says to the woman, "You had better go home; you had better get back to earth." He demands the sacrifice of two reindeer, a tribute that will make it possible for her to return to earth and to reenter life there. The sacrifice is necessary for to come down out of the clouds of fantasy into reality is charged with danger — all one's effort and work might be lost. Let me give you an example of how this looks in practice: One understands one's problem as presented in a dream, but what is one going to do about it practically? If one is truly committed to facing this problem, one soon realizes that one is being asked to genuinely participate in life. Experience shows that difficulties dissolve when one realizes one's own hidden potential in creative work. What looks so easy proves not to be when practical problems arise, compelling one to return from the adventurous quest in the unconscious. A problem also arises when one has developed

an individual relationship to a new value and then has to face the world's disapproval and hostility. There is always the danger that one will completely reject the experiences in the unconscious and regard them cynically as being "nothing other than this or that." Or, like the woman in this story, one becomes too dreamy: Instead of becoming conscious of reality, one tries to live out one's fantasies when, in fact, a realistic adaptation is required.

378   Often in primitive tales when a satisfactory ending seems imminent, the whole thing blows up. In this instance, the father and daughter die. There is no dissolution of their mutual identification. The entire problem of animus-possession thus remains unconscious. It is often imperative for a woman to escape from the baleful mastery of the animus. While our tale tells of such an attempt, the whole experience nevertheless remains stuck in the unconscious — similar to the South American tale of the anima that dances in the Beyond as a skeleton and the hero dies. Early primitive tales are filled with melancholy because many primitive tribes experience the unconscious as being dismal, doleful, and frightful. The unconscious has this dark aspect today for those who need to go into life, for young people, but also for those who are too sheltered and secluded from life. Thus, the hero's escape from the unconscious is as great a deed as his subsequent great deed of killing the dragon.

379   Another Siberian tale that illustrates the realization of the animus is "The Girl and the Skull." At the beginning of the tale, a girl, living with her elderly parents, finds a skull in the wilderness. She takes it home and talks to it. Her parents are horrified, decide she is a Kele, and abandon her. As in the tale of "The Woman Who Became a Spider," the animus appears as a skull in this Siberian tale, too. According to primitive beliefs, the skull contains the immortal essence of mortal beings, and from this belief came the hunting of skulls and skull cults. For the North American Indians, the scalps they took contained the essence of the enemy, and the alchemists used a skull as the vessel in which to cook the *prima materia*. In this Siberian tale, the skull again represents the animus in his death aspect. This negative aspect of the animus is especially connected to

his activities that relate to the head. As mentioned earlier, this takes the form of poisoning women with his noxious opinions or blinding their eyes to the treasures of the unconscious. The idea of a skull ghost has to do with the head or intellect becoming autonomous and, as a result, being separated from the instincts. In this separated state it can roll away from the body towards destruction. On the other hand, the skull is a symbol of the Self. This shows us that any particular aspect of an unconscious content is dependent upon the conscious attitude with which it is viewed. The Siberian parents ruefully conclude that their daughter has been changed into an evil spirit, a Kele, and that she is beyond redemption. They leave their home and travel across the river with all of their belongings. The distrustful attitude of the parents is typical of the primitive fear of becoming possessed by spirits, for as numerous, widespread, and ever-present as they are, they represent a constant threatening danger. When parents marry late or have no children for a long time, it often brings on tragic difficulties. The girl in our story is an only child; she grew up without any comrades to help her enter into life. By taking the skull, the girl calls forth hostile reactions and arouses the fear and hatred of her parents. An animus to which the woman is not related often attracts hostility without the woman in question suspecting the reason. The negative reactions of other people are a sign that one has not yet realized an essential part of one's personality. The environment seeks to irritate and prod one: One needs to recognize what one lacks. The forsaken girl reproaches the skull. He then orders her to gather faggots, to make a big fire, and to throw him — the skull — onto it: By doing this, he will acquire a body.

380   Fire generally represents emotion and passion, which can either burn one up or spread light. Sacrifices are burned in order to dissolve the physical part so that the image or essence of the body may rise with the smoke to the gods. When, however, a spirit creature is burned, the burning confers a body upon the formless matter. Passion compels one to sacrifice a too-independent, too-intellectual attitude, and it enables one to realize the spirit. When one undergoes

passionate suffering, the spirit is no longer trapped within an idea but is rather experienced as psychic reality. Therefore the skull implores the girl to throw him into the fire. "Otherwise," he says to her, "we are both suffering in vain." Behind this statement is the realization that one must fight suffering with suffering — that one must accept suffering. Torturing the skull in the fire means to fight fire with fire; the torture that the girl has suffered will be, as it were, paid back in kind. The animus awakens passion in a woman. His plans, purposes, and whims stir up self-doubt within her and cause her to drag her feminine, passive nature out into the world and to expose herself to the resistance of the outer world. When a woman has been successful in a man's world, it means acute suffering to narrow down the scope of her activities, or to give them up altogether, in order to become more feminine again.

381   In alchemy, fire frequently symbolizes one's inner participation in the work and is equated with the passion one gives to the different stages of the alchemical process. The skull tells the girl that she must cover her eyes and be sure not to look at the burning — once again, we have the motif of the danger of a too-early enlightenment: One must not grasp intellectually all that happens in the psyche, and by no means always define and categorize all inner happenings; often one must curb one's curiosity and simply wait. Only a strong person is able to control his or her impatience and to let the interplay go on without looking. A weaker consciousness wants to have the dream interpreted at once because it is afraid of the uncertainty and the darkness of the situation. The girl has to wait in the darkness while she listens to the roar of the flames and the confusion of horses and men rushing past. Being terrified yet remaining firm and untouched by panic denotes a strength beyond hope and despair. But many people cannot wait and prefer sudden decisions. In this way they disturb the inscrutable workings of their fate.

382   In the end, a man stands before the girl, dressed in animal skins and attended by a group of people and animals. This rich hero becomes the husband of the girl who, from now on, has a powerful positive animus and who enjoys life immensely. When her parents

later return on a visit, she serves them splintered marrow bones — which is more than they can swallow. The parents die, taking the old attitude with them.

9.3 The Motif of Relationship

There are many fairytales and fairytale-like tales whose leading characters can be interpreted as representing either the anima or the animus. They depict human patterns of relationship, namely, the processes that take place *between* man and woman, the fundamental facts of the psyche beyond what is masculine and what is feminine. Tales of mutual redemption are particularly of this type. Children often have the leading roles — for instance, the fairytale "Hansel and Gretel." Because children are relatively undifferentiated both sexually and psychically, they are much closer to the hermaphroditic original being. The child is thus an apt symbol of the Self — of an inner future totality and, at the same time, of undeveloped facets of one's individuality. The child signifies a piece of innocence and wonder surviving in us from the remote past, both that part of our personal childishness which has been bypassed and the new, early form of the future individuality. Seen in this light, the saying, "The child is father to the man" has a deeper significance.

Fairytales and fairytale-like stories are not concerned with human and personal factors but with the development of the archetypes; they show the ways in which the archetypes of man and woman are related, the one to the other, within the collective unconscious. There is a fairytale in which the coming together of the masculine and feminine psyches is presented from the angle of the unconscious; the reality of the feminine psyche is, however, more clearly revealed than that of the masculine psyche.

The White Bride and the Black Bride

A woman was going about the countryside with her daughter and her stepdaughter to cut some feed. God came towards them in the form of a poor man, and asked, "Which is the way into the village?" "If you want to know," said the mother, "seek it for yourself," and her daughter added, "If you are afraid, you will not find it, take a guide with you." But the stepdaughter said, "Poor man, I will take you there; come with me." Then God was angry with the mother and daughter, and turned his back on them, and wished that they should become as black as night and as ugly as sin. To the poor stepdaughter, however, God was gracious and went with her, and when they were near the village, he said a blessing over her, and said, "Choose three things for thyself, and I will grant them to thee." Then said the maiden, "I should like to be as beautiful and fair as the sun," and instantly she was white and fair as day. "Then I should like to have a purse of money which would never grow empty." God gave her that also, but he said, "Do not forget what is best of all." She said, "For my third wish, I desire, after my death, to inhabit the eternal Kingdom of Heaven."

386   That also was granted unto her, and then God left her.

387   When the stepmother came home with her daughter and they saw that they were both as black as coal and ugly, but that the stepdaughter was white and beautiful, wickedness increased still more in their hearts, and they thought of nothing else but of how they could do her an injury. The stepdaughter, however, had a brother called Reginer, whom she loved much, and she told him all that had happened. Reginer said to her, "Dear sister, I will paint a likeness of thee, that I may continually see thee before my eyes, for my love for thee is so great that I should like always to look at thee." Then she answered, "But, I pray thee, let no one else see the picture." So he painted his sister and hung up the picture in his room; he, however, dwelt in the King's palace, for he was his coachman. Every day he went and stood before the picture and thanked God for the happiness of having such a dear sister. Now it happened that the King whom he served had just lost his wife, who had been so beautiful that no one could be found to compare with her, and on this account the

King was in deep grief. The attendants about the court, however, remarked that the coachman stood daily before this beautiful picture, and they were jealous of him, so they informed the King. The latter ordered the picture to be brought to him, and when he saw that it was like his lost wife in every respect, except that it was still more beautiful, he fell mortally in love with it. He ordered the coachman to be brought before him, and asked whom that portrait represented. The coachman said it was his sister, so the King resolved to take no one but her as his wife, and gave him a carriage and horses and splendid garments of cloth made of gold, and sent him forth to fetch his chosen bride. When Reginer arrived on this errand, his sister was glad, but the black maiden was jealous of her good fortune and grew angry above all measure, and said to her mother, "Of what use are all your arts to us now when you cannot procure such a piece of luck for me?" "Be quiet," said the old woman. "I will soon divert it to you" — and by her arts of witchcraft, she so troubled the eyes of the coachman that he was half-blind, and she stopped the ears of the white maiden so that she was half-deaf. Then they got into the carriage, first the bride in her noble royal apparel, then the stepmother with her daughter, and Reginer sat on the box to drive. When they had been on the way for some time, the coachman cried, "Cover thee well, my sister dear, that the rain may not wet thee, that the wind may not load thee with dust, that thou may'st be fair and beautiful when thou appearest before the King." The bride asked, "What is my dear brother saying?" "Ah," said the old woman, "he says that you ought to take off your golden dress and give it to your sister." Then she took it off and put it on the black maiden, who gave her in exchange for it a shabby gray gown. They drove onwards, and a short time afterwards, the brother again cried, "Cover thee well, my sister dear, that the rain may not wet thee, that the wind may not load thee with dust, that thou may'st be fair and beautiful when thou appearest before the King." The bride asked, "What is my dear brother saying?" "Ah," said the old woman, "he says that you ought to take off your golden hood and give it to your sister." So she took off the hood and put it on her sister and sat with her own head uncovered. And they drove on farther. After a while, the brother once more cried, "Cover thee well, my sister dear, that the rain may not wet thee, that the wind may not load thee with dust, that thou may'st be fair and beautiful when thou appearest before the King." The bride asked, "What is my dear brother saying?" "Ah," said the old woman, "he says you must look out of the carriage." They were, however, just on a bridge, which crossed deep water. When the bride stood up and leant forward out of the carriage, they both pushed her out, and she fell into the middle of the water. At the same moment that she sank, a snow-white duck arose out of the mirror-smooth water and swam down the river. The brother had observed nothing of it and drove the carriage on until they reached the court. Then he took the black maiden to the King as his sister and thought she really was so, because his eyes were dim, and he saw the golden garments glittering. When the King saw the boundless ugliness of his intended bride, he was very angry and ordered the coachman to be thrown into a pit which was full of adders and nests of snakes. The old witch, however, knew so well how to flatter the King and deceive his eyes by her arts that he kept her and her daughter until she appeared quite endurable to him, and he really married her.

388 One evening when the black bride was sitting on the King's knee, a white duck came swimming up the gutter to the kitchen and said to the kitchen-boy, "Boy, light a fire, that I may warm my feathers." The kitchen-boy did it and lit a fire on the hearth. Then came the duck and sat down by it, and shook herself and smoothed her feathers to rights with her bill. While she was thus sitting and enjoying herself, she asked, "What is my brother Reginer doing?" The scullery-boy

replied, "He is imprisoned in the pit with adders and with snakes." Then she asked, "What is the black witch doing in the house?" The boy answered, "She is loved by the King and happy." "May God have mercy on him," said the duck and swam forth by the gutter.

389 The next night she came again and put the same questions, and the third night also. Then the kitchen-boy could bear it no longer and went to the King and disclosed all to him. The King, however, wanted to see it for himself and next evening went thither, and when the duck thrust her head in through the sink, he took his sword and cut through her neck, and suddenly she changed into a most beautiful maiden, exactly like the picture which her brother had made of her. The King was full of joy, and as she stood there quite wet, he caused splendid apparel to be brought and had her clothed in it. Then she told how she had been betrayed by cunning and falsehood, and at last thrown down into the water, and her first request was that her brother should be brought forth from the pit of snakes, and when the King had fulfilled this request, he went into the chamber where the old witch was and asked, "What does she deserve who does this and that?" and related what had happened. Then was she so blinded that she was aware of nothing and said, "She deserves to be stripped naked and put into a barrel with nails, and that a horse should be harnessed to the barrel, and the horse sent all over the world." All of which was done to her, and to her black daughter. But the King married the white and beautiful bride, and rewarded her faithful brother, and made him a rich and distinguished man.[22]

390 The woman, her daughter, and her stepdaughter can be regarded as a triad representing the feminine psyche. The woman represents the conscious attitude, while her daughter, who is negative, represents

---

[22] Cf. Grimm and Grimm, "The White Bride and the Black Bride," in *Complete Fairy Tales*, 589–93.

the shadow. Reginer, the stepbrother, stands for the animus. The stepdaughter is the fourth in the group, and she represents the true inner nature and source of renewal within the feminine psyche. However, she can only be realized and reach fulfilment when she unites with the discerning Logos principle personified by the king. The king does not belong to a foursome, but he is one of three masculine figures, the other two being the coachman, who makes the connection with the anima, and the kitchen boy, who leads him to the revelation of the inner situation.

391   God appears to the first triad of the woman and her two daughters. He rewards the one who shows him the way, but the woman and her daughter are cursed and made black, that is, they are covered over by the veil of unconsciousness. Their sin was their refusal to show God the way, and this suggests that God needs man's help. He asks man to be the instrument for reaching higher consciousness. In a deeper sense this scene says that the human psyche is the only place where God can become conscious. Because the two women fail at this task, they forfeit their human essence and become witches. Falling under the dark veil of unconsciousness, they step out of their role as representatives of female consciousness, which they had at the tale's beginning. Their role now is that of the king's negative anima. When this happens, one cannot discriminate between an unconscious woman and the anima of a man. Psychologically, there is no distinction. A woman who is lost in the sea of the unconscious is vague within herself and has neither critical understanding nor much will. Such an "undefined" woman easily plays the role of the anima for men. Indeed, the more unconscious she is, the better she can play the anima role. It is for this reason that some women are reluctant to become conscious; if they do, they lose the ability to be the witch-anima and thus lose their power over men. A man who is drowned in the unconscious behaves like the animus of a woman. A possessed man (Hitler, for example) has all the animus traits; he is carried away by every emotion, is full of unconsidered opinions, and expresses himself sloppily and didactically, often in an emotional uproar.

392　　The beautiful white bride is pushed into the water and swims away in the form of a white duck, while Reginer, the animus whose task it was to lead her to the king, is thrown into a snake-pit, presumably to make real contact with Logos. It is finally the lowly shadow of the king, the kitchen boy, who is instrumental in bringing out the truth. When the king beheads the duck, she again turns into the beautiful woman she once was. In psychological terms, if a psychic content is not recognized in the human realm, it regresses into the instinctual realm, as we saw in "The Three Feathers" or in the case of Snati-Snati. After the witch and her daughter have been destroyed, a mandala of four persons emerges: the king, the white bride, Reginer (freed from the pit), and the kitchen boy. While there is much more that one could say about this story, I cite it only to show how a factor that represents the consciousness of a woman can, at the same time, be identified with the negative anima of a man.

393　　Fairytales light up different aspects within a single context, and they always contain similar motifs such as witches, stepmothers, and kings, who are always subject to similar processes that unfold in similar ways. The fact that the threads running through the tales all follow the same direction — so that several tales can be linked up into a circular chain of rings of tales, each amplifying the other — suggests that the order they refer to is a single, fundamental one. It is my feeling that when fairytales are brought together in clusters and interpreted in relation to one another, they represent at bottom one transcendental archetypal arrangement.

394　　In the same way that a crystal may be illuminated from its various sides, so each kind of tale presents certain aspects and necessarily obscures others. For instance, in one tale certain archetypes can be seen particularly clearly, while in another story, other archetypes emerge. And because this is so, fairytales can be put into groups, or classified according to their similar configuration of archetypes.

395　　It is tempting to try to create an abstract model of the general structure of the collective unconscious that manifests in many different ways — in "ten thousand" different fairytales. I do not believe this to be possible because I assume that we are dealing with a transcendental order similar to the atom, which physicists say cannot be described as it is in itself because three-dimensional models inevitably distort it. While schemata can be invaluable, the four-dimensional event forever eludes our grasp.[23] Although the inner order refuses to be schematized, an exact description will render important hints concerning its structure. We are able to discern that very different fairytales at bottom circumambulate one and the same content — the Self. This type of fairytale that contains the problem of encounters with the Self is the foundation of all fairytales that revolve around the theme of surmounting great difficulties to reach a treasure. In my book *Individuation in Fairy Tales*, I have tried to interpret some of these tales that directly or indirectly are related to the problem of the Self.[24] This central connection is touched upon, for example, in the toad's ring in "The Three Feathers," in the name "Ring" of the king's son in the Snati-Snati story, and in the prickly fish on the altar of the mountain spirit. The hard-to-attain treasure is often present in the guise of simple things. When one is interpreting fairytales, it pays to always keep an eye open for this central motif.

---

[23] Cf. Jung, *Structure & Dynamics*, vol. 8, *CW*, §§ 951–53.
[24] Cf. Von Franz, *Individuation in Fairy Tales*.

Part 2

Animus and Anima
in Fairytales

Preface

396

"The animus is a cunning fox who knows how
to hide his footprints with his tail."

C.G. Jung

397   All fairytales represent something very much removed from human consciousness. Dr. Jung once said that if one interprets a fairytale thoroughly, one must take at least a week's vacation afterwards, because it is so difficult. The difficulty is rooted in the fact that the fairytale is based on certain functions of the psyche without any personal material to bridge it. What we have are just the skeletons of the psyche with the original coverings removed. Only that remains which is of general human interest. They are absolutely abstract patterns. In primitive tales, an element is present which has been lost in most of the later ones: that is, the element of awe, of terror, of the divine, which people experienced in meeting the archetype.[1]

---

[1] *Animus and Anima in Fairy Tales* was originally a seminar given by Marie Louise von Franz at the Los Angeles Society of Analytical Psychology in 1953. She described the spirit in which she gave these lectures when she returned to the Jung Institute of Los Angeles in 1976. "We were a group of younger pupils [Rivkah Kluger, Aniela Jaffé, et al.], and when we had these invitations abroad, Jung always said to us, 'Now, remember that by being close around me and hearing so much' — we went to all the lectures and all the speeches and so on — 'you know more than these people. So don't be shy. Your task is to hand on what the people who can't come to Zurich want to learn about, what you have learned to hand on.' And that gave one a feeling of a function, that one had something to give." Marie-Louise von Franz: "Confrontation With the Collective Unconscious" In *Psychological Perspectives*, 59/2016, 295-318.

Chapter 10

A Fairytale from Northern Germany:
Oll Rinkrank

398   The title of this fairytale, which has been handed down in Low German, translates as "The Old Red Knight."[2] It tells of a king, his daughter and a mountain of glass which the king has built to test the suitors of his daughter. Only a man who can walk over this mountain of glass shall receive her. A lover appears who wants to marry the girl, and so the two walk across the mountain of glass. The mountain cracks open — the girl falls in, and the rift closes again. Inside the mountain lives an old man with a cubit-long beard. He asks the girl to serve him as a maid and gives her the name "Mrs. Mansrot" (Man's Red); she is to call him "Rinkrank" ("Red Knight"). Every day Rinkrank disappears down a ladder through a small window, and every night he returns with a pile of gold and silver. One day the girl makes a plan to run away. To this end, she pulls down the window through which the old man leaves the interior of the mountain, dropping it on his beard. She holds Rinkrank until he is willing to give her the ladder he usually pulls up from outside. The princess then returns to the king and tells him what has happened. The king sets off to Rinkrank, kills him, and takes all the gold and silver. The tale ends with the marriage between the princess and the man who asks for her hand in marriage at the beginning of the story.

399   When interpreting a fairytale, it is important to look at the initial situation and ask yourself: Who is missing to make the family complete? Generally, the character who is not there at the beginning

---

[2] Jacob and Wilhelm Grimm, "Old Rinkrank," in *The Complete Grimm's Fairy Tales*, trans. Margaret Hunt (New York: Pantheon Books, 1972), 796 ff. Further commentary on this fairytale by Marie-Louise von Franz in *Feminine in Fairy Tales*. Vol. 12 of the Collected Works. (Asheville: Chiron Publications, 2022).

shows up later in some form. Something happens in the course of the story, and what was incomplete completes itself. An unsatisfactory situation prevails at the beginning, and the tale tells us how the completion comes about. The situation of a royal character having a daughter would, in a personal case, give us reason to suspect that we are dealing with a father complex. Generally, the animus develops out of the father. Moreover, there is no mother. In a personal situation, it is generally correct to say in such a case that there probably exists a weakness and insecurity on the feminine side, which exposes the woman to the danger of animus possession. However, the tale does not tell a personal case history. The male person is not simply the father; rather, it is explicitly stated that he is a king. Fairytales depict what happens when the archetypes are among themselves; that is, these folk tales depict processes in the collective unconscious that are much more fundamental than in personal material grounded on those processes.

400   So here it is a king and a princess who are at the center of the story. Fairytales are usually either about royal figures or about the typically ordinary, anonymous person. This indicates that the material refers to a suprapersonal or to a general human level. The king is the preeminent figure. In Egypt it was at first only the pharaoh who received the funerary rites which guaranteed immortality. Later, the priests claimed the same guarantee for themselves, and finally the ritual was accorded to everyone. In contrast, the king is God's representative on earth; he is an incarnation of God. In any case, kings in fairytales and myths are usually incomplete; they are either blind or infirm or they need rejuvenation, the water of life. The king, strictly speaking, represents that idea of the Self, which has become the fundamental representation of the collective attitude. Christ, in terms of the contemporary Christian world, may be looked upon as the central idea of a political state — but this is incomplete, for it represents only the dominant center of the collective system. That center may become old, obsolete, incomplete. This is the moment when renewal must take place, opening up the real meaning, the experience, which

underlies religious systems. Hundreds of fairytales are concerned with this process and tell us how it comes about.

401   In our fairytale, the king sets up a kind of glass trap for his son-in-law — not for his daughter. He represents a stage of the collective attitude which has become quite wrong, incomplete. The queen has apparently died — this means that the feminine factor corresponding to and connected with the king, the feeling, the Eros aspect of the old ruling attitude, has disappeared. Every system is linked with a particular feeling attitude. The birth of Christianity, as the old Roman Empire was declining, meant a change of attitude toward Logos, toward marriage, slavery, and the political system. And thus, generally speaking, all ruling attitudes are accompanied by a certain feeling attitude. If the queen has died, there is no longer any feeling attitude in the old ruling system. Therefore, the whole weight shifts to the daughter; through the princess, the renewal aspect emerges.

402   The trap of the glass mountain that the king sets suggests a mother substitute, insofar as mountains have long been revered as sacred sites, the home of mother goddesses. Certainly, Jung also says that mountains can represent the supreme personality, the Self. This is the case because mountains provide a safe point of orientation when one is on the plain. Certain church fathers have been referred to as "mountains" that rise above the plain. Going up or climbing a mountain is a symbol of becoming more conscious. A mountain is made up of a pile of earth and rock that has been thrown up by a volcanic eruption — the earth's interior has been thrown outward. The process of individuation is climbing and surmounting one's own worst, most resistant difficulties: this earthly mass. Now, by climbing the mountain, one becomes the mountain. The ego climbs that blind mass of material that we find within ourselves. That is why the mountain can represent the mother: Think of Gilgamesh's effort getting through this heap of matter.

403   Like a chalice, the mountain opens and encloses the girl, emphasizing its feminine aspect. However, the mountain is made of glass; it is not dark like matter. There are some fairytales in which

the heroine is confined in a glass coffin.[3] This state signifies a complete detachment from life, both emotionally and intellectually. You can look out of the glass prison and have a full view, but you are still isolated. Glass is, after all, also used as an insulating material; in our fairytale it alludes to the state of being shut off from emotional life. In this sense, "glass" people are brittle, stiff — you can come into contact with them intellectually, but they have no heart, and so there is no feeling contact with them.

404   So the king is trying to cut off all emotional contact with the future son-in-law. He wants to stop life so that there can be no future king to dethrone him. Every ruling system has a tendency to resist and petrify the flow of life. The various instinctive patterns, which higher species of animals have, come into conflict with each other — man is the only being on this planet who can control his instincts. That is why he was given consciousness. Compare this to the lemmings in Norway: They move in droves to another area, probably so they don't destroy the land completely and will continue to have food. But when the migratory instinct makes them head for the sea, the herd instinct forces them to keep the direction they have taken — until they are all drowned. Here we encounter the negative aspect of instinctual nature; and only consciousness gains control over such a destructive mechanism. But it is also part of the structure of consciousness to become one-sided. Consciousness is connected with willpower, and this involves the danger of becoming independent of instincts and going against one's nature. Such a one-sided attitude can be recognized by the fact that one just goes on and on, even when it turns out that the behavior that has been helpful so far will one day come out negatively. We face this problem in midlife when long-held beliefs or modes of behavior suddenly no longer satisfy or work. But in normal everyday life, too, the need for an adjustment or change of values is constantly present.

405   The old king's trick backfires, for it is the daughter who falls into the trap. The son-in-law, who would be destined to become king, represents the germ of a new attitude resting in the unconscious. In

---

[3] Of the Grimm's fairytales, *Little Snow-White* is the best known; cf. also *The Glass Coffin*.

this tale, however, he functions merely as a catalytic agent, for nothing is actually said about him. From the fact that the masculine element remains so completely pale, while the daughter has a real destiny and is truly characterized, we can deduce that our tale is probably the story of the anima. The girl wants to help her future husband get over the mountain and gets trapped as a result. We often see people fall into a complex, but it is not yet manifest at all. The problem becomes apparent only at a crucial moment, namely, when she has a chance to break free from the complex. It is only when the man wants to marry the girl in our fairytale that she falls into her father complex. It follows that a person with a neurosis has it because the chance to get out of the complex is being offered. When these people miss the right moment, some catastrophe occurs, for example, a disease, a sickness of some kind.

406   You know those mythical stories with the dragon — if you touch him, you gain possession of the pearl. Here, the girl could have simply married, and the king could have retired from his position. But instead, she falls into the mountain, into the trap. It is not the young man who falls in. Inside the mountain, she meets the old man with the beard. One gets the feeling that this old man does not earn the gold and silver in any honest way. He treats the girl as his wife and gives her the name of a married woman — but it is not the name he bears. And she must work for him. The beard, like hair in general, plays an enormous role in fairytales.[4] In our story, the girl captures Old Rinkrank by pulling the window down on his beard. Hair on the head represents unconscious thoughts — that's why hair has mana power. Sometimes we influence our environment much more by our unconscious assumptions than by our conscious thoughts. This is why hair, the spiritual power of our unconscious thoughts, is so important. Samson lost his power when his hair was cut off. As another example, consider the primitive tribe where boys must gather shells for their headdress, which they wear for the rest of their lives. After their coiffure is complete, they can marry. The hairstyle

---

[4] Thus in the *Bluebeard* fairytale; "Le barbe bleu" comes from the fairytale collection of Charles Perrault, *Histoires ou Contes du temps passé* (1697) and also found its way into the *Kinder- und Hausmärchen* of the Brothers Grimm.

here is synonymous with a worldview, a *Weltanschauung*, a philosophy that they wear on their heads. The beard, on the other hand, symbolizes the tremendous stream of unconscious talk, the blind chatter to which animus-possessed women are given. It flows out of their mouths — a lot of trash and a lot of pearls, but they are unconscious of both the trash and the pearls they spew.

407   In our story, the girl has pinned down the old man's beard — we know this trick from some ghost stories. If you can pin the ghost down, it disappears completely or turns out to be a pile of straw or something similarly worthless. Something like this happens in active imagination when we bring awareness to what is vaguely bothering us or what has too much emotional support. We then ask, "Do I really believe this?" and so on. You have to stop and pin down this flow. So who is the old man in the mountain, this sort of robber, the old red knight? It is natural to suspect that he is an animus figure. We have already said that the king represents a collective ruling attitude. It is not stated that the king put the old man in the mountain. If it were a personal story, we might claim that behind the king is the archaic figure of the old man. But we must consider the problem in a more collective aspect: There is the "red" in his name, a good reason to associate him with another "Red Beard" story dealing with Wotan slumbering in the German soul. According to one legend, Barbarossa famously became an embodiment of Wotan. So we can say that the Old Man in the Mountain represents an earlier image of God that goes farther back than the king. When a ruling figure or idea disappears, the first thing that appears afterwards is an older image of God. One can observe this truth throughout the history of religion. When the Greek gods lost their mana, the deities that arose after them were more archaic; they came from the pre-Greek period. But this does not imply a true regression — for the earlier figures of the gods contain the germ of the new and higher level of development. In this sense, for example, alchemy on a higher level returned as science.

408   The old man is an old pagan image of the Germanic god who reappears. This old demon gathers the values (gold and silver) to

himself so that there are no values left in consciousness. This constitutes a very dangerous situation. There is no thought of the old man becoming secret ruler of the land, for he is killed by the king in the end. The regressive aspect has to be killed, as it happens here. It is worth noting that it is not the daughter who kills the old man — she leaves that job to the king; his duty is to kill the one who has attracted the devil by his behavior. The daughter's only task is to *escape*. Women cannot fight the animus by killing him; they can only grab him — by pinning him by the beard and escaping. It is quite enough not to get caught. Rilke says, "Who speaks of victory? To endure is all."[5] The male hero always fights, overcomes and conquers the monster in the myths. The feminine, on the other hand, follows the path of individuation by suffering and escaping. It is enough if she can walk out into the human situation and there restore human relatedness, relationship.

409 The king kills the old Rinkrank — the opposites generally kill each other. The unconscious creates the conflict, it brings forth the two. If you can stay out of it and not take one point of view over the other, you can escape the evils of conflict. The princess simply suffers and then leaves. The only effort she makes is to pin down his beard. She turns Rinkrank into a helpful servant who provides the way to escape: the ladder. In Siberia they still tell of a spirit world where the gods dwell, but we in the West have lost that world. There is now only a rope ladder with knots in it that connects the ghost world with our world, and only a shaman or a medicine man can cross over to the other world by using the knots as he climbs. It is such a ladder that we build up every day in analysis — until we experience the feeling, "Now I am connected." The emotional representations are the knots. The oldest writings and calculations used cords with knots. The string, cord, or ladder is the meaning, the connection. We see the connecting links. The old demon provides the girl with a meaning, with connection. If the woman has not gone through the experience of being trapped by the demon animus, she has only unconscious thoughts. It is the demon who provides her with the

---

[5] Rainer Maria Rilke: *Requiem for Wolf Graf von Kalckreuth* (1908).

ladder. In all of this, we must remember that fairytales deal with archetypes — and archetypes cannot be killed. Our tale says that in this particular constellation, the negative aspect disappears. You can understand it this way: The devil will always reappear, but he will do so in a different form, a different constellation — this particular problem will not reappear.

410   From the discussion after the lecture

There is always a fairytale level going on in life. The myths develop out of it, and these sink into fairytales again. The princess who falls into the mountain falls into the mother, and there she is reborn. "Rinkrank," the red knight, is there — the passion is inside the mountain. The mother is represented not by a human being but by a mountain. That which is personified as a human being can be integrated. The mountain enclosing a person means that this content cannot be integrated by her — she can only relate to it. The positive thing here is that the values are rescued — the gold and silver are in the possession of the bride and groom in the end. We see here that the princess acquires her physical reality by falling into this mountain.

411   Often the negative hero is called the "Red Knight." This shows that there is an emotional link between the girl and the demon. Inside the mountain both names contain the "red": Rinkrank and Mans-red. The name "Mansrot" (Man's red) is a combination of the masculine ("man's") and passion ("red"). The demon gives her this name, which helps her realize who she really is. The great problem of the animus is this: If a woman is unconscious of her animus, it links up with the emotional side and becomes "a bull in a china shop." She is then able to develop a masculine mind, look at herself more objectively — but her feminine, passive feeling nature is pushed way down and melded with the animus. This causes many tragedies in life.

412   The old king does everything to prevent the renewal with his right hand, and everything to help the renewal with his left hand. Women are always spinning plots to catch someone and then fall

into their own trap. But men play with the anima, and she takes the key when they aren't looking. The evil old man robbed all that gold. But we can say afterwards, "Thank God he did, because now *she* has it." The fact that the girl goes through the transformation process of suffering, and takes action in pinning down the beard, causes the transformation in him so that he helps her.

413   The killing of the evil side, the wise old man, by the king may be compared to the "Christian habit" as king (dominant principle), in the sense of a killing attitude toward life. The demon in the mountain was like the Germanic Wotan as a seed of new life — but the Germans did not use in a positive way the libido that was released. Communism and the conventional Christian attitude are "damned near to each other" — the path for us to take is walking away from them both and letting them kill each other. That is how a conflict is always overcome — by walking out of it. In a conflict, the two sides come so near to each other that they use the same weapons. The process of individuation is never helped by taking part in the battle — but by walking out of it. The two sides hate each other because they are so similar and use the same methods. That is why the fairytale lets the king kill the demon — naturally, now the king will leave the throne to the princess and her husband.

414   Regarding Old Rinkrank as a robber: It is one of the activities of the animus life of a woman to steal, to suck life from people. Such a woman becomes a vampire because she has no life in herself. She needs life, and she must take it where she finds it. This animus kills every feminine aspect in life.

◆

Chapter 11

A Turkestan Fairytale:
The Magic Horse

There once was a king who had a beautiful daughter. When she was grown up, he devised a clever trick to test her suitors. He fed a flea until it grew as big as a camel. Then he killed and skinned it, and announced that the man who can guess to whom or to what the skin belonged shall have his daughter. One day his slave, who had gone to fetch water from the pool, exclaimed to himself, "Oh, they are fools for not guessing that this is the skin of a flea." He was overheard by the Div who lived in the pool, and this Div changed himself into a beggar and went to court and told the king, "I know what that skin is — it is the skin of a flea." The king was very unhappy but had to keep his promise to give the beggar his daughter. He didn't want to, but the Div threw his cap up in the air, and a black fog covered the sky like night. This frightened the king so that he gave up his daughter. Then the Div threw the cap on the ground, and there was light over the land again. Naturally, the daughter was very sad and miserable, and she went out alone to the king's stable to cry. A little horse or pony in the stable spoke to her: "Take me with you, and also bring a pink flower, a comb, a mirror, and some salt." The princess obtains these items and begins the journey with the Div, taking along the little magic horse and a large retinue of slaves and animals. But along the way, the Div begins eating first the slaves and then the animals, until they are all devoured.

416   The princess is full of terror, as they are approaching a cave.
The little horse advises her to tell the Div to go on in and that
they will follow him. As she and the pony enter the cave after
the Div, she sees that it is full of skeletons. The pony tells her
that the Div is going to eat her too, so she must beat him and
get on him (the pony). This she does, and they make their
escape. The Div is furious when he sees they have left, and he
makes a snowstorm so powerful that they cannot proceed.
Then the magic horse tells her to throw the pink flower
behind her. As she does this, all the plain between her and
the Div is immediately transformed into heavy thorn bushes.
The Div calls to her, "Oh, dear little bride, you are so far away.
What did you do to get through these thorn bushes?" She
answers, "I took off all my clothes until I was as naked as the
day I was born, and then I came through." The Div removes
his clothing, and, of course, he has an even more devilish
time. While he is working his way through, the princess and
the little horse continue their flight. But at last, the Div does
get through, and soon he is close behind them again. Now
the magic horse tells the girl to throw the salt behind her. This
is immediately transformed into a great sandy desert and a
salty sea between the Div and the fleeing pair. Again the Div
calls to his bride far away, "Oh, dear one, how did you get
through this sand and sea?" She answers again, "I took off all
my clothes until I was as naked as the day my mother bore
me." Again the Div removes his clothes, which makes his
progress through this forbidding wasteland even more
difficult, and again this gives the princess and the magic horse
time to get away.

417   But, of course, it is only a breathing spell, because the Div
does eventually cover the distance between them and is
nearly upon them for the third time when the magic horse
tells her it is time to throw the comb behind her. This time it
is a giant mountain that rises between them and the pursuing
Div. When the Div asks his bride how she got through it, she

tells him she pulled out two teeth and tried to make a hole through the mountain. Following the procedure, the Div is naturally delayed a long time, and the horse and the girl get far ahead. But as before, the Div finally gets through, and now he is very angry as for the fourth time they are almost within his reach. Prompted by the horse, the girl throws the mirror behind her, and the land transforms into a wide and roaring river. The Div calls to her, "Oh, dear bride, what did you do to get across the river?" She answers, "I put a big stone around my neck and plunged into the waters." The Div does this and then disappears from the story for the time being.

418 The girl and the horse finally come to a hut in which live a little old man and a woman, who invite them to stay. The next morning the girl falls asleep near the hut. The king of the area has meanwhile been out hunting and become lost. His servants find the king's hawk sitting on the princess's head. The king asks who she is. The girl had asked the old couple to say, if anyone asks, that she is their daughter, which they do. Although the king believes them, it doesn't make any difference to him that she is of such lowly birth, and he asks her to marry him. So they marry and are very happy. One day the king decides to go out hunting again and to stay away for eight or nine months. The young queen doesn't much like this and is even more concerned when he wants to take her little horse with him. But the horse tells her not to be afraid; she must take some hair from his mane, and she should burn it when she is in danger, and he will be there. In the meantime, the Div has escaped from the stream and is bent on vengeance. He assumes the form and wears the clothes of a humble laborer and waits for his opportunity. While the king is away, the queen gives birth to twin sons, and a messenger is sent to the king with a letter telling him about the event. This is the chance the Div has been waiting for. He sends a terrific rain storm to hinder the messenger, and in

the confusion, the Div changes the letter so that the message reads that the queen has given birth to a dog and a cat.

419 When the king receives this message, he is dismayed and sad but sends back a letter saying not to harm the queen. This message too is intercepted by the Div, who arranges that the court receive an order to set the queen backward on an ass, together with her two sons, to blacken her face and send her out of the city in disgrace. The Div comes upon her in this predicament, as she is sorrowfully leaving the city, and laughs at her. He says that he will now eat her but will torture her first by eating the two children before her very eyes. The queen thinks quickly and says that at least he should make a proper feast out of them by building a fire to cook them. The Div builds the fire, which gives her an opportunity to burn the hair from the mane of the magic horse. The magic horse promptly appears. He tells her that this is very serious and that this time he will have to fight the Div. If blood or red foam appears in the stream, she will know that he has been killed by the Div; but if white foam appears, it will mean that all is well and the Div has been destroyed.

420 The fight takes place between the magic horse and the Div as the young queen watches anxiously. Red foam appears, and the girl faints. But when she wakes up, she sees that the foam is white, and the horse is alive. He tells her that she is now safe from the Div forever, but he also tells her that now the time has come that she must kill him, the horse. She must throw his head away, place his four legs in the four cardinal directions, throw the bowels away, and then sit with her children under the ribs. The queen protests against killing the horse, but he convinces her that it must be done. She follows all his directions and finally sits with her children under his ribs. All the dismembered parts of the horse now transform themselves into a paradise: The legs turn into emerald trees; out of the bowels spring beautiful villages; the ribs turn into

a golden castle; and out of the head comes a beautiful crystal river.

421 Meanwhile, the king has returned from hunting and discovered that his wife is gone. He is very angry as he realizes what has happened. In his fury and grief, he kills all the people in the town and very nearly goes mad himself. After this holocaust, he becomes a wandering dervish and sets out to look for his wife. Eventually, he comes upon the beautiful paradise which had come into being by the sacrifice of the magic horse and is delighted with the landscape and the golden castle. A maid is drawing water at a well, and he asks her who lives in the golden castle. She tells him that it is the home of a widow and her two sons. He suspects that his search is at an end — that it is his wife who lives in this paradise — and while the maid is not looking, he puts his ring into her water bucket. The queen recognizes the ring and rushes out with her two sons to meet him. The rejoicing family is reunited, and from then on, they live together in this beautiful city.[1]

422 Here the trap set by the king is not a glass mountain but the flea and its skin. Fleas and bugs in general belong to the devil. To the peasants, the devil is the master of the rats and bugs and fleas. The general feeling that these are devilish and demonic is due to their being parasites, autonomous things which suck our blood — an autonomous complex. There is an anecdote that tells of a psychotic who said that "crazy people are covered with lice." The flea is also a vulgar term denoting a whore. In German there is the expression, "To make an elephant out of a fly" or "out of a flea," and in English you have the expression "to make a mountain out of a mouse" or "out of a molehill." In *Faust*, Mephistopheles sings of the king who loved his flea and had him clothed by a tailor, then decreed that the

---

[1] The original tale "Das Zauberross" can be found in Gustav Jungbauer, Märchen aus Turkestan und Tibet, *Die Märchen der Weltliteratur* (Jena: Diederichs, 1923). Additional commentary by Marie-Louise von Franz on this story appears in *Archetypal Dimensions of the Psyche* (Boston: Shambhala, 1999), 93 f; *Shadow and Evil in Fairy Tales* (Boston: Shambhala, 2017), 248 ff.

lords and ladies must let him — the flea — have his way without hindrance.[2] He makes his heir and successor a flea, who only bites the ladies. Making the heir so silly keeps him from being a serious threat to the ruling order. One makes a big thing out of a trifle in order to prevent life and growth. This is a typical attitude of dying religions or political systems. When the flow of psychic energy leaves, then come the endless theological and philosophical quarrels; or, in academic life, silly dissertations over unimportant questions while vital issues are ignored. That is a typical symptom, a sign that the real spiritual life has vanished, and therefore all the fleas come up.

423   Here again, we have no queen, so the feeling life is not present. When the feeling life is gone, then it degenerates into just sex as the only way of relating to an object. In cases where catatonics are being helped toward relating again to life, the first forms of relating come out in the most primitive expressions of sex. In the same way, wherever feeling life has degenerated, in all decaying civilizations, you see this very visible and tactless display of sexuality. In living civilizations, it is more hidden and is mixed with feeling. This confirms the theory, proposed in my talk on "Old Rinkrank," that the king is a reversion to the old Wotan in the German soul. We can say that the word "Div" is a degenerate form of "divine." In Abyssinia, the same figure is called "Zar"; possessed women are called "brides of Zar," and there are dance rituals for the curing of such possessed women. They have the feeling that it is not good for a woman to be alone, and if she is, she generally picks up some Zar as a "ghostly lover," and they should stay away from her.

424   In the beginning of our story, the slave at the king's court betrays the secret of the flea's skin. In fairytales, the slave is a frequent carrier for a projection: he portrays the naïve, the lowliest, the uncivilized. This betrayal of the secret by a slave or something lowly is a common motif — the murmuring of what is going on, and its being overheard by a ghost, etc. Sometimes the slave murmurs into a reed, and the

---

[2] Cf. Johann Wolfgang von Goethe: *Faust. Part One* (1808). The "Song of the Flea" can be found in the scene "Auerbach's Cellar," lines 2211-2240.

reed gives it away; or a shepherd cuts a reed for a pipe, and the pipe betrays it. If one's unconscious complex is activated, you cannot stop it. It creeps through doors. People may even dream about it who cannot possibly know about it. This is the penetrating force of unconscious complexes, the infectious quality of which needs more research and studying. This reminds me of a bit of "research" done by a friend of Dr. Jung's, who found a "familiar style" of dreaming in his own family — certain similar motifs. He also discovered that friends who stayed with them in their new situation became invaded by these motifs in their dreams, too. There is such a thing as an "atmosphere of the house." This is connected to the mythological motif that if there is a content of vital importance, something that should be known, it will somehow come out. In this story, it is not coming out of the unconscious into the consciousness, but a Div picks up this secret flow of energy to the unconscious which cannot be stopped.

425   When the ruling attitude is no longer adequate, there is this loss of libido into the unconscious. It constellates the compensating figure. In this case, it constellates the beggarman, the Div, and the king is forced to give his daughter away as he promised. He wants to keep his position, but at the same time, he wants to undermine his position. There is an old German tale where the king's daughter is very haughty and she rejects all who woo her. The king becomes angry and says, "Well, you'll have to accept the next beggar who comes along" — and then he has to keep his promise.[3] Here the king tries not to keep his promise, but the Div shows his power, and the king gives in. At this point, the darker, more archaic form or image of God appears. The daughter belongs to a form of civilization. The anima is generally or always one step behind, and therefore the animus is also represented by a very primitive, pagan god. The anima of ancient Greece was generally represented as a foreign slave, a foreign princess of a more primitive tribe. In medieval times, the anima became pagan, appearing as a Greek or Roman goddess. We might speculate that she may become Christian. This is a fairytale

---

[3] This is the fairytale *King Thrushbeard* by the Brothers Grimm.

of Islamic times, so the animus would be a pre-Islamic, pagan demon.

426   The Div now produces a clever trick — not a beard, but a cap which, when he throws it up to heaven, becomes or creates a black fog. Then he throws the cap down, and it creates light. He can use the cap to create storms; he is a weather demon — creating "weather moods" (We speak of someone being "under the weather"). There is rather a difference of style in the tactics used by the anima or animus: the animus produces an emotional, stormy king of arguing, whereas the anima is subject to subtle, female moods, not saying much, other than making "spoiling remarks." The animus likes very much a brutal demonstration of his power, brute force. The anima has more cunning little ways to get where she wants.

427   The cap covers the head, and so refers to the "top Weltan-schauung" (worldview) — one's ultimate concepts. There are various kinds of caps. If it is a cap of concealment, it produces typical confusion.[4] In dreams we often see disorderly hair, which indicates animus confusion. "Her head was just a nest of plots" — wanting to play all sorts of tricks at the same time. "She got into a sort of snarl of confusion," wanting to say "just the right thing," and so in the end she could say nothing. The animus loves to create an atmosphere of mist, in which nobody can find any orientation. The spreading of a cloud over a country is also attributed to dwarfs and giants — because they disturb consciousness. The king is so frightened by this demonstration that he gives in and gives his daughter away. She goes into a stable where there is a magic horse who later becomes the saving factor. Here, it is interesting that the saving factor is in the stable of the king, the same place where the whole difficulty begins. We take the horse here as a bisexual force, although in the end, it turns into the beautiful city, which is feminine. The missing mother is probably in this horse. In fairytales where the mother is dead or has disappeared — regressed into the animal layer of the psyche — she typically becomes the helpful instinct for the daughter.

---

[4] A cap of concealment produces a fog-like effect, as the German term "Nebelkappe" ("Nebel"= fog) suggests. It refers to the dwarf Alberich's "Nebelkappe" in the German "Nibelungenlied," "The Song of the Nibelungs"; translated as "cap of darkness"; "cap of invisibility"; "cloak" or "cap of concealment."

428   Jung interprets the high pointed caps of dwarfs as meaning that the contents are trying to push up into consciousness. One might call it a phallic symbol in the sense of an activity that wants to shoot up. If caps appear with such points, we don't need to do anything about the matter — there is enough energy in them that they will come up on their own. There is an animus thinking about love which destroys a woman's real feeling. For example, she thinks, "Shall I or shall I not go to bed with him?" rather than, "Do I love him?" The wrong conscious attitude calls forth a counterreaction from the unconscious, and then there is a panic. The king must now give in to the Div's demonstration of power. He represents a conscious attitude which is completely helpless towards the unconscious. Had it been adequate, the king would have called in a magician of his own. Panic attacks are always a symptom of weak ego consciousness which cannot cope with the unconscious.

429   The helpful animal here is not a wild animal but is a domesticated animal in the stable underneath. This would indicate that the split between the animal layer and the civilized layer is not too great. This story comes from Turkestan. You can read the cultural situation of a land from its fairytales. In the Christian civilization there is much more of a split, and thus much more tension. Orientals have developed their civilizations so slowly and gradually that there is not the kind of split that is found in Western civilization. They have a deeper "wisdom" — but because there is not much tension from splitting, there is a negative side to this situation: There isn't much potential of energy in them either. The one time they had a big *élan* was when Mohammed created monotheism in their land of polytheism, but now again they have a low potential energy.

430   The symbolism of the horse generally falls into the bisexual category, as is the case with a tree. When we speak of "masculine" or "feminine" symbols, it is only a nuance we are indicating, anyway. The horse is one of the most difficult animals to interpret. The fox usually represents cunning, as well as some cruelty — cold hate and grim rage — but the horse is just horse power. Horses are very

sensitive to the ghost world, very much given to panic, they can take the bit in their mouth and run. But mainly the horse is *force*, and a carrying force — if we know how to treat it. Then there is the beggar motif. The Div, then the girl, and then the king go through the beggar stage. There is a German fairytale "King Thrushbeard," where the haughty girl must marry the beggar — and after she is completely humiliated, he reveals that he is a king who only appeared as Thrushbeard in order to provide her redemption through the necessary first step of humiliation. There the king and the beggar are the same, compensating sides to the same. The Div comes out of the pool as a compensation to the too-high-up position of the king.

431   We have a tendency to think of "high" and "up" and are referring to consciousness, with unconsciousness as "down." But looking at it from the natural viewpoint, that is obviously wrong. In the primitive view there is the world, the middle level, which is consciousness. And both the heaven above and the underworld are different realms of unconsciousness. Certainly one who is "up in the clouds" is not conscious. The subject matter is much too complicated to speak simply of "up" and "down." The primitive picture or point of view generally refers to the form or pattern of the instincts: the upper realm contains the archetypes as spiritual elements, then our conscious world in the middle, and below it, the archetypes as physical instincts. The upper and the lower worlds are both in the unconscious, they are two archetypes of the same thing. Early Christianity came up in a decaying civilization where people were living a lower-than-animal life, in a perverted swamp. Hence the dreams of the early Christians contained images of going up towards spirituality. This was a necessary compensatory process. Today, where we have gone too far "up" and away from the instincts, compensating dreams involve going "down." We cannot even speak of mother goddesses as always below — as they were in Greece. In Egypt the earth god was masculine. And spiritual things in Egypt were concrete because the earth god was a male god.

432   When the Div comes out of the pool below, it means that the ruling principle has gone too far from the instinct. Therefore, it must

be the horse that is the redeeming animal. They have all been too high — therefore, they must all be humiliated into beggars before redemption. We have experienced the new sense of power that comes when we have sunk down in the sea and finally our feet touch the ground, and we can now get the spurt of energy to rise again. They must all go down and become "Div-ified," acquiring what he had, and then they can come up again. Here the Div is specifically only negative, devouring human life and leaving nothing but the bones (as in the cave). Here again we have the motif of running away, escaping. We have other, shorter fairytales where the successful running away from the demon is the only solution. In many instances, to escape the unconscious in a certain aspect is just as heroic a deed as conquering the dragon. It is quite difficult enough just to run away, escaping again into the human realm.

433   Throwing things backward without looking is the pagan gesture of sacrificing to the unnamable, the untouchable chthonic god, the gesture of worship to the dark powers which you cannot look at, cannot face. This is important to know psychologically, because we are so caught up in the Christian attitude of having to face everything. There are dark things which have numinous qualities which we cannot face; we can sacrifice to them, which is to recognize them. In psychotics, for instance, there are things too dark which it would not be wise to pull out and look at. One can only sacrifice to them but not look back at them. The princess cannot face this terrible Div, but she sacrifices to him without looking at him. She sacrifices the three instruments which affect her feminine persona: the flower, the comb, and the mirror, as well as salt, which we will discuss later. It is said that roses have thorns because there is no love without thorns. Thorns are negative remarks and the like.

434   The shadow is a positive function, a vital instinct which could help. We can say the shadow is positive as long as it stays in the inner world and doesn't act up in the outer world, where it is the province of the persona to move and act and serve as a protection. The Div comes up against the girl's own negative, feminine side, which stops him for a while, "gives him a lot to chew on." What does that mean

practically? Animus possession may take the form of criticizing everybody and everything outside. A way to stop that arguing — and the damn thing about the animus is that he is right, but that he is likely to be wrong in the specific situation — is for the woman to say to the animus, "If you are so terribly fanatical about what is wrong and what should be, let's look at my shadow." Then there is an impact inside which is very helpful. Women don't have such a desire as men to be perfect. But if there is a strong animus, then there is a strong shadow, and in this way, they have a chance to become conscious. If she has a strong animus, she overcomes this indifference toward knowing her shadow and can have a male objectivity in becoming conscious about it. There is always one step in the individuation of women where she must give up the magic power she possesses as the anima. She must sacrifice it if she wants to acquire an individual personality. Dr. Jung once said that where love is lacking, power jumps in.[5] A woman with a strong animus has a prestige persona which she protects.

435   Salt has a double aspect: In alchemy, salt is the symbol of wisdom, but it also has a stinging quality of bitterness — the bitterness of the sea comes from the salt. Wisdom, wit, bitterness, and Eros — all that is salt.[6] Jung says this has to do with a specific feminine feeling of love — when love disappoints her, a woman either becomes bitter or wise, developing a sense of humor or a certain wit.[7] Eros is always combined with disappointment — everyone who really loves must risk disappointment. The wisdom of love comes in accepting disappointment without bitterness. The comb has to do with putting one's hair in order — an objective instrument for putting one's thoughts in order. The comb

---

[5] "Where love reigns, there is no will to power; and where the will to power is paramount, love is lacking. The one is but the shadow of the other: the man who adopts the standpoint of Eros finds his compensatory opposite in the will to power, and that of the man who puts the accent on power is Eros." C.G. Jung, "On the Psychology of the Unconscious," in *Two Essays on Analytical Psychology*, 2nd ed., vol. 7, *CW* (Princeton, NJ: Princeton University Press, 1967), § 78.

[6] Cf. C.G. Jung, "The Personification of the Opposites," in *Mysterium Coniunctionis*, CW 14, § 330.

[7] "Disappointment, always a shock to the feelings, is not only the mother of bitterness but the strongest incentive to a differentiation of feeling. The failure of a pet plan, the disappointing behavior of someone one loves, can supply the impulse either for a more or less brutal outburst of affect or for a modification and adjustment of feeling, and hence for its higher development. This culminates in wisdom if feeling is supplemented by reflection and rational insight. Wisdom is never violent: where wisdom reigns there is no conflict between thinking and feeling." C.G. Jung, Ibid., § 334.

transformed itself into the mountain, and the animus must chew his way through that. The mirror is an instrument of reflection. And that is what the animus gets drowned in, dissolved in, while we save ourselves from drowning through conscious reflection. Did she sacrifice these? There is a difference between throwing away and sacrificing. Sacrificing, for pagan people, had a ritual meaning. The horse tells the girl to take these things with her and tells her when to throw them back. Dr. Jung says that only by sacrificing can we have — and can we see what we have.[8] *Real* sacrifice should be made with the same definiteness and lack of bargaining that there is in throwing things away. We can do this only if we are forced by a stronger power in us — not our ego — that gives us the strength to sacrifice. At such a moment, we experience the Self as we realize the power in us which tells us "we must." The sacrifice and what is sacrificed is always the Self. When the girl sacrifices, she realizes her real meaning.

436   Let me add something to what I said about "walking out of the conflict." This can be misunderstood. This is not meant as a cheap escape in order to avoid going into the conflict. This girl is running for her life. We naturally presuppose that you are *in* the conflict before the question arises concerning walking out of it. There are people who avoid conflict by shutting themselves up in a rational system and by not facing the darkness of a conflict. But here what is meant is that the girl is already in this terrible conflict. In practical life, there comes the opportunity to save one's life by stepping aside until one recovers. This is, in the end, not a definitive solution, for eventually she must face the conflict. Women can be tortured by the animus, who tells them they are a complete failure, their life is finished, and now it is too late. The thing to do then is to say, "OK, I am a failure, let's not discuss it anymore." This is a sort of stepping out of it, and thus one saves energy and can turn to something else. This is like throwing a part of ourselves to the animus — let him eat it and in this way stop him from hindering our further action.

---

[8] Cf. C.G. Jung, "The Psychology of the Mass" in *Psychology and Religion*, Vol. 11, *CW*, § 390 ff.

437   In our tale, we have here the motif of recovering. She arrives at a hut and finds the poor old man and woman who allow her to stay for the night. She is so exhausted she falls asleep outside the hut. But the king's hawk alights on her head, and thus the king finds her. And that is how she comes to marry the king. In the old beggar couple, she has for the first time a positive father and mother — the wisdom of the spirit and the wisdom of the earth, so to speak. Think of the Greek story of Philemon and Baucis, who entertained Zeus and Hermes in disguise and who, because of their piety, were spared by the gods when everyone else was destroyed in the flood. In Goethe's *Faust*, Faust kills this old couple due to his inflation.[9]

438   Every possession by the animus is a secret inflation, like every possession by the anima in a man. The anima and animus are suprapersonal to a great extent; they belong to the divine realm. The shadow does belong to the personal unconscious. If you check on the standards used by the animus for his constant criticisms, you find they are always a collective truth, something much beyond the individual. Therefore, every identification with it is a secret inflation, different from the visible inflation that can be so annoying. That is why the humble couple provide a sort of cure — that is where she receives her cure and recovers. This is one more form of escaping animus possession — this humiliation, the humble attitude. When you are going around saying, "You should do such and such," it means, "I am the person who is in a position to tell people what they should do." The way to walk out of a state of possession is to accept humbleness, to admit that you might be a failure, that you might not know.

439   As soon as the girl is low enough — a beggar's child — she falls into a state of unconsciousness, and through this, new life comes to her again. When people put themselves high up, it is like standing on a mountain, and all the water of life flows away from them. But down in the valley, the water can reach them. It is the king's hawk which sits on her head. In the Orient, the hawk is a divine bird, a royal bird. She is chosen by the spirit to be the king's bride. The king

---

[9] Johann Wolfgang von Goethe: *Faust. Part Two*, Act 5.

represents, in the very end, also the animus, if we take this whole tale from the feminine standpoint. But he would represent a spiritual attitude which is more than just a contrast to the feminine life. We are inclined to think of nature and spirit, Logos and Eros, etc., as total opposites, but this is not really so. A real spiritual attitude which lacks the negative character of the animus does not oppose real feminine life. It is what gives objective understanding; it is a creative, inspiring force, providing inspiration for men. This is the true, positive animus, which gives the woman the possibility of sharing with the man the objective and creative attitudes toward life. If a woman is "only" a woman, this implies a certain amount of inertia; but the positive animus enables her to be creatively enterprising, to be active. This is the king, in a positive aspect on the personal level.

440   So now, with this new king, there is the dominance of a new collective attitude. Thus, we can say that whenever a woman overcomes her animus problem, then she will belong to the new spirit of her time, taking part in it and even bringing it about. In Christianity, for instance, it was the women who provided the larger number of earliest converts. Women have this tendency to take up new ideas, new movements, because their mind (the animus in them) is less bound by traditions. In a way, no theory about life is quite as important to women as it is to men. In the negative sense, it means also that they are not completely committed to it. This is because love means more to them than any theoretical questions. But, on the other hand, they can pick up a new idea more easily than a man who is committed to a particular *Weltanschauung*. I once knew a professor of physics who was frightened when he listened to some of the new speculations. He said that if he thought they were true, he would go out and hang himself — because "all is lost if I must now find out that everything I have been teaching is wrong." This is a natural attitude for a man, who is so much more committed to his concepts. Men really feel it as an earthquake if some part of their *Weltanschauung* is falling apart. Women have no definite sense of commitment to an idea, and that is why women help build up the renewal of the attitude of their time. That is why, in general, if a

woman has a father complex, she is somehow better able to come to terms with the spiritual problems of her time — she cannot live just the physical side of her life. That is why the wife who leaves the traditional path of the superficial form of feminine life becomes the queen.

441 The girl marries the king — but the story starts over again. The Oriental fairytales like to end their stories with a link — done in just the right way — which starts a new story. Here the queen becomes pregnant, and the king goes away hunting, asking to take the magic horse with him since he can't see that she will have any use for it while she is pregnant. At first, she is afraid, but the horse reassures her, giving her some hairs of his mane which she can burn if necessary. Why must the king go away? We don't really know, but we can assume that the solution of the first part of the tale — their happy marriage — is not in accord with life. There are still certain parts of their life that are not integrated. This happens to people in analysis who feel "finished" for a time and then find the parts later that still need integrating or feel the need to amplify their consciousness. Here we cannot explain why the king goes away but can say that the king is possessed by a passion for hunting. Perhaps, too, he is not satisfied with his home or is bored with his pregnant wife. There has been a certain solution, but there is still a restlessness going on. The animus does this to compensate for natural feminine inertia.

442 The king, by taking the horse, is taking with him the vital, carrying powers. Certain individuals have the need for enlargement of their personality. Such a person is more liable to fall into difficulties than a weaker person might experience. Something in him wants to get into trouble because of the need he feels to use this energy and realize himself. So, the life force is on the side of restlessness, expressed in the form of hunting for a new adventure. Meanwhile, the woman is brooding something in her pregnancy. We can be pretty sure that when people are as restless as a prancing horse in a stable, that now the psyche is pregnant. But on the other hand, if the animus breaks loose ahead of time and hasn't the

patience to wait, then the negative side of the animus comes in, too. If the king had stayed back, had not been impatient, then he could probably have met and fought with and disposed of the Div. The animus frequently is too impatient; a woman feels she must make up her mind immediately, cut through the situation, act one way or another, instead of waiting for the pregnant psyche to bring forth the proper new development.

443   So, the Div is waiting for his revenge and twice intercepts the letters regarding the birth of the children and the treatment of the queen. Here the negative animus appears in a new function — that of falsifying the messages which come from the unconscious to the conscious, and from the conscious to the unconscious. Practically speaking, a woman can understand with her heart what was really meant by something that was said to her — and later in the evening she begins to think of *just how* it was said and to get suspicious about it, about just why it was said this way and so on. The animus has intercepted the message and put his own poison into it. The first letter he changed to read that the queen has given birth to cats and dogs. And the second letter he falsified to arrange that the queen shall be humiliated. This is, in a word, the "nothing but"-animus who destroys what should be born from the inside. He disparages it as "nothing but" and then makes her feel completely humiliated. He turns one against oneself, and against the future life one is carrying within oneself.

444   In medieval times it was a common custom to put women who were accused as whores on an ass, seated backward, and to drive them out of town. Here the animus is trying to make the girl think like that about herself. Out in the desert, the Div shows his hand and says, "Now I am going to eat you." But she is clever enough to trick him, giving him some cooking advice. She says he might as well have a good meal by building a fire and brewing up a good shashlik out of the boys he threatens to eat first. In practical life, this also works — trying to accept what the animus says. For example, he may say, "My man doesn't love me anymore." One tries to accept and says, "Well, perhaps I don't deserve it," and then one can find peace.

Through this appeasement of the animus, one may find oneself and may discover that it was all animus talk.

445   The burning of the horse's hair and the consequent immediate appearance of the horse bring up the idea of the relativity of space and time in the unconscious so that what seems far away can actually be present if one sees the connection. It is something on the order of mental telepathy. The horse appears and explains that the time has come when he must fight the Div. And that the girl will not see the fight but will know if red foam appears that he has been killed by the Div, but that if white foam appears he, the horse, will have killed the Div. The fight takes place. The girl thinks she sees red foam and faints dead away. When she wakens, she sees it is white foam, and the horse is there to tell her that her troubles with the Div are now permanently finished. Then the horse tells her it is time that she must kill him, the horse, and tells her how she must dispose of his various parts. At first, she resists but finally does as told.

446   We see here that she is not engaged in the battle. The real fight goes on between two supernatural powers. This is a common motif in fairytales. There is one northern tale which tells of a woman who was expelled from her home.[10] First, she marries the moon god but commits sins, so he sends her away. Then she marries Kali, an evil, spirit-eating man. When she realizes he has eaten her brother, she escapes with the help of a fox. She goes toward heaven, till she reaches the polar star, which represents the supreme and good god in this land where the real polar star is so necessary to the people. The Kali follows her and demands his wife back. The polar star puts him in a box and stirs up a wild snowstorm, then opens the box and asks, "Do you still want her?" The Kali says yes, so the process is repeated, in ever-increasing severity until the Kali finally says, "No." When the Kali is disposed of, the polar star says she may now go back to earth — but she still fails to sacrifice to the polar star and so she dies, unable to go back to heaven.

---

[10] "The Woman Who Married the Moon and the Kele," in János Gulya and Ruth Futaky, *Sibirische Märchen,* Die Märchen der Weltliteratur, ed. Friedrich von der Leyen (München: Diederichs, 1995). For further commentary see Marie-Louise von Franz *The Interpretation of Fairy Tales,* xxx.

447 Every animus conflict, if it goes deep enough, seems to touch these deepest, archetypal layers of the conflict between the light god and the dark god. That is why we should try to stand outside the conflict and at the same time watch it, try to realize it objectively. If a woman tries to step into the conflict between good and evil, she can only get caught in the animus. Her task is just to take part in life itself, to guarantee the continuity of life outside. In Persia, only the men are required to pledge themselves to fight against the dark god. The women must only keep life going and preserve human relatedness. It seems as though to suffer fate is the right attitude for a woman, not to try to take action in it. Here in our story, in the decisive event, the girl faints and doesn't even witness it. Previously, the time hadn't yet come when the horse felt it was the moment to fight. This seems to have to do with the fact that the queen now has children — now the future form has been born. The old quaternity looked like this:

King	Princess
Horse	Div
In the end we have this situation:	
Second King	Queen
Boy	Boy

448 This is a new form of the *Auseinandersetzung*. The horse and the Div cancel each other out in the end. The horse could not risk the fight until there was a new possibility, in the boys, of carrying the life force. It is only the animal form of the horse which is linked with the Div, and when the Div is killed then the horse is transformed into its true nature, the garden. This was the same situation in the Siberian tale where a big mouth chased the girl until she came upon the three princes, who were waiting for her and who give her a choice of which one to marry. Here the Div has the positive aspect

of goading her on until she comes to the place where she meets herself. Women go through the process of individuation mainly by suffering, when it is done in the right way — in the unconscious, there seems to be a shifting then of the libido. If one can adapt to the devil without being eaten by him, he makes for consciousness.

449   The horse tells her that after she has killed him, she is to put one of his legs in each of the four cardinal points, throw his head away to one side, throw his bowels away, and then sit with her children under his ribs. This is a general motif in fairytales — the killing of the helpful animal after a given time.[11] One such tale tells of the helpful fox who then asks that his head and paws be cut off, and when this is done, he turns into a prince who had been bewitched into fox form.[12] Generally, the one restored to human form explains afterward that he had been cursed — that the animal was a curse and that he had wanted that form of himself to be killed. He had once been a human being and had been transformed into an animal. If a woman dreams of her feminine nature as an animal, say a cat or a cow, she cannot integrate this but can only relate to it. But if it appears in human form, it has reached a level where it can be integrated. If it appears as a god, again we cannot integrate it but can only relate to it.

450   A content which has been a human shape but, by a curse, has been changed to an animal form means a regression. The erotic life in late antiquity had reached a relatively highly differentiated level. But this period came to an end, and further development was cut off by the arrival of Christianity. This meant an enormous progress in consciousness, on a much higher level. But in the field of the anima, of Eros, it was cut off completely. In antiquity, there was a much higher level of relationship to the anima than in the Middle Ages. There is an Irish tale about mermaids: A chief heard of the approach of the Christians and swore that "those damn Christians" would not get hold of his daughters. So he threw a net over them

---

[11] On the motif of the helpful animal in need of redemption, see Marie-Louise von Franz, *Archetypal Dimensions of the Psyche* (Boston: Shambhala, 1999), 91f.
[12] See "The Golden Bird" in *The Complete Grimm's Fairy Tales*, trans. Margaret Hunt (New York: Pantheon Books, 1972), No. 51.

and turned them into mermaids — who now splash around trying to lure men. These mermaids had been human but, through a wrong attitude in consciousness, have been kept in an instinctive form. Eros in the Middle Ages, for example, regressed into pure sex without feeling — just the animal act. The spiritual implication of sexual relations wasn't seen; that regressed into the mermaids, fantasies, witches, etc.

451   If an animal asks to be redeemed, it is an act of discernment, a realization that in the physical instinct, there is a spiritual and human implication which could be humanized. With this discernment, one has to attack something which has previously been a help — that is, the overcoming of self-pity or self-indulgence in a field where one has been going along fine before. People with a sound inner instinct can move smoothly through life for years and years, as simple peasants do, for instance — their horse carries them through. This is an enormous advantage to a certain extent; but it then becomes a disadvantage because if people are too sound, they remain very unconscious, because they have never dissociated themselves enough from the animal to become conscious of what it is. That is why the human instinct itself sometimes asks for the neurosis — asks for the deviation, for the split, in order to become conscious. When Jung realized this, he stopped working for three months, having written: "Freud will never realize that the instinctive drive is not a one-sided drive but that it contains its own counter-drive and its own sacrificial drive in itself." It does contain its own sublimation, its own counteraction, which comes forth.

452   *Discussion*

The battle between the horse and the Div is the natural split of the libido. The psychic libido is an antinomy, its own contradiction. Since this story is from Turkestan, which shared some symbolism with India,[13] it is important to understand the Indian attitude toward

---

[13] Turkestan ("Land of the Turks") is the Persian name of an undefined Central Asian region. It stretched from the Caspian Sea in the west to the Gobi Desert in the east. Today it is part of the states of Kyrgyzstan and Uzbekistan, among others; today's Afghanistan forms its southern part.

the horse. According to the Upanishads, the horse represents the whole world and is a sacrificial horse: "Verily, the dawn is the head, the sun is the eye, the wind his breathing, universal fire his open mouth. The hair [of the horse] is the Atman, the sky his back. The atmosphere is his belly, water his flanks, the seasons his limbs, day and night his feet. His voice is creative speech. The horses place is the eastern sea. Verily the night is the sacrificial vessel which remains behind; its place is the western sea. The sea is his relative, the sea is his place."[14]

453   Note that in our tale, the battle takes place in the water. As an illustration of the secret relationship between the Div, the spirit of death, and the horse, the Uphanishads continue: "In the beginning was nothing; all was covered with death, with hunger, for hunger is death. He is greed (hunger is greed for life) and death. Then He said, 'Would that I had a Self.' And so He went on praising, and water was produced. The water was brightness. Out of the water the earth was formed. Then came death, then fire and wind." Notice that in the first chapter, the world *is* the horse. In the second chapter, hunger and death become the world. The world as horse is creative power, which is the symbol of the libido. East is the head, and West is the tail. "Then He sacrificed greater, after which came glory and strength. Then He thinks: 'Would that this body of mine were fit for sacrifice.'" So then He wants to become his own sacrifice, in order to realize Himself. (Before the horse is brought to the sacrifice in India, they let it run as it wishes, unconfined for one year). After this, He sacrificed Him for Himself. This is followed (still in the Uphanishads) by a description that those who sacrificed the horse transcend the world and live in the wind, which is a little space

---

[14] In what follows, Marie-Louise von Franz gives a brief summary of her source, the *Brihadaranyaka Upanishad I*: "Verily the dawn is the head of the horse which is fit for sacrifice, the sun its eye, the wind its breath, the mouth the Vaisvânara fire, the year the body of the sacrificial horse. Heaven is the back, the sky the belly, the earth the chest, the quarters the two sides, the intermediate quarters the ribs, the members the seasons, the joints the months and half-months, the feet days and nights, the bones the stars, the flesh the clouds." [https://www.sacred-texts.com/hin/sbe15/sbe15053.htm] Jung comments on the horse sacrifice of the Uphanishads in *Symbols of Transformation*, vol. 5, *CW* (Princeton, NJ: Princeton University Press, 1967), § 657–660. Cf. on this topic also: Marie-Louise von Franz, *Creation Myths. Revised Edition* (Boston: Shambhala, 1995),128 f., 135.

between heaven and the world, no bigger than a razor blade. (There's the idea of the smallness of the Self.)

454   Looking at our fairytale from this Indian angle, we see now what the horse sacrifice means: the animal, instinctive libido turns into its own contrast, its opposite — that is what leads to the process of individuation. The process of individuation is, to Jung, a natural growth which comes forth — all we have to do about it is not to disturb it, to accompany it only with understanding and with suffering. It is given to our nature. To be oneself is the most natural process which can exist. That is why the horse turns into this natural paradise. But what is not complete is that the garden is a symbol of the mother, a symbol of the womb. The horse turns into a containing vessel. The killing of the horse is the Indian solution, which leaves the animal, leaves the world, transcending the instinct. But it is not complete, because it is outside reality.

455   The other incompleteness is that the queen gives birth to two twin boys. At this point, we have four human beings — an advance over the first quaternity which included the horse and the Div — but there is an overbalance on the male side. The sons are only germs, and since the majority is now male, this means there is no balance. The earth belongs to the female, and if the earth is missing, it remains a spiritual solution only. This is the Indian solution but is not the satisfactory one for us. The Greeks also knew the twins motif. The twins are a double impetus in the libido, a new movement toward the development of consciousness which is still a germ and has not completed itself and is still outside the bounds of reality. According to our tale, the twins are brothers and no longer animals. But I have never found any fairytale yet that is complete in the end. However, they could not represent completeness, because there is no individual in them. Only individuals can experience completeness, individuation.

456   A fairytale is a *pattern*. A pattern can only be a sketch, can only illustrate or bring to light certain laws of functioning. It cannot represent the complete goal, because for the realization of the completeness, the individual as the carrier of the process is needed.

And that is the feminine aspect, the earth, which is lacking in this process. The *solution* is always individual. We cannot read a fairytale and have the complete solution; the tale only shows how the libido is flowing in the collective human psyche. There is, then, no completeness in this tale of the animus problem, though the tale ends with two boys, representing a higher level. The feminine Self must be present. The Self is represented in the story as the horse, and then as the city which is a paradise, that is, only the light side. The dark aspect, such as a witch, is missing. With the exclusion of the dark witch, there is excluded also the physical reality of the woman, the physical earth.

◇

Chapter 12

A Norwegian Fairytale:
Kari, the Girl with the Wooden Frock

⁴⁵⁷ In this Norwegian tale:

> there was a widower king who had a beautiful daughter.[1] He
> married a second time, and the stepmother was very jealous
> of the girl, abusing her relentlessly. Among the king's cattle,
> there was a big blue bull who was very clean, and so the
> daughter would run away from the palace and spend most of
> her time with him. In his ear, the bull carried a magic
> tablecloth, which the princess would spread out, and then it
> would provide her with food. When the stepmother
> discovered him, she was very angry and hysterical. She went
> to bed and pretended that her illness could only be cured by
> eating the flesh of the bull. The girl and the bull learned of
> her intention to have him killed and made their escape
> together. By and by, they came to a forest made completely
> of brass. The bull said to the girl, "Don't touch any of the brass
> leaves, for if you do I will have to fight the troll with three
> heads who lives in the forest. But if you can't avoid touching
> the leaves, and the troll does come out and fight, then take
> the ointment which is in my other ear and use it to heal me."
> The girl couldn't help touching the leaves, and the three-
> headed troll came out and fought with the bull. The bull won
> but was exhausted and injured; however, the girl cured him
> with the magic ointment, and they continued on their way.
> The second forest they came to was all of silver, and the

---

[1] The original tale can be found in: Klara Stroebe, *Nordische Volksmärchen: Norwegische Volksmärchen*, vol 2. (Jena: Diederichs, 1940), 146.

situation was the same except that the troll was six-headed. The third forest was all of gold, and the troll there had nine heads. In each case the girl could not avoid touching the leaves, so the fight with the troll had to take place, followed by the magic curing of the bull with the ointment. Finally, they arrive at a castle, and here the bull says, "This is the end of my help. You must sleep in a pigsty and wear a wooden frock. But first, you must kill me, skin me, and then put into the skin one brass leaf, one silver leaf and one gold apple. Roll up the skin and put it under this rock, and if you are ever in difficulty, knock on the rock and you will get help."

458   The girl does as she is bidden and then begins a period of servitude as a lowly maid in the castle. She is given a wooden frock to wear and told to carry the bath water up to the prince. She clumps and bumps along in her stiff wooden frock, and the prince is infuriated by the noise and her clumsiness. He kicks her out, throwing his towel after her. Upset and distressed, she goes and knocks on the rock. Immediately there appears the spirit of a man who gives her a frock made of brass, which she wears to church. The prince goes to church and sees her in the beautiful brass frock and on a brass horse, and his mind is not at all on the church service. After church he tries to catch up with her, but she repeats a charm:

459   *Light before me*
Darkness behind me.
So that the prince shan't see where I am going.

460   The prince loses sight of her then, though he does catch one of her gloves. When he asks her later where she came from, she replies, "Towel Land." The same drama is repeated twice more, the next time involving a silver gown, the charm as before, and the prince catching her comb, with her again naming the land she came from after the towel he had thrown

at her. The third time it is a golden dress she wears, and a golden shoe she loses to the prince. Always she uses the same magic charm to prevent him from catching up with her. As in the story of Cinderella, the prince then sends out all over the land to find the lady whose foot fits the golden shoe. The stepmother tries to trick him by cutting off part of her foot, but the blood is discovered in the shoe. Finally, the rightful owner, Kari, is found in the kitchen in a wooden frock. She reveals her royal background and she marries the prince.[2]

461   Having a stepmother means that one is cut off from the feeling function, which is replaced by something else. Stepmothers are always characterized as a "Frau Welt," a feminine personification of the outer world in its aspect of falseness, jealousy, vanity. Wherever Eros vanishes or fails, then up comes this prestige psychology. Wherever there is a real power drive, there is a crippled Eros life. And also, wherever a ruling system stiffens because it has lost its Eros life, then there is sure to be the power attitude — because it feels the earth slipping from beneath its feet. Here the helpful animal is a bull, which is one form representing primitive masculinity, brutal emotionality which is often linked with the negative animus, who can really be like a bull in a china shop. But describing the bull as "blue" and "clean" means that here he is not destructive. Blue refers either to the sea or to the heavens. He is also a magic bull, with the food content in one ear and the healing ointment in the other ear. Sometimes the Self and the anima are one and the same thing, the figures are compacted into one personification. Here it is the feminine Self and the animus. And here again, the fight is carried on not by the girl, but by the bull and the trolls. The numbers three, six and nine are considered male, representing force, the flow of energy which is increasing more and more according to the number of heads on the trolls. There is also an increase in the value of the metals: brass, silver, and finally gold.

---

[2] Additional commentary on this story by Marie-Louise von Franz appears in *Archetypal Dimensions of the Psyche*, 155–159.

462   The fight is always brought about by the fact that the girl touches a leaf. If she could have avoided touching the leaves, no fight would have been necessary. Tree leaves generally represent a human individual as a mortal creature. In Homer's *Odyssey*, the human beings are represented as the many leaves of a tree — the family or clan which goes on living although the individual leaves (i.e., people) fall in the autumn. Leaves are the individual in the aspect of something transient and mortal. If the girl could keep away from the individual human reality, then they would not be in conflict. There are women who are so afraid of this battle that they stay out of this world — they seem to have no animus and no conflicts. They are like princesses going through the forest untouched. But they remain untouched because they themselves don't touch the reality of the mortal individual, the drama of human relationship. If they do touch it, this princess's life stops, and the trolls and bulls break loose. Here the girl cannot avoid touching the leaves of mortal reality in herself, and then she is in the conflict — the greed and death power against the positive power, the chaotic versus the ordering forces.

463   There is always the fourfold pattern in these tales. Here we find three of the same general thing: the forest of copper (brass), silver and gold, and then a breathing space until the fourth appears — the castle. Then there are the copper (brass), silver and golden frocks, with the fourth event being the prince. There are always three similar, parallel things, and then one different one, the fourth, which is now inclusive of the whole thing. Copper (brass) is transient, ambiguous, decaying easily. It is associated with Venus, Eros. Silver is associated with the moon. It is easily blackened; it is weak and eventually wastes. Gold is the sun; it is incorruptible, resists everything, withstands every destructive, undermining influence. Regarding the wooden frock, it is as if — just when the occasion demands that she be articulate, that she express herself in feminine form — she only clomps along in a stiff wooden frock.

464   Then comes the most interesting motif in this story: She always runs away from the prince when he tries to find her. It is only after

the incident when the stepmother is cut out of the story, when she is made ridiculous and without any more power — only after this can the girl marry the prince and reveal her identity. This secrecy may be because of the danger posed by the stepmother. In the charm the girl asks for "light before me," so she can see where she is going, but he who follows her cannot see. If she did turn back to the prince, the stepmother would get her. This shows the feminine relationship to the animus: by facing too directly what is desired or wanted, there comes this power drive — the stepmother is constellated. Therefore, to keep the feminine integrity, one must not look toward what one wants, but look inside oneself and try to find the light. The danger comes when one touches reality, because the witch — the world, the woman who represents the world, the prestige drive — this witch comes in and destroys everything. For a woman, it often seems like a long incubation, encouraging the process until it can come out from inside.

♦

Chapter 13

An African Fairytale:
The Magician of the Plain

465   This Bantu fairytale is another animus story which will lead over to the anima problem. It illustrates the more numinous and uncanny background of the anima figures.[1]

466   In a Bantu family there is a son who doesn't want to marry any of the girls in the village, as his parents wish. Instead, he wants to go to a foreign country to look for a wife. His parents warn him, but he won't listen. While traveling through foreign places, he finds a girl with whom he falls in love and decides to marry her. The parents of the girl advise her to take along a large group of female slaves and other helpers as a sort of wedding present, but she doesn't want to take anything except the bull of the tribe — the Magic Bull of the Plain. This is a buffalo bull, which possesses a thousand magic arts. Her tribe is upset about this and tries to prevent her, but she insists and finally manages to take the bull along with her. She also carries some magic roots, herbs and medicines. Her husband is never able to see the bull, because it is always hidden behind her. Back among the husband's tribe, the couple establish their home. The bull magically does all the work for her, plowing, planting, and cooking, and she is very much admired by the village because everything is done so wonderfully. But one day the bull comes to her and says he can't go on working like this because he is so very hungry —

---

[1] The original tale, "Der Tausendkünstler der Ebene," can be found in Carl Meinhof, *Afrikanische Märchen* (Jena: Diederichs, 1921), No. 20.

he must have something to eat. However, the girl can't feed him without her husband knowing, and so she tells the bull just to go out and steal peas from the fields of the village. The villagers become angry and thoroughly aroused when they realize that someone is stealing their peas. One day the husband is able to see the bull who was previously invisible to him. He shoots the bull and kills him. When the girl sees what has happened, she cuts off the bull's head and hides it along with the bull's skin in the garden. Then in the night she secretly takes them out of hiding, puts them in a pot together with some magic elements, and sings this song:

467

> Oh my father, Magician of the Plain,
> Indeed they told me thou shalt go into deep darkness,
> in all darkness.
> Thou art a young sprout of the miraculous tree
> which grew out of the winds,
> devoured before the right time has come,
> devoured by the worm.

468

Then the skin starts to come back to life, and the head moves. But at that moment the husband steps out of the door and sees what she is doing; the whole process ends, and the bull is dead again. The next night the girl goes out and tries again to bring the bull back to life, using the same magic formula, but again the husband appears and intervenes, and the bull falls back dead. The third night the girl tries, but there is no more power left in the magic — it doesn't work anymore. So now the girl picks up the remnants of the skin and the head and puts them in a basket which she carries on her head. Without saying anything to anyone, she returns to her own tribe. Here she tells the people that the bull is dead. They are in a panic of despair at hearing this news; there is no longer any meaning in life for them. So they all kill themselves, even the children, until no one is left. Meanwhile, the husband had been searching for his wife and has followed her to her tribe; he now finds them all dead, including his wife. Heartbroken, he returns to his parents, who tell him he should have listened and obeyed them and taken a wife from his own village. They say it serves him right, and now he has lost all his money.

469 The animus figure appears here as a totem animal of a tribe: he is the life principle of the girl's tribe, the guarantee of their prosperity and meaning of life, and therefore when he is dead, there is no more *raison d'être* left. The story also shows why in primitive life there are such stringent marriage taboos, which prevent one from marrying the projections of one's own anima or animus. Any individual choice is therefore made impossible, for that reason. This precaution is necessary because their ego consciousness is not strong enough yet to deal with the whole problem of the anima and animus. All the stories dealing with the anima or animus end tragically: Either the woman disappears, the mermaid returns to the sea, etc., or there follows a complete catastrophe. It is important to understand this because we can see it in people today who blindly marry an anima or animus projection: This leads to a situation where the people are not able to deal with the problem.

470 Here the girl calls the buffalo bull "father," which shows that the animus is derived from the father figure. But there is a mutual incompatibility between her family god and the tribal atmosphere of her husband's people. In "Psychology of the Transference," Jung speaks of one of the most primitive means of dealing with the anima/animus, the so-called cross-cousin-marriage.[2] There are a great many instances of marriage laws following this pattern. For instance, there may be two divisions within a tribe — the "Night people" and the "Day people" or the "Grass people" and the "Water people," etc. A man cannot marry a woman within his own totem group. For example, if he is a Grass man, he must marry a Water

---

[2] C.G. Jung, *The Practice of Psychotherapy*, 2nd ed., vol. 16, *CW*, (Princeton, NJ: Princeton University Press, 1985), § 422 ff.

woman. But when he does this, then the brother of the Water Woman must marry the sister of the Grass man (the groom of the Water woman):

Grass man's sister	Water woman
Grass man	Water woman's brother

471   This mirrors the fact that they do not experience any separateness of identity between inner factors and outer reality. There has always been this endogamous tendency, but the incest is committed between the Gods and Goddesses (cf. Zeus and the Olympians; in our story the sister of the groom and the brother of the bride). But the exogamous tendency overcomes the former, making a break between the divine realm and the human realm and reinforcing it by taboos. Very often among the primitives the god and goddess were first a human man and his sister who committed incest. Many primitive stories have this theme. Then the two leave the tribe and go over the river and become figures of the "beyond" — gods and goddesses. From then on, you have the supernatural realm where the endogamous tendency is lived, and the human realm where the exogamous tendency is lived. There are terribly severe laws against endogamy in the human realm because of the danger of being overwhelmed by the unconscious.

472   Our story concerns the god (the buffalo bull) who is drawn into the human realm. When this happens, a tragic catastrophe is bound to occur. One must respect the tribal god as something belonging to the divine realm, and not try to take it into human life. So historically, we have: (1) first the primitives, where the endogamous tendency — incest — is lived only in the divine realm, between the gods and goddesses, figures of the unconscious; (2) then in Egypt the god and goddess appear in human form — the Pharaoh and his sister are the only human beings who may commit incest; (3) the next step appeared in alchemy, which probably derived its symbols from the Egyptian ritual. But in alchemy, where the quaternity was expressed as

King.. Queen

- -

Man... Woman

the king and queen are also chemical substances, so at this stage, it appears nearer the human being because now it becomes part of the elements of our body; (4) the next step is Jungian psychology, with the concepts of anima and animus. The next step would probably be human beings.

473   In all the above quaternal relations, there are the possibilities of relatedness of various kinds. For instance, a man may relate to his anima but not to another woman, or to a woman but not to his anima, and so on. Sometimes the relationship involves only the anima and the animus and not the human beings at all: Animus and anima are attracted to each other, but when the two people are thrown together, they may not be able to stand each other. In past times, these factors, anima and animus, were projected into the realm of kings and queens. In our tale, the animus figure in the form of a bull cannot be made to live again when the husband sees the ritual; the very fact that the husband sees it is what kills it. We see this happen today in the human scene, in everyday life. When a woman makes an attempt to develop her animus, the husband makes a natural attempt to shoot down the effects; and the wife likewise tries to destroy the development of the anima in her husband. There is a legitimate secrecy during this process, which is necessary because of the incompatibility of these elements. For example, you often see a woman make a beginning towards developing her interests — she starts in a typically feminine way, perhaps beginning with a quite second-rate book, but becomes absorbed in it, really excited. The husband notices that and says, "Well, if you are going to take that up, you should begin this or that way, read this or that book," and so on. He wants to organize it systematically — and the whole interest is killed. On the other hand, when the husband is trying to develop his feeling function, he may begin by doing very silly things, sloppy and sentimental, and the natural Eros of the

woman resents it, causing her to intervene and kill the whole development. The path of these archetypes meanders like a stream in a swamp, and the partner in whom the function is developed naturally wants to make order out of it in his mate.

474   The woman in our story wants to draw this totem god, the buffalo bull, into the ordinary human realm, using him to plow fields and so on, and in this way she destroys it. The food of the husband's tribe is not for the buffalo bull, so when he eats the peas, he becomes visible and is killed by the husband. The tribe of the girl, before killing themselves when they learn of the bull's death, sing the same song she had sung to it, addressing the bull as the *Magician of the Plain*, a sprout out of the winds, dying before the right time had come. This woman has tried to touch the animus problem too soon. It was an attempt toward consciousness too early and therefore took on a negative aspect. The villagers of her tribe also sing, "He is the one who spreads flowers and fruits on his way" — all the qualities which later appear in Osiris, the god who dies too young. This early-dying sun-god of the Great Mother later became the typical personification of the female animus. In our story, he is under the Osiris aspect, and he is a typical African god.

⟡

Chapter 14

Anima Stories

475 Now we start the anima stories with a few primitive examples. There is a South American story in which a man catches a female ape and takes her home into his hut with him. He discovers while she lives with him that whenever he goes out, all of the work in and around the hut has been done upon his return. So one day he decides to find out what happens, and instead of leaving, he hides and watches. He sees a beautiful girl appear out of the ape skin, and it is she who is doing the work. He reaches into the hut and snatches the ape skin and burns it. Then he speaks to the girl and asks her to remain with him. She agrees to stay, on the one condition that he never call her an ape or remind her of her people. He is glad to accept this condition, but there comes a time when his anger is aroused against her over something, and in his fury, he does call her an ape. She then immediately resumes her ape skin, takes their child — which had been born in the meantime — and runs off. The man is so angry that she took the child that he burns down his whole hut.

476 In another story, almost identical, the woman is a bitch, a female dog, and when the man calls her a bitch, she runs off. Another story, slightly different, concerns a hunter of jaguars, who finds that the jaguar he brings home is a beautiful woman. She agrees to stay with him if he will never betray to his tribe that she is a jaguar woman. He promises. But his mother is a persistent, nagging woman, who asks indiscreet questions until, at last, he tells her the secret. Later, during a festival, his mother gets drunk and tells the whole tribe. Then the girl, "growling from being ashamed," resumes the jaguar shape and disappears forever into the forest. In still another story, the animal form of the girl is a bee. As long as the husband keeps

his promise not to call her "bee," he finds bee-hives wherever he goes in the forest, and he becomes a wealthy man. But when he betrays the secret, he finds no more bee-hives, and his fortune is destroyed. In another story concerning an ape-woman, the man cuts off the tail and then keeps the woman under the same conditions as in the other stories. One day he sees the family of his wife sitting in the trees and making merry. They invite him to come up and have a drink. The party becomes wild, and he gets drunk and tells them that his wife is an ape. Then they and his wife all run away from him — and he is left sitting up in the tree with the problem of how to get down.

477   All these stories illustrate the primitive problem that the animal side is the divine side. Man cannot deal with it; the only way to go is to accept the animal as a divine and secret mystery. If this attitude is lacking, if there is an attempt to draw the divine into the human realm, there can only be a catastrophe. But to keep such a secret is absolutely isolating. When the girl in these tales tells the man to keep her secret, she cuts him off from the collective. Generally, even in our society, the secret leaks out. We are out of contact, are isolated from the *participation mystique*, when we keep the secret. That is why there are stories which say that one shouldn't look at the anima or animus — it is transcending the human boundaries to look at them.

478   Another story illustrating the problem deals with a young man living in the communal bachelor's hut. Through a hole in the roof, he sees a beautiful star, which he watches night after night. He falls in love with it. One evening he wakes out of his sleep and finds a beautiful woman at the foot of his bed. She says, "But you called me." She agrees to live with him, and every night she appears in this form, as a woman to him, and they have a wonderful time together. In the daytime, however, she becomes very, very small, so that he can put her in a little bottle, and no one knows her identity. People look into the bottle, but they see only a very disgusting-looking animal with mean little eyes. That is, in the banal light of day. To the eyes that can see in the daytime, it is all nonsense, but the eyes that see in the night are able to discover the beautiful woman. For the primitive

unconsciousness, this is an intolerable situation — they couldn't stand the paradox. They have a terrific awe of the unconscious on the one hand, and on the other, they have a banal, down-to-earth attitude: "And now you have lost all your money." The tension would be too great for them to try to unite the two aspects: Day — the animal mystery; and Night — goddess of the stars.

479   Continuing this story of the star goddess, the young man is consumed with curiosity about where she goes when she leaves him. Against her warnings, he insists that she take him along the next time. He goes up to heaven with her, and there he sees what she does: She dances among skeletons, and she herself is one. The impact of this discovery is so great that he asks her to let him go back down to earth. So she does, but the shock has been too great, and he dies from meningitis. That is why the North American Indian stories say, "Don't look up at the stars — they are death, and we shouldn't look at them." They are projections of the unconscious, and the primitive stories say, "Keep away from it, because you haven't the strength to look upon them or to stand them." For us who are so cut off from the unconscious, it is good to read these stories. Many people have chosen not to marry the one they first love, and then later in analysis, this first love appears as the anima or animus. Had they married, it would have been a dangerous situation, creating a lot of difficulties. This unconscious wisdom which blocked them from marrying is the same instinct which drives the primitive to tell such stories and say, "Don't look at the stars."

Chapter 15

A European Fairytale:
The Black Princess

480 There are two versions of this European fairytale which illustrates the dark aspect of the anima. When the anima appears in such a way, we must remember that both versions come from Catholic countries, which means that there the light side of the anima is already recognized and projected onto the Virgin Mary, and so in compensation, the emphasis is on the dark side, the black side of the anima.

481 The Austrian version of "The Black Princess" starts with an old king and queen.

482 They had no children, and the queen terribly wanted to have a child. A river ran through the town, with a bridge spanning it. On the right side of the bridge stood a crucifix, and on the left stood a stone figure of Lucifer. It is common in Europe for a crucifix to stand near bridges in order to protect travelers, because the devil lives under the bridge and tries to pull people under. The queen went regularly and cried and prayed to Christ to give her a child, but after a while, she got tired of doing this and of getting no results, so she decided to turn to the devil. After three months she found herself pregnant. The king felt himself not responsible for this pregnancy, but he didn't say anything about it. At the end of six months, he gave a huge festival; and at the end of nine months, a coal-black girl child was born. This child grew as much in one hour as any other would grow in a year, and so in twenty-four hours, she was an adult woman. At this time

she says to the king and the queen, "Oh, you unhappy father and unhappy mother, now I must die. Bury me behind the altar in the church, and always keep a guard in the church during the night, or I will bring a terrible catastrophe on the land."

483 The South German parallel of this story says that:

a witch gives the old couple tea, which makes the queen pregnant with the black princess.[1] The witch tells the king to drink it "in the name of God," but the king is so excited that he blurts out: "in the name of God and the Devil." The black child is born and calls out, "Father." The king answers, "Yes, my child." She replies, "Now I have talked for the first time." This happens three times, after which she says, "Now I have talked for the third time." Then she says, "Now you must make an iron coffin, because I must die," giving instructions as in the other version for her burial behind the altar and for the guard. And so the black woman is buried behind the altar because she is dead. Every night a soldier guards the coffin. But every morning when they open the church at 4:00 a.m., they find that the guard has been torn to pieces. Naturally, the people strongly resist being drafted to stand guard in the church, only to be torn to bits, and they come near to starting a revolution because they don't want to serve. And so the king finally brings a regiment of soldiers in from a foreign country where the news of what happens in the church hasn't got around.

484 Among the foreign regiment, there are three brothers, one a major, one a captain, and the third a common soldier who is apparently never going to amount to anything: He lives light-heartedly, carouses, and spends his money freely, frequently getting into trouble and serving time in a prison. When it is

---

[1] *Der Soldat und die schwarze Prinzessin [The Soldier and the Black Princess]*, in Friedrich von der Leyen, Paul Zaunert, *Deutsche Märchen aus dem Donaulande* (Jena: Diederichs, 1926).

the major's turn to serve as a guard, he tricks this common soldier into taking his place. The soldier goes into the church, prays first, and then goes into the pulpit, making crosses on all the steps leading up to it. At midnight the black woman comes out of her coffin, enveloped in fiery flames. She goes into a rage when she finds him in the pulpit, but she can't climb the steps to reach him because of the crosses. She goes mad trying to get to him, overthrowing the seats, throwing down the statues, even stacking up chairs near the pulpit, trying to reach him. But he is saved because the clock strikes twelve, at which time she must return to her coffin. The next morning the people are astonished to find the soldier alive. They tell him that since he is so clever, he had better stand guard again the next night. But he is afraid. It seems to him that he has done enough, and he tries to escape. While he is trying to get away, he meets an old beggarman[2] who tells him to go back and stand guard, but this time to hide behind the statue of the Virgin Mary. The soldier does as he is advised, and this time the black princess goes even more raging mad. It takes her a long time to find where he is hiding, but then just as she is about to catch him, the clock strikes again, and he is saved.

485 The people rejoice to find the soldier alive again the next morning, and now, naturally, he is elected to return for the third night. Again he wants to run away, but the old beggar intervenes, telling him that this time he should climb into her coffin as soon as she leaves it. He must lie there with his eyes closed, as if he were dead, and make no answer when she discovers him, for she will be alarmed if he doesn't get out — she will shout at him, rant and rave; then she will beg him, but only when she says in just the right way, "Rudolph, get up," should he come out of the coffin. The soldier does as he was told by the beggar, and everything happens as the beggar

---

[2] In the original it is a "Zitherschläger," a musician with a stringed instrument (zither), who gives advice.

said. When the princess quiets down, she turns into a white maiden, and in the morning when the church is opened, the two lovers are found. They marry, and later he becomes a king. In the other version, it is God, not an old beggar, who intervenes — God becomes tired of all these tricks of Lucifer's daughter. He can't stand them anymore and teaches the soldier how to redeem her.[3]

486   These stories have a compensatory aspect for modern Christian man — it is the modern situation of the anima problem. The anima in fairytales is very often represented as the devil's daughter — her father is the devil. This is because the feminine principle in Protestant countries is lacking: We have no goddess, and so she has fallen into the unconscious, and therefore has that dark side. So in Protestant countries, it is the entire drama which is lacking, but in Catholic countries, it is the dark side of the anima. Dr. Jung points out that the introduction of the cult of Mary in the thirteenth century enabled Christian man to project his anima, but that it had the disadvantage that the individual choice of an anima projection was gone: There was the one, identical anima for every man. In the days of chivalry, every knight chose his own lady to serve. Then, as Christianity and the cult of Mary took hold, there came the increasing persecution of witches as men experienced the individual fascination of a specific woman. The element of the real, the individual woman is not represented in the goddess.[4] To put together all these paradoxical aspects of the feminine and to know how to relate to them is one of the great difficulties.

487   The initial situation in "The Black Princess" is that the king and queen have no children. This means that the ruling attitude, personified in the king, has become sterile. Though there is a balance between the masculine and feminine powers, there is a certain sterile situation, because the darkness is excluded too much. The queen

---

[3] The original tale, "Die schwarze Königstochter," can be found in Friedrich von der Leyen, Paul Zaunert, *Deutsche Märchen aus dem Donaulande* (Jena: Diederichs, 1926).

[4] Jung elaborates on this connection in *Psychological Types*, vol. 6, *CW* (Princeton, NJ: Princeton, 1971), § 399.

wants desperately to have a child, and that is why she eventually prays to Lucifer when she has had enough of praying to Christ without result. In a similar Austrian tale, the devil has a wife who is also his grandmother, and at the same time, he has a daughter who lives with them. Thus there is an incestuous relationship. So we have the double set-up:

in the Christian religion:	God	Son	Holy Ghost
and below:	Devil	Grandmother	His daughter

488   In Christianity, the Holy Ghost is a necessity to man. It enters man and enables human beings to do things even beyond Christ. On the dark side, it is the devil's daughter who has the true feeling for mankind, who loves men. This devil's daughter is the link between the dark side and the light. In our story the king feels that he isn't responsible for the pregnancy; it is really Lucifer who has impregnated the queen. There are medieval legends that the devil will have a daughter and will commit incest with her, and her child will become the Anti-Christ.

489   There is the queer fact that the devil's daughter, the Black Princess, grows so quickly: She speaks only three times, and she grows as much in one hour as a natural child does in a year. This characterizes her as being inhuman, with magic powers, especially concerning the aspect of living outside our world of space and time. We are in the habit of speaking of the unconscious as having no time and space boundaries, and thus we cannot understand the unconscious because we ourselves are imprisoned in space and time. But this tale tells us that the archetypes in the unconscious cannot see, cannot understand, our life either, because they live *outside* space and time, that is, in another rhythm of life. So the black princess lives life in a much faster rhythm, which probably refers to a fact that we observe in everyday life — that the anima in anima-possessed men acts on age levels quite unconnected with the actual age of the man himself, and her timelessness prevents him from getting into the "here" and, especially, the "now" of the present

moment. There is always the anima outside time, pulling the man outside time, disturbing the whole normal rhythms of his development. Then you have these "wise" young boys and "childish" old men.

490   In the story, the black princess appears in fiery flames; she is full of energy and libido, but it is destroying life. It is a vitality which doesn't carry one into life, but somehow carries the man outside of life. In the German parallel, she doesn't tear the men to pieces, she eats them. She is always hungry. This anima contains the element of impatience that you find in anima-possessed men — their unwillingness or refusal to do what is necessary *right now, at this moment.* That is also seen in the fast growth of the black princess, because she is living in this unnatural rhythm. She belongs to eternity and to the gods, and it is illegitimate to pull her into human areas of life.

491   Three times she calls out, "Father," and then she says, "Now I will die, and you must bury me behind the altar; and every night there must be a guard in the church." Here she reveals who she is — namely, the shadow of the Christian dogma. She is *behind* the altar, the shadow side. Thus she tells who she is by asking to be buried there. In a way, she has taken a step toward her redemption by revealing her divine nature, dark as it is. Regarding the iron coffin, iron is the metal of the planet Mars and is associated with the god of the same name. Iron has to do with conflict, because Mars is the god of war. Also, in alchemical writings it refers to the mortal, decaying body, because iron rusts so easily. Therefore, it came to represent the decaying mortal matter of the body, that which is corruptible in our nature. This was probably also on account of the biblical reference to treasures which rust cannot eat (Mt 6:19). Therefore, the black princess is now in prison — she is in the iron coffin — because what we reject psychologically very often becomes imprisoned in the body. She is dead during the day but alive at night — which shows the shadowy aspect of this anima figure. Now she starts to kill human beings and threatens to bring about a catastrophe in the land. For the most part, she destroys simple men,

namely soldiers — not the rulers, but the simple people — which shows how the anima attacks the emotional side, the inferior side. In the collective situation, we see this occur in populist movements, such as Communism or Nazism, where this aspect of anima possession is at work. She doesn't attack the ruling system yet. It is particularly the "inferior" man who redeems her — a light-hearted, socially inferior type, spending money, drinking too much, and ending up in jail. But he has the gift to redeem the princess. He is not afraid of the dark. Often in stories it is the silly man, the fool, who becomes the great hero. That is because he is naïve — and spontaneous. The relationship to the unconscious is given by that human element which is spontaneous and able to expose itself naively to the new fact. The naïve one has the gift of being spontaneous. He climbs up the pulpit, making little crosses on the steps. And the second night, he hides behind the Virgin Mary. Thus, twice he escapes by climbing up.

492   The first escape is very subtle: He goes to where the priest talks to the community, and that is where he saves himself. Though it is true that the priest usually carries a collective role as a collective spiritual leader, here the soldier is taking the priest's role as a leader of the collective, the teacher and truth-teller, to the community. He takes on this leadership, takes on a spiritual activity in order not to be overcome by the unconscious. He tries to take on the role of the one who knows and who has leadership. There is a hint here that one way a man can deal with the anima is not to become overwhelmed and simply passive, but rather to try to take action in some way, so as not to be thrown into a completely feminine attitude. The real essence of a priest is that he has renounced experiencing the anima in its earthy aspect, and he keeps himself above the situation as much as he can. At all costs, he must keep his head above the threat and not be overrun.

493   Of course, this only puts off the solution for our hero; it is a temporary solution, too near the old attitude to be the final answer. It is a form of escape — but then, for a soldier to play the role of a priest means he is trying to get above the situation. You very often

see intellectuals "dancing up and down with their brain." If we ask, "Why don't they ever come down to earth, touch earth?" the answer is that they have the fear that if they ever do touch earth, then the black anima will get them — therefore, they must keep "in the upper story." Sometimes, for the time being, nothing else can be done. This is at least a putting off of the problem. The pulpit also represents that part which is relatively intellectual. It is only a putting off, because the fiery black princess pulls up chairs and would have got him except that midnight comes. This does indicate that she is bound to a certain time rhythm here and appears in that time rhythm. She is bound and not bound. That is the great problem with the unconscious. It is only a *relative* time and *relative* space. The unconscious is not *completely* outside time. As the figure of a human person, the princess has come into the human realm to this extent. The striking of the clock, or the crowing of the cock, which ends her activity for the night, may be connected with the turn toward morning, when consciousness begins increasing again.

494   One could say that the anima is also affected by the fact that if a man tries to relate to her, the poor anima gets bound to the human. Animus and anima are not always happy to have this relationship — they lose part of their power when they are made conscious. They would prefer to remain gods and goddesses and keep their power. That is why there is a certain amount of energetic resistance to their integration. This cage of space and time can also be helpful. In the case of the clock striking midnight, the soldier is saved by time. Thus, a man should fight his own impatience which the anima brings in and should accept the boundaries of space and time. If he would take the attitude that "this is a helpful thing, this prison of space and time," then just waiting, putting off, using time as an element sometimes helps to bring about a progress in consciousness. When one is possessed, then he has the feeling that he must *immediately* do something about the situation — it is terribly urgent to send off a letter, for instance, or telephone and speak his mind. The tip-off to this state of possession is often just this feeling of urgency that it "has to be done this minute."

495   There are primitive stories among primitive tribes and in northern Europe which revolve around a competition as to who can annoy the opponent into exploding first. The one who endures the annoying and tormenting the longest without losing control of his temper wins the contest, and the loser must become his servant, obliged to do the most demanding things. But this servant plays his tricks, too, and one day the other will explode, and then the servant can cut off his head! If one doesn't allow such a panic or rush to get the better of oneself, then the figure in the unconscious will begin to change. This happens when the soldier gets into the coffin and plays dead; he won't listen or answer or pay any attention to the black princess's threats. I know an analyst whose patient came to say goodbye, since he intended to commit suicide immediately afterward. She didn't discuss his decision with him — she couldn't have answered the threat directly — but just persuaded him to first drink a glass of wine with her ... and another ... and another. Thus, time intervened, and the suicide didn't happen. If one can delay the excitement, delay acting on it, one finally becomes tired, which is a good way of dealing with such a destructive emotional outburst. Therefore, time is a terribly important factor in dealing with the anima.

496   Next time, the soldier wants to run away because he thinks he has done enough, but he meets the old man (or, in the German tale, God, who is fed up with the devil's tricks) who tells him to climb up behind the Virgin Mary. This is the place of the shadow, the dark aspect of the feminine, the aspect that has not been included in the collective. When he goes there, it is already the same thing as later when he gets into her coffin. That is, he takes her place away from her, as though saying, "I know you, know where you belong, where you come from." A man threatened by the anima could get conscious by going into the place where the anima is and then resisting her. This is a double trick, to follow the fascination and at the same time to deal with it. Some men always try to escape when they see the anima situation coming up; or else they say, "To hell with it," and go straight into it. But to go into it without falling into it, that is the

difficult thing. It is a slap in the face to the usual male attitude, because it goes against the grain. A man wants something to be either *this* or *that*, not to go into such a paradoxical situation. This "following the fascination but dealing with it at the same time" is not the *puer aeternus* situation, where the attitude is to have the whole experience, but not to commit to anything.[5] It is rather the struggle for the light, to find out the meaning of it, keeping the moral responsibility.

497   In the animus situation, his destructiveness takes the form of an inner argument, destructive arguing, which makes it necessary to give him something to chew on. But for a man, if he goes into a place where the anima herself is, it would mean that here he takes a step into life. This has to do with the fact that the anima is an archetype of life, and the animus is an archetype of death. There is a romance told among the Roma people in which a woman marries Death. He disappears from time to time, and she begs him to tell her where he goes. He tells her she wouldn't be able to face it, but she wears him down, and he finally reveals himself as Death. The shock of this discovery kills her. While he stayed with the woman, Death would forget to kill people on the earth, and then the people would multiply until there were too many. It is necessary that he perform his duties as Death. In the human realm, men do the actual work of death in the outer world, as hunters and warriors, etc., while women do the work of life, giving and preserving it. That is why it reverses itself on the inside — why animus possession makes a woman fall out of real life, while a man possessed by the anima gets entangled into life. The anima's darkness is that she wants to entangle man in the doubtful ambiguities of life, while the dark side of the animus is a demon who would pull women away from life, cut them off from it. So the man must take a step into real life, into the dark side, in the place where the anima is. In the case of the woman, she must run away and not step into death.

---

[5] See Marie-Louise von Franz, *The Problem of the Puer Aeternus* (Toronto: Inner City Books, 2000), 8 ff.

498   Naturally, these comments refer to this particular story: If the anima appears like this, as a dark power, and sleeps like this in an iron coffin, then we must say that the man will not get away without doing certain things in life. It is from the hint of darkness and fire that we must conclude that he must step into life. This compensates the Christian consciousness where very often a man doesn't want to step into a situation because he might get some spots on his white shirt. The third night, the soldier actually has to go into the black princess's coffin. The coffin has to do with the place where the dead body, the corpse, lives — the rejection of the physical. In the Christian dogma, it is the rejection of the "natural man." The average Christian attitude in Christian countries considers the body as sinful, and it is rejected. That is why here he must step in, realize what she wants. He goes into the coffin, shuts his eyes, doesn't move, and goes through a symbolic death. He lets himself be killed symbolically. He is "Osiris in the coffin." He must give up completely in order that the anima can show a different aspect.

Chapter 16

A Russian Fairytale:
The Virgin Czarina

499   In the fairytale *The Virgin Czarina*, the anima does not appear exclusively in her dark aspect; rather, dark and light facets combine in her image.[1]

500   A czar had three sons, two of them intelligent, but the third one was very silly, generally drunk, and thoroughly despised by everyone. The czar had become old. One night, at a dinner party with his generals, he gave a speech in which he said, "I wonder which one of my three sons will pick my flowers and follow in my footsteps?" The eldest son, Teodor, said, "Father, give me your blessing and permission to pluck your flowers and follow in your footsteps, and I will try." The czar was pleased and commanded that he be given the best horse in the stables. It was saddled and bridled, and the brave lad rode out into the open country. After some distance, he came to a crossroads, where a sign read: "He who takes the road to the right will get plenty of food but his horse will remain hungry; he who rides to the left, his horse will find food but he himself will go hungry; he who rides on the middle road will suffer death." After considering a while, Teodor decided to take the road to the right. This road led him to a mountain which he climbed, and there at the top, he found a brass snake. He picked it up and brought it back to court to present to his father. Upon seeing the snake, the czar was thrown into

---

[1] The original tale can be found in Reinhold Olesch, *Russian Folktales* (London: G. Bell & Sons, 1971), 119 ff.

consternation and cried, "What the hell have you brought here! This is a horrible thing — it will destroy our whole empire!" In a rage he threw the boy into prison.

501   Sometime later, in a better mood, the czar was again at dinner with his generals and again asked the question: "I wonder which one of my three sons will pick my flowers and follow in my footsteps?" Dimitri, the second son, said, "Father, I will try." So he takes the best horse in the stables and rides out. He too comes to the crossroads and reads the same sign: "He who takes the road to the right will get plenty of food but his horse will remain hungry; he who rides to the left, his horse will find food but he himself will go hungry; he who rides on the middle road will suffer death." He thinks, "Well, if my horse is well fed, he will find the way. I will take the left road." The road leads him eventually to a house with golden columns. Inside, he finds an attractive woman lying in a great bed which continually turns round and round. He promptly gets into bed with her — but she presses a button, and he is dropped into the cellar, where he finds a lot of other men who have gone before him. There he is stuck, and never goes home.

502   The czar is very sad for a long time at the disappearance of his son. But eventually he organizes another feast and muses again to his generals: "I wonder which one of my three sons will pick my flowers and follow in my footsteps?" His third son Ivan, the idiot-hero, speaks up: "Father, I would like to try." The czar ridicules him, saying, "You? — you are completely unable; you can only sit on the stove, that's all you can do." Ivan answers, "Father, with or without your blessing and permission, I will go." So the czar commands that he be given the best horse. But in the stable, there is a small, almost worn-out mare, the worst horse of all, used only for carrying water to the court. Ivan gets on her, facing the tail, and the whole town laughs at him, calling him a simpleton as he starts out on his journey. Ivan comes to the same crossroads

as his brothers and reads the same sign: "He who takes the road to the right will get plenty of food but his horse will remain hungry; he who rides to the left, his horse will find food but he himself will go hungry; he who rides on the middle road will suffer death." The boy begins to weep, saying, "Oh, am I not a poor fellow that I will have to die!" But he starts down the road that leads straight ahead, pulling so violently on the horse's bridle that he takes off the whole skin of the horse. He hangs it on a post, saying to a crow nearby, "There you are, crow — now you will have something to eat!" Then he roars like an animal and whistles like a dragon. A fiery horse appears. From its mouth blaze flames, from its nostrils flash sparks, from its ears rises steam, and fiery apples shoot out of its behind! Ivan takes this steed by the bridle and strokes it until it is calm.

503 Before continuing his journey, Ivan goes down into his grandfather's cellar where he eats a lot to strengthen himself. His grandfather (apparently a ghost, an ancestral spirit) gives him a beautiful saddle and whip for his horse and teaches him how to tame and control the horse. Ivan then jumps on the horse and rides until he comes to a little hut which stands on chicken legs and continually rotates like a spindle. He sings out, "Little hut, stand still, turn your face to the woods and answer me!" Then he sees the old witch, Baba Yaga, combing yarn with a long finger, scratching in the ashes with her long nose, and watching with glittering eyes the geese in the field. She says to him, "Tell me, child, do you come here voluntarily or involuntarily?" Ivan answers, "Shut up, you old witch! You shouldn't question a hero. Bring me something to eat and drink or I'll chop off your ears and knock off your head, and sand will come out of your arse!" She then serves him a beautiful supper, and he asks her, "Has my father ever come this way?" "Yes," she says, and then he asks her the way to the Virgin Czarina, Maria with the golden tresses. She can't give him this information but tells him to travel on till he

meets her sister and to ask her the way. He goes on to the second witch, who also asks him, "Do you come here voluntarily or involuntarily?" He shouts at her as he did with the first witch and again is served a good meal. She too says yes, his father has passed this way. He asks her how to reach the Virgin Czarina, but she says he will have to go on to the third witch who will tell him that he will have to go to the Kingdom Under the Sun, where he will find a beautiful garden. In this garden are the rejuvenating apples, and there he will also find the waters of life and death. Nearby is the castle of the Virgin Czarina, Maria with the golden tresses, who rules the Kingdom Under the Sun.

504   Ivan travels on until he comes to a great town. He finds the rejuvenating apples and the two wells, the waters of life and death. He takes a great crow and tears it to pieces, and then sprinkles water from each well on it. When he sprinkles it with the water of death, it disappears; when he sprinkles it with the water of life, it comes back to life. In this way, he finds out for himself which is the water of life. Now he goes to the castle of Maria, taking with him the rejuvenating apples and a vial of each kind of water. He finds the Virgin Czarina asleep. She is beautiful beyond all belief, and quite transparent, so that he can see her heart and the marrow flowing in her bones. He rapes her as she sleeps and quietly leaves before she wakens. Ivan is terribly exhausted now, and his horse, too, is nearly dead with weariness. But he sprinkles it with some of the water of life, and they hurry on. In the meantime, Maria with the golden tresses has woken up and is furious that a thief has been in her garden. She takes off in pursuit of the boy, and he flees before her. In jumping over a wall, the left foot of his horse strikes a little bell — Maria has such hidden bells all over the town to sound the alarm against intruders. All the people in the town wake up and race after him, led by Maria.

Ivan's flight back leads past the huts of the three witches, and each one in turn calls out to Maria as she appears in pursuit: "Oh, Maria come on in and have a cup of tea — you can catch that idiot later." Maria stops in with each of them, thus giving him a chance to escape again. He comes to the crossroads before her, and there she has to turn back. But Ivan himself now turns back too, for he has an impulse to look for his brother Dimitri who never returned. He finds the house of the woman with the turning bed and gets in with her, but he presses the button first, and she falls down into the cellar with all the previous would-be lovers, who tear her to pieces. Ivan frees them all, including his brother. Now he is so exhausted that he goes to sleep. Dimitri steals the rejuvenating apples and the waters of life and death, and takes them back to the court, saying he is the one who found them. When Ivan returns home, he doesn't say anything about his adventures or Dimitri's deception.

505   A year later, a ship draws up near the town, carrying Maria herself, the Virgin with the golden tresses. She shoots off big cannons and muskets against the court, demanding the father of her two sons, at once. The czar looks out at the bombardment. He is puzzled — who is the guilty one? The shooting continues, and the situation becomes crucial. Finally, Teodor, the eldest son, goes out to the ship, but Maria sends out her slaves who beat him back. Dimitri then tries and gets the same treatment. She still demands the guilty one, the father of her two sons. Everyone is wondering. Then one of the generals says, "Ivan is always going around the inns, getting drunk and telling funny stories. Let's try him." They find Ivan in his dirty and rumpled uniform, half drunk, and send him out to meet Maria. Her two sons immediately run out to meet him, shouting "Father!" — and they take him by the hand, and all go into the ship.

506   Since Maria is very powerful, the czar now changes his attitude toward Ivan and offers him the whole kingdom of

Russia. But Ivan says, "No, thank you," and he walks away with Maria and the two boys into the Kingdom Under the Sun.

507   The story begins with the quaternity of four figures — like the story of the little magic horse, where there were first the king and his daughter, and the Div and the horse. Here we have the czar, Teodor, Dimitri — and then Ivan, the fourth. Ivan comes to the crossroads as his brothers had before him. On one side is a road that leads to the mountain, with the brass snake; on the other side is a road that will take him to the house of the whore with the turning bed. Going straight ahead, where it is said he will suffer death, he comes to a group of women — another quaternity: three similar witches, and the fourth one is Maria. They are all one family, that is three aunts and a niece. In each quaternity, it is the fourth one who is the uniting factor. The end result of the story is that the old court is left with no feminine principle, and the youngest son, the new life, is lacking. That is, the situation is destroyed in its totality. And on the other side, in the Kingdom Under the Sun, we have the quaternity of Maria, Ivan, and the two sons. The beginning quaternity (in the court) is completely masculine, and the compensating quaternity (the three witches and Maria) is completely feminine. The end situation in the Kingdom Under the Sun contains at least one feminine figure, so that is an advance.

508   The story opens again with the theme of the old king who is worn out. The two eldest brothers are opposites: One of them goes too much to the right, upward; the other goes too much to the left, downward. One starves the horse, going astray into the upper realm of the intellectual; the other starves himself but feeds the horse, giving in too much to the instincts, to the animal. The third son, Ivan, who goes straight ahead, "dies" between the opposites. The king has once been the lover of Maria too, given his own words: "Follow in my footsteps and pick my flowers." But now he is old. The czar represents a dominant collective attitude which was once near the well of life, that is, in complete union with the psychic flow in

the unconscious, but through growing old has lost contact with it. He is no longer the symbol of the Self but has become a collective ruling system. So he puts this question as a test: Which of his three sons can go back to the source of life, where he has once been himself? His directive to "pick my flowers" has erotic connotations, in line with expressions used today. So, though it may be squeezing too much meaning out of that phrase, perhaps it is not too much to assume that Maria is the mother of the czar's sons. The old king has once flirted with Maria — she is a mother anima in the daughter aspect.

509   The description of the court makes us think of the scheme of the four functions.[2] The developed, or superior, function is the czar, now worn out, no longer in connection with the inner psychic life. He has two intelligent sons, the auxiliary functions, which are opposite to each other, and then there is Ivan, the typical inferior function. But we have already said that the czar must represent a ruling collective attitude, so does that mean we can't consider the court set-up as a pattern of the functions? We can only remind ourselves that we must have an actual human being when we talk about functions — but we *can* talk about a pattern of functions which is in the structure of the human psyche. It is quite possible to draw certain deductions about a person when you know that person's type. Thus, there are patterns. No matter what the inferior function might be, it is always linked with emotions. It is always a handicap in the outer world, and it is always linked with the mystical (in mystical religions, for example). This typical behavior of the inferior function can be deduced because there *is* a pattern in the human psyche. So we can say that this court shows a basic pattern on which the four functions of a human being develop. It is a pattern of the conscious world, while Maria and her three witchy aunts would be the pattern of the unconscious world, seen from a masculine angle.[3]

510   The interesting thing in this story is that the main function — the czar — doesn't do much harm to Ivan. The czar simply despises

---

[2] Cf. on the theory of the four functions cf. C.G. Jung, *Psychological Types*, vol.6, *CW*.
[3] On the functions in fairytales see also: C.G. Jung, "The Phenomenology of the Spirits in Fairy Tales," in *Archetypes and the Collective Unconscious*, vol. 9/I, *CW*, §§ 431–34.

him, with the attitude, "You're hopeless." There is the same thing in "What good can come out of Nazareth?"[4] But the two brothers are disturbing factors. Dimitri is even dangerous to Ivan, stealing his treasures. The two are doubtful figures because, although they reflect the pattern of the auxiliary functions, at the same time they represent what is meant by the expression "neither fish nor fowl." The superior function, for instance, may be an outstanding personality. Then the inferior function is below the average but has all the mystical qualities of the inferior function: enabling the individual to turn to the field of the unconscious. This is a bad thing only when it is turned toward the outside world. The two auxiliary functions are just average, not outstanding in any way, and just so, it is the *average* personality that can be the greatest disturbance in an individual's adventure — it doesn't want to risk itself in the great adventure. These brothers want security — they don't want to go down the path that leads to death. The czar has been there; he is not a coward. And Ivan goes — he is not a coward either. But these two brothers are dangerous enemies of the main hero — they are the reluctant, undifferentiated, average person. They don't go so high as the main one, and they won't take the risks of the inferior one. These two are differentiated — one goes to the mountain, and the other, in a silly sense, falls into the animal (the whore's cellar). But when they become constellated — after the second auxiliary becomes developed — then there is too great a weight on the conscious side. Consciousness becomes very strong, and that is a moment of danger, where a split from the unconscious may occur, because the ego has so much power. Tension arises with the development of the third function, and this tension is not relieved because the fourth is undeveloped and therefore cannot provide a balance.

511   The fourth function is less concretistic than the others; it conveys an experience on the symbolic level, while the others convey it either in an intellectual way or in a concrete way. Thus, from the perspective of the conscious, it seems like an inner death to risk sacrificing the security of the concrete. In the field of consciousness,

---

[4] "And Nathanael said unto him, Can there any good thing come out of Nazareth?" (John 1:46).

there is always an "inner" and an "outer" — the "concrete or the symbolic," the "spiritual or the physical" — but the fourth function generally leads into a reality where this split does not exist. That is, the anxious question of consciousness — "Is *this* real or is it *that* which is real?" — is not there. This is intolerable from the standpoint of consciousness. Therefore, a symbolic death is necessary in order for the inferior function to develop.

512   Let us consider the symbolism of the brass snake. In the Bible, Moses lifted up the brass snake before the people of Israel in order to free them from a certain evil (Num 21:9). The Church Fathers have always interpreted this as a prefiguration of Christ, as did the Gnostics. It possessed the highest saving qualities. But in our story, the czar is horrified. "Don't bring this monster into our kingdom," he says, "it will destroy everything!" This shows how any symbol in time may turn too much to the right side and become destructive. That which has once been a saving factor — the lifting up of the serpent into the spiritual realm — this gesture, which was emphasized in Christianity, as it also was in the earlier times, a symbol which *was* saving, has now lost those qualities and has become destructive. Dimitri had followed the road which led only into the animal experience, without the inclusion of the spiritual. Teodor took the other road and found the copper (brass) snake.[5] Copper belongs to the planet Venus, the goddess of love, and the ordinary Aphrodite. So Teodor falls into the opposite aspect of Aphrodite — it is sublime but it is dead!

513   Both the older brothers are looking for the anima. They both find something that has to do with Venus, but they found it in a too one-sided aspect. This would be like trying to experience love, from the very beginning, as something only symbolic. A person lands in the cellar, in a collective, among other fellows who fell into the same blind trap. A cellar means darkness; one is enclosed in the darkness of the instinctive drive and its collective elements, all because he had not the courage to say: "I just don't know which way it is. Let me simply go where I must go."

---

[5] Brass is an alloy of copper and zinc.

514   Ivan doesn't behave like a hero going to his death. He is completely human and bursts into tears of despair. He is an ordinary human being, naturally unhappy about having to die. This natural, spontaneous, ordinary human being is the one chosen to be the hero. He is typical of the hero of that time, compensating for the knightly ideal peculiar to Christian countries. It has only been since the era of the Christian knight and the English gentleman that natural man has been rejected. This led to the development of the spiritual, but it splits people from the ordinary human being. Ivan takes with him the little horse whose previous function was to carry water. The little horse (the instincts) is still alive, but it is practically worn out. Ivan symbolically asks himself, "What will best carry me?" and answers, "That which works for the collective unconscious will best carry me." The little mare carried into the court the living powers of the psyche, symbolized by water. People in analysis often ask, "Where shall I start in active imagination?" I say, "One must start where there is still a flow of energy, even if it is just a thin flow, even if it is in the silliest part."

515   Ivan is the natural man, so he has the spontaneous instinct to take the right horse. But he sits on it the wrong way round, with his horse looking in the right direction and himself looking back toward the town. Everybody laughs at him — but he turns the whole situation around. This is a subtle symbolical motif: As long as we turn our inferior function in the same direction as the world of consciousness, it is just a fool. Feeling will be heavy, slow, mystical, inarticulate, as long he looks at it from the viewpoint of his extraverted thinking world. He will be afraid to trust his feeling, afraid he would just fall into a complete mess. He must confess and realize that although his other functions may be well developed, in the use of his inferior function he is just a schoolboy. Many people are constantly trying to turn their inferior function in the same direction as their conscious interests take them. If they are extraverted, they try to develop their feeling function (if that is their inferior one) toward the outside world, also. Neither can the introvert work out everything on the inside. For him, it is absolutely

important that he work out a relationship with the inferior functions in the outside world, just as the extravert must recognize the inferior function in the inner world. Thus, the inferior function of feeling, for instance, not only *looks* foolish, but it *is* foolish. But as soon as it faces toward its own realm of functioning, it is no longer foolish. The inferior function has the ability to become the connection between the unconscious and the outer world. In the realm of the ruling function, it is just foolish, awkward, making one be ridiculous, childish, silly.

516   Ivan has no doubts about taking the path straight ahead — and that is one of the principal qualities of the inferior function. He is sure that he has to go straight ahead, and with a natural, instinctive knowledge, take the path of death. There is a completely simple straightforwardness about the inferior function — it is not sophisticated, argumentative — it simply wants to break through. It is turned in the right direction, that leads to the goal, and it is no longer awkward and foolish. This crossing point leads to the realm of the women. From such a structure in the unconscious, this means crucifixion, death. Like the simple soldier in the previous tale, he has to enter the coffin, a voluntary form of death. As soon as he has crossed this dangerous point, he pulls at the bridle of his horse and tears off its skin: he throws it to the crows, saying, "There, you can eat it." Then he whistles, and the heroic horse comes. The new horse is like a transformation of the old horse which has been killed. Here, he gets rid of the old horse and thus gets a new one; or, more likely, through the killing of the old one, it is revived in this new form. He sort of turns the old horse inside out (tearing off its skin), and then what looked so miserable outside becomes the fiery, heroic horse. First, Ivan had turned himself: He had started out looking regressively toward the world he is leaving instead of forward to the unknown; but afterwards, he turns around; and then he forces the horse that carries him to make the same turn.

517   A feeling type may complain that he just gets too tired, he has no libido when he tries to force himself to read: "I would like to do it, but I just haven't the strength." But his whole approach is from

the wrong direction; he is looking at the thing with worldly eyes, probably as if he were a schoolboy confronted by a textbook. If he could turn his attitude by saying, "Well, I do think for foolish reasons; so let me really think just what I think, and not mind if it is silly," and if he would then go on with it, he would suddenly become terribly fascinated by it. It is only when he is looking at the matter with conventional eyes, then there is no libido. Feeling types have an enormous philosophical thinking which is not thinking as we learn it in school. It has the gush of energy which characterized early Greek thinking — an unspoiled thinking which dares to ask the last questions, something which the sophisticated thinker has lost the power of doing. When somebody can do this, then suddenly there is generally an enormous libido which transforms, and then this miserable water-carrying horse turns into the golden heroic horse carrying him into the most amazing new experiences. This happens only by turning the inside outside in the human part of the function, and even in the instinctive part of the function. It is naturally a sacrifice — with all the painful implications of a sacrifice because one has to sacrifice all mapping out, every program as to what one thinks about it. When you try to bring people to develop their inferior function, they generally agree with the experiment, but they want to map it out with the main function, to decide where it has to go — a sort of patronizing of the inferior function. When the inferior function starts to work on its own initiative, this moment is experienced by the whole personality as a complete crucifixion, a complete, symbolic death.

518   An extravert came to me for analysis. He had overdone his extraverted intuition in a most successful, but at the same time, most destructive way so that his whole physical makeup practically gave out. He had become impotent sexually, so in analysis his amazing extraverted intuition — his excellent dog-nose — ran ahead, finding out where the thing would go. He decided that to be cured from his impotence, the best thing would be — to fall in love with a woman. But — he fell in love with a woman whom he couldn't possibly get, for outer reasons. It was a devilish trick of the unconscious to put

him like this, up against a wall. His dreams would not let him get away without accepting this fact. Yet, if he tried, as his unconscious seemed to insist, it looked like sure catastrophe. He had been chased into an impossible situation; it could lead only to disappointment. Yet his unconscious finally impelled him to try. It was a shattering experience; but through the shock, an introverted feeling attitude came up in him for this woman — which cured him from his impotence. Here, he realized how real the inner world is, that it can even cure him. Naturally, he had wanted to map it all out on the extraverted side. Had he been an introvert, the pattern of the cure would have been the opposite. That is the moment when the inferior function reveals itself in its mystical aspect (meaning: in a shocking way, not understandable from the conscious standpoint). That is a terrible, terrific moment.

519   This inferior function also has the naiveté to bring up the courage to face such a situation, to risk things without hope. The effect is that after this, Ivan goes into the grandfather's cellar. This is a typical fact you find in many primitive initiation ceremonies — before setting out on a great adventure, they integrate the ancestral souls: otherwise, these inherited tendencies and parts are elements which would work in a destructive way later; therefore, they must unite themselves.

520   There is an Eskimo initiation story:

> There was an orphan boy, rejected by everyone so that he had to live alone at the very edge of the village. One day he hears a voice and goes out into the snow to see who it is. It is a bear, who says to him: "If you have the courage to stand while I beat you, you will become a great medicine man." The boy stands, and he is beaten nearly to death. All during the beating, tiny bones fell out of him until finally there are none left. After this, he goes out into the world and becomes a healer. The name of this bear means "The Great Ancestor"; and this beating means both a uniting of oneself and, at the same time, a getting out of the system those things which do

not belong to one. Sometimes we have picked up particles of the milieu which do not belong; therefore, we must integrate the ancestors, but sweat out what doesn't belong. There is the same significance in those primitive rites where medicine men insert medicine stones in the body of the new Shaman. There are parts of the personality which do not really belong, and other parts which do belong and should be integrated. Down in his grandfather's cellar, Ivan drinks — i.e., from the ancestral power he gets the old means of taming the instincts and taming the horse.

521 *Discussion*

Question: How does it look, from the standpoint of an introvert, that the inferior function links up with the outer world, when at the same time we see it leads into the unconscious?

522 This is subtle, but one can say — it is a symbolic experience of the unconscious *but* linked with the outer object. The outer object cannot be scratched out by the introvert. This can be illustrated by the experience of a famous French poet, who fell terribly in love with a common little midinette. He experienced her as a goddess and wrote poems about her as his Beatrice. Then, with his very French intellectual attitude, he couldn't stand the paradox that she was an ordinary woman of our time. So he said to himself, "I must keep this completely inside and have nothing to do any more with the ordinary little midinette": he cuts off the relationship, not being able to stand the paradox. But then he began having psychotic episodes. He had a dream: In a garden he found her, but she was a statue, broken in two, the upper part of her body lying on the ground. His soul had died from an inner split. And, in the end, he actually hanged himself.[6]

---

[6] Gérard de Nerval (1808-1855). His love experience is dramatized in the story *Aurélia ou le Rêve et la Vie* (1855). See also Jung's Lecture on Nerval's *Aurélia* in Craig E. Stephenson ed., *On Psychological and Visionary Art. Notes from C.G. Jung's Lecture on Gérard de Nerval's "Aurélia"* (Princeton, Oxford: Princeton University Press, 2015); Marie-Louise von Franz: *The Golden Ass of Apuleius. The Liberation of the Feminine in Man* (Asheville: Chiron Publications, 2022).

523   This is an extreme case of trying to work out everything inside, and by doing so, funking the opportunity for individuation, shrinking back from facing it. He tried not to include the outer object into his inner experience. It was an ordinary love affair and, at the same time, the mystical experience. It is interesting that during his psychotic phases, whenever he traveled in Germany, and especially in the Black Forest, he always felt all right. For Germany is the land of romanticism.

524   *Question*: Can you amplify on the third (auxiliary) function?

525   When the main function and then one of the auxiliaries is developed, then this second function is what sort of colors the main function. For example, we speak of intuitively colored thinking. The development of just the two makes an average man. If the thinking is more accurate, scientific thinking, it is colored by an auxiliary sensation function. One rational function cannot function alone. A thinker must have one other function to provide the thinking with an object — either the intuition helps, or the sensation; both are irrational functions. If one is a feeling type, combined with intuition, then there is an intuitive coloring of the feeling; if it is combined instead with sensation, then the feeling is linked with the objective facts. There is always the irrational background of the rational, or the rational background of the irrational.

526   The third function is more damaging, insofar as it is already deep in the unconscious. It functions irregularly. One doesn't have it always at hand. It requires a certain amount of effort to get it going. It doesn't flow by itself. And it creates a tension: Intuition and thinking would be getting along O.K., but the third function quarrels with them. The ego, which is identified with the main functions, can swing it by making the switch; it is tiring, it creates a certain tension, but it is not a tragedy. But the fourth function can be assimilated only by a complete assimilation of the whole personality. And that is the death experience. It is so incompatible with the main functions.

527 You can also say, in this fairytale, that Dimitri *falls* into the cellar — he follows the horse, who leads him down a narrow way which leads to being imprisoned. It has all the qualities of the inferior function without its redeeming aspects. People sometimes confuse "going into the cellar" (drinking orgies, sex orgies, etc.) with "going into the unconscious." But the horse doesn't get him into the right place at all. There is a difference between just letting the animal, the instinct, run off, and exploring the unconscious. If the attitude of the crucifixion is not part of the process, going into the unconscious turns into a cheap letting oneself go for the sake of it.

528 Another Siberian story concerned with the integration of the ancestors — related to the going into the grandfather's cellar — is as follows:

529 A man named Wolf is called upon to get rid of a giant eagle who is a great killer, especially of the children of the community. Wolf sets out on his journey, crossing the plains until he comes to the mountain where the eagle lives. At the foot of this mountain, he meets an old man and woman, who greet him: "Oh, Wolf, have you come, grandchild? We knew you would come..." They are his ancestors. They give him some talismans which he takes with him in the killing of the eagle. Then a huge round stone rolls out of the slain eagle — this is called "Rage of the Eagle," and it chases Wolf, threatening his life as he flees from it. He reaches the grave of his grandparents, jumps in and hides, while the great stone rolls on by, now getting smaller and smaller until it is nothing but a pebble lying on the ground. And so it was that the ancestral spirits helped him.

530 *Continuation of the lecture*

In the *Virgin Czarina*, after eating and drinking in his grandfather's cellar, Ivan comes to the three witches (the Baba Yaga). These are wonderful figures, a complete image of the great devouring mother in her positive and negative aspects. As soon as he doesn't allow the witch to ask the wrong questions — "Do you come here voluntarily or involuntarily?" — she feeds him. It is his attitude that determines the situation. The witch's hut stands on chicken legs (sometimes the story says cock's legs with a cock's comb on the roof). The chicken represents the primitive, promiscuous, feminine Eros. The hut rotates like a spindle. The only direct parallel is in Plato's *Timaeus*, where he represents the cosmos as a sphere surrounded by the world soul, which is divided into four parts. The whole thing is rotating on an axis, a rotating spindle, spinning around in the womb of Nemesis, a goddess of justice or vengeance. The whole Platonic system turns around and around in her womb. Here the autonomous movement of nature is linked with the goddess of fate, who spins the thread of human life — "spinning" belongs to fate. The yarn of human life which fate spins: the illusion-spinning of the mother-anima figure. The cocoon of fascinations and illusions which this figure spins makes up a man's life.

531   Spinning represents the aimless, circulating movement of the psyche. An anima-possessed man goes spinning round and round the same experiences — he is in the cocoon of the spinning goddess. He must say, as Ivan does to the spinning house: "Stop! Don't mill around — turn your back to me so that I can go." There is a spinning of nature which leads to nowhere if consciousness does not break the movement of the unconscious. There is a spinning and milling around of symbols, a building up and tearing down in fantasies, a huge symbolic system building up, and then a breaking down. The conscious ego must say, "Stop!" and must make a straight line out of this circular movement. To a lesser degree, one sees this in people who are caught in a fate dictated by their unconscious. For instance, such a person may go through a series of marriages, all to the same type of man or woman. The spinning factor always creates the same fate. That is one of the witch aspects of the unconscious. "Child, do you want to come voluntarily, or involuntarily?" — that is a devilish question, raising eternal doubt. It is the Sphinx-question which the unconscious likes to bring in. Oedipus replied to the Sphinx that it

is the human being, meaning that you must live it out.[7] Or you can try another tactic and say, "Shut up, you old witch! That is not a question for you to ask. You just run along now and bring me something to eat!" That is the primitive masculine, who cuts out doubt and isn't vulnerable to insoluble conflict. It is better to take the attitude, "I know what I'm doing and I take responsibility for it." One of the Baba Yaga's tricks is to depotentiate the hero. In another version Ivan answers, "Shut up — I come voluntarily and involuntarily." Then she can't say anything more. It mirrors how this negative aspect can be stopped.

532   The Baba Yaga has a very long, phallic nose with which she scratches around in the stove. These witches often have a certain phallic aspect, sometimes a huge thumb or toe or nose, as is the case here. The male in this primitive realm is just the phallus. That is why the Baba Yaga is so dangerous — she is everything, father and mother, male and female. Those monstrous symbols of totality which are the complete symbol of the Self — they are the preconscious totality, the Uroborus, from which the male has to break free in order to get into life. This is especially the case with men in the first half of their life: They have a certain preconscious totality which they cannot give up for the sake of becoming more one-sided. This is quite legitimate; what they have *is* completeness — but it is paradise behind instead of paradise ahead. Only the hero who has the courage to cut this totality off can find it again as a *personal* experience, not just an inborn experience. But cutting off the old witch, Ivan reaches Maria, the Virgin Czarina with the golden tresses. Just those three goddess-witches who thought to stop him end up giving him food and showing him the way. This is the pattern of how a man can break free from the devouring mother image and assimilate the feminine principle.

533   There is a collective aspect in this story: The Russian man has the typical problem of someone tied to the Earth Mother. He likes to drink tea and vodka and discuss doubts; he likes to start

---

[7] The riddle of the Sphinx reads: "It is four-footed in the morning, two-footed at noon, three-footed in the evening. Of all creatures it changes only with the number of its feet; but just when it moves the most feet, strength and speed of its limbs are the least to it."

something, and then he gets lazy about carrying it through. There is no solution, no directedness by a disciplined consciousness. The Russian fairytales have the most beautiful descriptions of this figure appearing in many fairytales. That is perhaps why Communism is as it is today (1953), overdoing the perfectionist ideal, with any breaches of discipline in any area being punished in harsh, exaggerated ways — by killing, etc. It is a compensation to their unconscious.

534   Back to our story. Ivan then jumps into the "fourth dimension." The fourth witch is Maria, the Virgin Czarina, who is a niece of the other three. There is a kinship, a connection. She is indirectly connected with the other three. Ivan comes to the Kingdom Under the Sun. Here the anima is combined with the sun and not with the moon. Only in the German and Russian languages is the sun designated as feminine and the moon masculine. In Russian, "Maria" is often the name of the sun. This feminizing of the sun and masculinizing of the moon is likely connected with the different makeup of these two nations, referring to fundamentally different attitudes. The sun generally represents the source of consciousness, while the moon is dimmer. Perhaps the main source of consciousness in those two nations is in the unconscious. Their deepest thoughts and experiences come via inspiration, from "the source of consciousness which is in the unconscious." However, this is just a speculation. Ivan now comes to the castle and finds Maria, so beautifully transparent that he can see the marrow flowing in her bones. (In another version of the story, she is only transparent, but "one could encompass her body with two fingers, it is so small, but when one lets it go again, she fills the whole world.") She is the world soul, fills the whole cosmos. She is the soul of matter. This figure appears in stories from the Caucasus way up to the far north — but nowhere else but in Russia.

535   These stories are a continuation of antique Greek Gnostic ideas which survived in these areas, although the Gnostics were aggressively persecuted in the Christian world. The Gnostics taught of a Sophia figure, a bride of God. In the tenth and eleventh centuries

A.D., this goddess was described as the world soul who fills the whole cosmos. This bride of God is his feminine aspect, which completes the male aspect of the ruler of the world.[8] Her name, Sophia, means "wisdom." From the male god comes the wisdom found in revelations. But this goddess, this bride, reveals herself through experience — not through reading the Scriptures, but through experiencing the unknown, experiencing reality. So we see that the tendency is toward assimilating this Sophia figure. This anima has the fantastic, antique character of a highly spiritualized world soul which, in the Western world, appears only in alchemy and in certain sects but in the Eastern world survives in this complete form.

536 *Discussion*

Question: Could you amplify for us the motifs of "the spinner" and "the spindle?"

537   The witch Baba Yaga is living in a little rotating house, she lives inside a rotating spindle. One cannot approach her unless one knows the magic verse: "Little hut, stand still, put your back away from me and the front towards me." This motif of the spindle, and of spinning, is always associated with the fate goddesses. In India, it is Maya who spins the illusions. These illusions make a man's fate, the fascinations, attractions, which entangle him into life. In Western psychology, it is the "Norns" (the three Fates, past, present, future, who in Norse mythology live by the well at the foot of the mighty ash tree, Yggdrasill) or the three Greek fates, one of whom spun the thread of life, one who held it and fixed its length, and one who cut it off. In the Platonic concept, it is the goddess Nemesis — a Great Mother goddess whose meaning is justice, vengeance — in whose womb is the axis of the cosmos. This conceives of the mother goddess as

---

[8] In the Old Testament, Sophia appears as Yahweh's consort. "The LORD possessed me in the beginning of his way, before his works of old. / I was set up from everlasting, from the beginning, or ever the earth was. / When there were no depths, I was brought forth; when there were no fountains abounding with water [...] / Then I was by him, as one brought up with him: and I was daily his delight, rejoicing always before him." (Prov 8:22-30)

being the *container* of the spinning movement, whereas in our fairytale *she* is *inside*, sitting within the spindle.

538   This spinning has certainly to do with the autonomous movement of the unconscious psyche. We always try to interpret a dream as a *compensation* of the conscious situation. But besides this, it seems as if the unconscious psyche is a living system by itself which can move by itself. This is very difficult to prove, because one can always say, "This has been called forth by the conscious." So we cannot prove this point. But it is revealed here, in the mythological field, that we must reckon with arbitrary, autonomous events. This is a factor parallel to the situation in modern physics, where we know now that there is a spontaneous, arbitrary movement in matter, too, which breaks the law of causality and which cannot be predicted. For example, you cannot predict when a particular uranium atom will fall apart. We do know the exact, definite number of years for a uranium atom to become lead — in that length of time, one-half of the atoms in a piece of uranium will have disintegrated. But we still cannot answer, "How does each atom know when it is its turn?" The physicist cannot explain that, cannot predict *which* atom will disintegrate.[9] So, if the material world has this possibility of a spontaneous movement, why should the unconscious psyche not have it, too? This has to be taken into account: There is a development in the collective unconscious which cannot be explained as only an answer to consciousness. Probably there are the two systems affecting each other, both of them having the possibility of a spontaneous movement.

---

[9] Wolfgang Pauli, the theoretical physicist and one of the pioneers of quantum physics, comments on this in a letter to Jung: "The physical phenomenon of radioactivity consists in the transition of the atomic nucleus of the active substance from an unstable early state to its final state [...], in the course of which the radioactivity finally stops. Similarly, the synchronistic phenomenon, on an archetypal foundation, accompanies the transition from an unstable state of unconsciousness into a new stable position. [...] The moments in time when the *individual* atoms disintegrate are in no way determined by the *laws of nature*." In Wolfgang Pauli and C.G. Jung, *Atom and Archetype: The Pauli/Jung Letters 1932–1958*, ed., C.A. Meier (Princeton: Princeton University Press, 2001), 41.

539 *Continuation of the lecture*

The inner rotation is always linked with a symbol representing the deepest layers within the collective unconscious — where it somehow melts with the physical processes of the body, activating emotions. Baba Yaga is very close to the physical. Maria, too, has a wall around her town, with hidden bells — and when the horse jumps over it, he touches one of these bells (it "rings a bell"), which brings about the movement of all the people. She herself is walled about within the town. In practice, one sees this a lot when we have to do with "women witches" — women possessed by the witch archetype. These women seem to have to stir up emotions purely for the sake of stirring things up, even if it is destructive. Such women, when they see a blind spot in one of their neighbors, just have to put their finger on it and stir it up. They can't leave it alone. The witch anima in men has this tendency, too. Normally, it is a shadow figure in women that has this element — but in psychotic people it is sometimes an actual possession, and very destructive. A little bit of this stirring up doesn't matter because sometimes having to talk about it can help bring out shadow elements which can then become conscious. So in a way it is positive and works toward bringing out the light. But when it becomes autonomous, as happens in certain psychotic cases, then it can actually destroy people. With these psychotics, you get the feeling that they do it just for the sake of having something destructive to do — an autonomous pleasure in keeping the devil going. There is a lust for destruction in it.

540 Baba Yaga is the feminine personification of a devil. If somebody approaches this hut, he faces dissolution, an eternal milling around. But it is also interesting that Ivan uses magic, an incantation. That shows us that here we are dealing with elements of the unconscious which can be affected only by magic. Sometimes an element, a psychological content, cannot not be touched just by analyzing dreams: something magical is needed to make this hut stand still. If we are up against such elements, it takes more than bringing things up in the unconscious. Then we are faced with the question: Do we have tools by which we can *do* something to the unconscious, not

just bring it up into consciousness? The only means Dr. Jung has discovered up to now is "creative imagination."[10] That is the only means by which *we* can have an effect on the unconscious. It is a technique of "bewitching the unconscious." These things cannot be assimilated just by making them conscious. It needs more than that.

541 That is why Dr. Jung feels that if an analyst must treat psychotics, he must know how to use "creative imagination" for his own protection.[11] Because a psychosis is a very infectious disease — it affects from behind. Often one sees this happen in a group in society, where personalities that are half-psychotic, borderline, are able to stir up the whole group — wherever something in such a group is unconscious, then bang! they hit on it, they sit on it, so to speak. The analyst needs "creative imagination" in order to disentangle himself from the psychotic effects of a patient. Otherwise, sooner or later they get the analyst, on a day when he is tired, overworked, or has fallen into his own black spots. But there are also other threats to the analyst besides the psychotic infection. He may be exposed to such terribly vile materials coming up from the unconscious of the patient that he himself gets poisoned by it. The very fact that one has to listen to such things, or look at such drawings, has an effect on one's soul. That is why primitives are afraid to look at certain things. But — if one *has* to look at such material, then the necessity is to de-poison oneself. And active imagination is the most direct way to get rid of it. Understanding is not enough; one needs a more effective tool to touch it, deal with it. Ivan knows how: with his magic verse. He interferes with consciousness. In the Platonic image, the mother goddess is outside, and the spinning wheel is inside, but here the spinning wheel has covered everything. There is nothing you can talk to, relate to: It is the most destructive abyss of feminine nature.

542 The witch is stirring the stove, i.e., stirring up the emotions. The "stove" has to do with the stomach and intestines; that is where we

---

[10] The term "creative imagination" is a synonym for "active imagination."

[11] See C.G. Jung, "The Transcendent Function," in *The Structure and Dynamics of the Psyche*, 2nd ed., vol. 8, *CW* (Princeton, NJ: Princeton University Press, 1970), § 400–403; Barbara Hannah, "On Active Imagination," in *The Inner Journey. Lectures and Essays* (Toronto: Inner City Books, 2000), 24 ff.; Marie-Louise von Franz, "Active Imagination in the Psychology of C.G. Jung" and "On Active Imagination," in Marie-Louise von Franz, *Psychotherapy* (Boston: Shambhala, 1993), 119–142.

"cook" food for assimilation. So the kitchen and the stove refer to everything that has to do with affects. The nucleus of the emotional psyche gets hit — then we have to run to the toilet, for example. Jung remarks on how the center of consciousness has climbed up the body during the course of history: Among primitives the belief is common that the psyche is in their belly (Jung likes to say that dogs have their consciousness in their bladder, because they only think when they have to go out). Practically speaking, only what affects their intestines exists as a psychological factor. Anything which is more subtle than that, which doesn't hit their belly, they are not aware of. The Greeks thought the center was in the diaphragm. Our word "schizophrenia" comes from that: "split diaphragm."[12] Heracles, when in dire straits, "talked to his diaphragm." Later, the heart was considered to be the center: Many Indian tribes "think with the heart"; only those things are psychological factors which make the pulse beat faster. Then the center moved to the breath: those factors which make us breathe irregularly are the only psychic contents we are aware of. Thus the center moves up.

543   The stove always refers to the belly-psyche and those awarenesses connected with it. This type of witch must always stir up an emotional fuss with her animus. She can't leave a situation to develop on its own — she must bring everything up into the light. That is how witches are driven, always stirring around in other people's emotions. But Baba Yaga is not only scratching in the stove with her nose. At the same time, she is combing yarn with her claws; that is, she does make a certain order of "disheveled" life, so that everything goes in the right direction. Also, she watches the geese; that would be positive — she takes care of the instincts. That is why when Ivan talks to her in a certain masculine, independent way, she becomes completely positive, becomes the goddess of fertility, feeding and taking care of him.

544   The most striking thing about geese is that they are organized in such a military fashion, wild geese always flying in chevron

---

[12] From ancient Greek σχίζειν (s'chizein) = "split, cleave, fragment" and φρήν (phrēn) = "spirit, soul, mind, diaphragm."

formation, and tame geese always marching in single file. Animals have a pattern in their behavior. Geese let themselves be invisibly organized. That is why the goose is the animal of the goddess Nemesis, and of Aphrodite in her aspect as a mother goddess. In the Chinese book of wisdom, the I Ching, hexagram 53 (nine at the top), says: "The wild goose gradually draws near the cloud heights. Its feathers can be used for the sacred (or ritual) dance."[13] The utmost fulfillment is that the human ritual follows the order of wild geese. There is this absolute harmony with nature; the greatest conscious-ness is like a return to the animal, but on a higher level. The wild goose has to do with a secret order within nature itself. That is why geese are associated with goddesses of fate. Baba Yaga rules all the secret orders of nature. These drives are not chaotic but follow a secret pattern. But in Maria, the Virgin Czarina with the golden tresses, the anima aspect comes out more. The Kingdom Under the Sun contains the rejuvenating apples and the waters of life and death; that is, it is a sort of paradise, the Hesperides of the Greeks. "Hespera" means evening, when the sun sets, the end of the world. That is where Heracles went for the golden apples. So, Maria is the goddess of the setting sun, therefore actually a goddess of death, an aspect of the anima quite outside the human sphere, in the beyond. She is surrounded by the town wall. This again refers to the town goddesses of antiquity, most of whom were represented with the walls of the town as their crown — the familiar crenelated walls.

545   There are certain quite interesting speculations about this during late antiquity, in which the goddess represents the World Soul and the wall is matter which encloses it — her girdle or her crown is the outer part of her world soul. So the outer shell is the actual matter, and inside there is the symbolical, psychological fact. On a higher scale, this same representation is made as the *matter* of the cosmos — that is the anima in her deepest aspects, which have to do with the actual secret of the world.[14] How is the unconscious psyche

---

[13] Hexagram 53 "Chien / Development (Gradual Process)," see *The I Ching or Book of Changes*, trans. Richard Wilhelm (London: Routledge and Kegan Paul, 1968), 208.

[14] In this sense Jung speaks of the "anima mundi" as an "expression of the 'life spirit' and the 'filius macrocosmi,' the Anthropos who animates the whole cosmos." C.G. Jung, *Memories, Dreams, Reflections*, ed. Aniela Jaffé, trans. Richard and Clara Winston (New York: Vintage Books, 1989), 211.

linked with physical matter? That we don't know, though we do know there *is* a link. We can even compare this with the spinning, round sphere — that would be the dynamic aspect of nature — and on the other side, matter has this mass aspect. Energy and substance are the two aspects of matter. We can look at matter as consisting of *particles*, or we can see it as *magnetic fields*. The anima is "the archetype of life itself,"[15] and therefore she must somehow have to do with the actual physical consistency of the cosmos, with the secret of the physical life in this world. She is dormant in it; she sleeps there. This matter aspect is only a shell — she is not matter but is only *inside* the wall. From the psychological angle, we are, with our consciousness, observing our psyche, and then we may come to an element of the unconscious where we have the feeling, "That is no longer psychological, it is material" — the psychosomatic aspect. The two are linked, there is a parallelism; but we haven't yet an adequate amount of knowledge of what it is. And so, in working with the unconscious, we come to a border of the psyche where it becomes somatic.

546   Physicists start from the other direction: They look at things pragmatically, and then they come to a borderline where the metaphysical (beyond their physical data) begins. The study of atomic physics has made it clear that we can no longer exclude the consciousness of the observer from the results of an experiment. All material phenomena can be studied either as radiation phenomena, waves, or as atoms. This is the great contradiction, that when we want to prove that light consists of *particles*, the only way we can prove this is that we *move* the light source. A screen is made with a little hole in it, and only one quantum of light is allowed to go through; then only one molecule on the photographic plate is disintegrated. If you keep the light field static, you can say, "Now we know that light is all particles, they go back, the light is reflected psycho-somatic aspect the waves are an illusion." Then you move the light so that only one particle can move through, so there is no possibility of its shooting back and forth.

---

[15] C.G. Jung, *Archetypes of the Collective Unconscious*, vol. 9/1, *CW* (Princeton, NJ: University Press, 1969), § 66.

547   On the other hand, the wave theorists make a crystal screen, and they break (diffract) the light. Then they get the phenomena of interference. When waves chase each other, they either get bigger or they level out, depending on how they hit each other. Wherever you have an interference pattern, you get waves. So they say, "Light is waves." In order to get this phenomenon, the light source must be constant, and there must be a great amount of it.[16] Thus, in one experiment, you cannot settle the time and space norms exactly, although the energy factor is exact — you can send off just one quantum of light, but space and time are the vague factors. In the second experiment, the amount of energy is the vague factor — it is not exactly measurable.

548   The interesting conclusion is that it is the way the experiment is set up that determines the result we get. Whether we want to prove that light is waves, or that it is particles, then we set up the experiment to prove *this* and make it impossible to get the *other* answer. We *have* to do this in order to get a pure result; we have to corner nature, have to ask a question in order to get an answer — but it ends all hope that we will ever be able to find out what matter really is. Therefore, we can only say, "If we create this phenomenon with this hypothesis, nature will answer in *this* way; if we create this other phenomenon, nature will answer in *that* way." Therefore, the question a man has in his consciousness becomes a relevant factor — we have to include both the observer and the experiment he sets up. When we want to find out one thing, we must sacrifice another factor, such as space-time exactness or the energy factor. We have to realize that "in order to acquire one piece of knowledge, I have to sacrifice another; I cannot get a complete picture."[17] Also, then I get

---

[16] Marie-Louise von Franz refers here to the so-called double-slit experiment, conducted with light by the physicist Thomas Young in 1802. He thereby refuted Newton, who thought that light consisted of particles ("corpuscles"). With the birth of quantum physics about 100 years later, it was discovered that light does indeed consist of tiny indivisible energy units (quanta), the photons. Under certain circumstances, however, light behaves like a wave. In quantum physics, the double-slit experiment is often used to demonstrate wave-particle duality.

[17] In a letter to Jung, Wolfgang Pauli describes this problem from the physicist's point of view: "It rests with the free choice of the experimenter (or observer) to decide which insights he will gain and which he will lose; or, to put it in popular language, whether he will measure A and ruin B or ruin A and measure B. It does *not* rest with him, however, to gain only insights and not lose any." C.G. Jung, "On the Nature of Psyche," in *The Structure and Dynamics of the Psyche*, vol. 8, CW, § 440.

a contradictory result: One cannot say that light is both a particle and a wave. Instead, we get two results which absolutely contradict each other. That is behind the scientist Niels Bohr's theory of complementary aspects.[18] For us, what is interesting is the fact that the people who have tried to study matter completely objectively have been forced back to psychology: the observer and the hypothesis in his mind have to be included along with the physical factors. In this way, scientists are discovering the unconscious. They have started working on the material aspect of nature and have pushed through to where they meet the borderline of the unconscious. The psychologist has started working from the other side, from the unconscious, and finds himself meeting the borderline of the somatic, where the psyche seems to mirror itself in material facts.

549   It is a sort of sign of our times that even in mathematics the same thing has happened. In what is called "fundamental mathematics," it is recognized that even the basic axioms cannot be proved. Sensory experiences on the one side, and archetypal experiences in the psyche on the other — that is the basis of mathematics: For example, "two parallels meet in eternity (infinity)." That comes from sense experience, where two parallel lines meet in the distance, but also from certain inherent laws of the mind — and hanging in midair between these two experiences is mathematics. And so the whole of natural science has shifted over to being a description; that is, *if* you look at it this way, then you get these results. The observer and the inherent activity of the human mind have to be taken into account. Natural science has the advantage of being able to measure its phenomena to a certain extent and to demonstrate results which are statistically true. Its experiments can be repeated exactly and are not dependent on the subject too much. But this is only true in microphysics. As soon as you deal with millions of atoms, then you

---

[18] Niels Bohr developed the theorem of complementarity on the basis of the realization that the properties of classical waves as well as those of classical particles must be attributed to the objects of quantum physics. Bohr and Werner Heisenberg encapsulated the facts of two apparently contradictory, irreducible modes of description or experimental arrangements – which in their mutual complementation are necessary for understanding a phenomenon as a whole – in the concept of the principle of complementarity. In 1927 they introduced this principle of complementarity into quantum physics under the title "Copenhagen Interpretation."

get laws which are relatively true, which are average reactions. In the study of the unconscious, the archetypes are the fundamental factors. Their activity is the only place where you can predict with a degree of certainty. Case material is always strictly individual.

550   In our tale, Ivan goes over the wall, he transcends it, and comes to something beyond which we can call the psychic reality, the hypothesis that the psyche has in itself an actual reality (We have to have a name for the unknown stuff we are studying, so we call it "the unconscious"). Ivan comes to this reality of matter, and there Maria is asleep. When he turns back (after raping her), she wakes up. So, Maria lives in a countermovement to his rhythm. We can say that when our ego consciousness is focused, then we cannot be aware of the unconscious. When we are aware of the unconscious, then our consciousness has to be dimmed. The best phenomena of this sort are dreams, where consciousness is just barely awake, but not enough to stop the unconscious; the borderline of the unconscious meets it. The concept of the "highest consciousness" is where we always quarrel with the Eastern philosophers. They say that *samadhi* is the highest state of consciousness, whose absolute reality is the dimming out completely, the extinction of the ego complex. Jung argues that this state represents complete unconsciousness, but to them, it is the highest state of consciousness.[19] So, there are these two complementary qualities: You cannot be conscious and unconscious at the same time. Active imagination is an attempt to keep the whole ego complex intact and at the same time to get the borderline phenomena of the dream into it, too. That is why it is the technique for bringing together the opposites.

551   The understanding of the dream also requires a dimming down of our consciousness in order to get the meaning of the dream. The Eastern way would mean to us the giving up of ego consciousness, and that is not a valuable thing to us because then we lose the

---

[19] "There is no doubt that the higher forms of yoga, in so far as they strive to reach samādhi, seek a mental condition in which the ego is practically dissolved. Consciousness in our sense of the word is rated a definitely inferior condition, the state of *avidyā* (ignorance), whereas what we call the 'dark background of consciousness' is understood to be a 'higher' consciousness." C.G. Jung, "Psychological Commentary on *The Tibetan Book of the Dead*, " in *Psychology and Religion: West and East*, 2nd ed., vol. 11, CW (Princeton, NJ: Princeton Press, 1989), § 775.

possibility of scientific description. When Jung was in the African bush country, he determined to observe the natives' psychic phenomena scientifically, with careful notes and records. But then he had some of the experiences — but when he looked at his notes later, they were lacking! So it is, if you keep the scientific mind, then you walk through the bush and don't have the experiences, nothing happens. If you go through the bush as the natives do, then the light of ego consciousness is extinguished, and you can make no scientific notes. It is our consciousness which distinguishes between the outside and the inside. If our consciousness is extinguished, there is no longer this distinction — everything is simply an *event*, with the inner phenomena actually occurring outside. There is an anecdote of a missionary, who once watched all night the body of the medicine man who was in a trance but who said he had gone to a mountain far away for a meeting of all the medicine men — a sort of ghost meeting. The medicine man had been asked by the missionary to deliver a message to a friend living in that mountain area, such as, "Please return my rifles." Some days later, the missionary received a letter from that friend saying that he had been wakened on the night of the trance by a voice outside, saying, "Please send me my rifles." Such a thing can only happen if you are in a trance — then it is experienced as an outer reality. But you who try to watch are excluded from "going to the mountain." These are complementary qualities — you either experience the reality, or you keep a scientific account. You cannot have both.

552   In *The Virgin Czarina*, Maria was transparent. In the parallel story it is said that she could be picked up between two fingers, but at the same time fills the whole world. Obviously, she has a subtle body, with no density. She doesn't have the qualities of ordinary matter. Transparency also refers to the ghost world — you can put your hand through ghosts but not touch them. Ivan could see the marrow flowing through her bones; that is, she was also a skeleton. In some stories the anima figure appears as a beautiful woman from the front, but when she turns her back, she is a skeleton, death. This aspect was in the story about the star goddess, who also was a

dancing skeleton.[20] The star-maiden's home was a misty dominion. And Maria is living on the borderline between life and death. This makes her a supernatural being. She is not material; her body is like a shell which you can look through. Ivan rapes this figure in her sleep, and then he runs away. She wakes up when his horse touches the bell. When Ivan went in, his horse didn't touch it; going out, he was in such a rush that he set off the alarm.

553   This motif of touching was also in the story where the girl rides successively through the copper (brass), the silver and the gold forests, and is told by the blue bull not to touch the leaves or the troll would come out.[21] In that story the leaves signified the mortal side of experience. In the present story, the wall is where the physical quality is touched, where the thing becomes real. That is the danger point. The anima is from the spiritual realm, not a concrete woman. The image of the anima must be realized as a psychological aspect — but there is this human experience, too, because there is always a hook attached: Otherwise, the question is, why has the man fixed on this particular, real woman? That is the dangerous point, where the anima is linked with a human being, where it becomes a problem in concrete life. We touch this problem not only in connection with the anima — it is a general problem whenever the dream speaks: "Must I do this concretely or symbolically?" It is a very difficult problem, one of the ethical, touchy points of the whole analysis. In general, if one has the patience to wait long enough, one learns from the dream whether it wants to be realized completely, in fact, or only symbolically. But it takes a lot of great reading of the dream to see it. Very often there are dreams where you just don't know; you must try one way, and then another. If you have not taken the right track, the dream will insist again.

554   Here Ivan touches the bell — there is a vibration going through him. It is the feeling of emotional reaction. One of the main effects of archetypal symbols is that they have an enormous dynamic load or charge, they are explosive factors. Therefore, they are responsible

---

[20] See above, 38.
[21] *Kari, The Girl With the Wooden Frock*, see above, 28.

for dynamic movements like Nazism, for instance, and for what goes on in the insane. Archetypes release the most overwhelming emotions. The image and the emotion are the two factors we are aware of — but what is behind it, we don't know, that is, the archetype as an entity we don't know. We only know that it occurs repeatedly as a similar picture, and we know that it has this enormous, dynamic effect. This effect is the moment when the archetype touches the fringe of the physical being. The archetype has to do with the instinct; the instinct has to do with physical activity. The archetype is a common way of experiencing things in a psychological manner. It is linked with the instinct, it is the pattern of the instinct. The way it is realized instinctively, that's where the emotion arises.

555   People sometimes have an archetypal dream and experience no other effect than to think, "All this mythology is very interesting." This lack of affect isn't because the analyst hasn't been able to convey the significance — it is just that it is too far removed. But it can happen that even a year later the patient gets a huge emotion and comes running in a panic to the analyst — because now it has come through, now they understand; up to now, the archetype was unapproachable. This borderline where the realization comes to the point where the field of the physical and of the psychological link up — that touches a bell, there is a vibration. We know the Eastern image of the Kundalini: This snake is dormant; the Yogi concentrates and makes her rise, and the first thing is that a gong sounds — that is the awakening of the Kundalini. That is what we mean when we say "constellated." This wonderful word comes from astrology and astronomy. The stars have moved into a certain constellation. That is one of the most mysterious words. What does it mean that a thing is suddenly "constellated?" It is a wonderful word to cover up something we don't really know! It is the moment of touching human reality. Before, it slept, as a possibility within the human being. That is why this is also the borderline between life and death — it is dormant, it is not real.

556   Ivan's animal — the left hind foot — is the thing which touches, which makes the fatal-yet-hopeful mistake. It is like the sin in Paradise. Like all the wrong acts of human beings, by which a step forward in consciousness is made. Every step in consciousness is always seen as a fatal mistake, a violation of nature. That is why a person who is "too sound," like certain peasants who live in a very sound relatedness to reality, may have all the archetypes in them but it is not constellated; it exists in their life, but it is dormant. You couldn't talk with them about it; they are moving in this world, but it is not constellated as a reality. It must first be split off, which causes some emotional disturbances, and then he can realize the inner nature. The animal impulsiveness of Ivan does this — drags the hind foot a little, it clings downward a bit — a tendency to the Dimitri side. But that arouses the possibility of realization.

557   Maria then puts wings on herself and on all her servants, and thus reveals her ghost nature, her spiritual nature, in response to the fact that he has touched the physical. It brings forth the other aspect: She was dormant, she was at first both, and he has now brought about this countermovement. What rings a bell touches a complex, hits the inner life. At that very moment, he gets the most terrific fright. She is off after him. That is a typical representation of dealing with the anima when consciousness isn't yet strong enough. Perhaps it concerns the Russian problem: He can rape the anima only when she is asleep. When she awakens, he is terrified. This terror is a symbol of a weak consciousness. But now the Baba Yagas delay the anima, invite her in for a cup of tea. With all this stopping and talking with her aunts, she is delayed. This is also an image of what the Russians actually do: When they are frightened, they delay the problem so that it can't become really crucial. This old-woman talk is very helpful — it protects against the realization. The mother figures act like a shock-absorbing bumper, a protective buffer ahead of the realization of the anima. This situation in the story is represented as positive — but this need for the mother to help, to interfere, it really shows the Russian problem.

558   Ivan returns to the court, and apparently nothing has happened to him. His brother takes the golden apples and the water of life and death and goes boasting to the court that he had actually been where they came from. Ivan doesn't even try to disprove this, doesn't state that it was only he who was there. He just starts getting drunk again. It looks as if nothing has happened. That again is an image of the Russian soul. They have the greatest inner experiences, but when it comes to a real way of life in this world, the old, eternal way takes over again. The creative gifts dormant in their psyche are of the greatest value, but they regard them always with a sort of primitive attitude, so that all gets lost again. Ivan simply does not trouble himself about the matter. This is an effect of the mother complex again, which always sweeps away what has been gained. This is the puzzling thing with the Russians, who we know have really been confronted with religious experiences, as revealed for example in *The Brothers Karamazov*.[22] This problem must be connected with the sun's being linked with the anima: The possibilities of consciousness are still in the unconscious. That is, experiences are experienced as inspiration, they are being *owned* in this form but not handled, they don't become a quality of ego consciousness — their ego only *receives* the experience, remaining in the receptive state. In Dr. Jung's *Psychology and Alchemy,* he tells of the man who dreamed that the anima is the sun goddess: The whole spiritual genius of the man is still in the unconscious, still linked to the animal.[23] Such people make great discoveries, but only because they got them via the unconscious. They haven't worked it out themselves, they just got it in their mind. This is when the sun is in the unconscious; but the thing discovered is not acquired. Then the data can again get lost. It is just a gift from the anima, and it is taken away again, falls back into the unconscious.

559   At this point in the fairytale everything seems to be lost. Dimitri, who is doing the boasting, is actually only the man who had been

---

[22] *The Brothers Karamazov* (1880) by Fyodor Dostoevsky. Philosophical novel and theological drama that enters deeply into questions of God, free will, and morality.
[23] C.G. Jung, *Psychology and Alchemy,* 2nd ed., vol. 12, *CW* (Princeton, NJ: Princeton University Press, 1993), § 110 ff.

in the cellar of the woman with the turning bed. She can be compared with the Greek goddess Circe, who touches with her wand every man who comes to her island and makes them all into pigs — that is, in the image of the blindness of their instinct. And it is now this Dimitri who takes over and says, "I'm the one who has had the experience." But the real mystic experience is denied in the unconscious. This is like the situation when people have tremendous experiences in analysis — then they have difficulty bringing them into their real life. They feel, "So, what shall I do now, *practically speaking?*" — and the experience is all gone. People can have a wonderful analysis, but in the conscious field, nothing moves. It was like a bath, but nothing has happened. The technical term for this in mythology is the difficulty on the return, "the way back difficulty." The hero has overcome great obstacles, slain the dragon, etc., but on the way back, he either falls asleep and everything gets lost again, or someone steals it from him, as in the Gilgamesh story. It seems to be just as great an achievement to make the transition back, to reconnect with one's own life, as it is to get into the unconscious. But if it isn't accomplished, then the whole business is like an intoxication, and then one wakes up and has a hangover, and afterwards everything is as it was before. This is why Jung is against hypnosis — it doesn't last, unless it is done step by step, really fastened in the conscious realm. In the long run, these quick techniques do not work because the unconscious and conscious have not really been linked.

560   The difficult achievement of bringing it back into consciousness is too much for Ivan: When he goes back to the court, where all the old experiences await him, he can't carry that other experience with him. He takes up his old way of life, and the experience of his journey seems to be lost. This danger of losing everything is illustrated in the story of the man who wins and marries a princess in another realm, but after a while, he wants to go back to his old home for a visit. The princess is very anxious about this and says: "Don't forget me — and whatever you do, don't kiss your mother!" He promises — but once back in his old home, he forgets and does

kiss his mother, and the whole experience with the princess is gone, he has lost all memory of it. After a lot of complications in the story, he finally does get his wife again, and this time forever.

561 　　When you have a reductive interpretation of the experience, you can say, "Oh, that was nothing but" — i.e. the Devil gets in and interprets something that you haven't experienced in exactly that way — and then all is lost. That is the third function, showing the "nothing but" interpretation which is always put over by consciousness — consciousness, which has always the difficulty of linking the two worlds, realizing something that has both aspects. But it is not true that everything is lost, because Maria is pregnant, and Ivan is the father of the two boys. Only *apparently* is everything lost. Something which has once happened is never lost forever. Something has been constellated, has been moved in the unconscious itself, and that is why the whole experience is not lost. The psychic movement has been activated, the anima is impregnated by the fact that he, Ivan, has been there. The two boys growing up lend the conscious enough dynamism so that now an irruption of the unconscious into the conscious world occurs. Maria appears, firing guns, threatening to shoot down the whole town if the father of her two sons doesn't show himself. She brings the same brutal force as Ivan had when he entered her town and raped her.

562 　　The Russians have gone into an overenlightened movement now: Nothing irrational is admitted. They now apply thoroughly the materialism and mechanical world of the 19th century, which we have rejected — that is "raping Maria." Thus, there is a very brutal counterattack — suddenly the unconscious attacks. People living in an old culture have a more balanced relationship; there is always a movement and countermovement, but it doesn't take this violent form in these old cultures. The dreams of nations reveal a lot of their individuality. "Shooting with a gun" means rousing terrific emotions. An explosion produces the attack. One really feels like having been shot in the back. So, shooting is an emotional approach — it means being charged, loaded. That is what the anima does now. She just shoots down the world of consciousness. This is the dangerous thing

about sudden, undisciplined emotions. They can overrun reason, make people go berserk. Then the whole conscious program is shot down. That is her vengeance — because she had been raped.

563   The king's court must find out what had happened. After trying some wrong solutions, they resort to Ivan. The anima is then satisfied, and the Czar then recognizes Ivan as the one who "followed in his father's footsteps." He offers Ivan his kingdom, but Ivan says, "No, thank you," and goes into the Kingdom Under the Sun — which means that the whole thing goes into the unconscious. In spite of this great creativeness, this richness in the unconscious, you often find that the conscious town is only shot down. Among other peoples, similar stories relate that the czar keeps half the kingdom and gives the other half to his son and bride. So, even from the standpoint of the collective, this story has a sad ending. The greatest values still disappear into the unconscious — which means that the possibility of realizing consciousness is pretty small. Before in this story, we had here a male world and a female world. The end result is still completely unconscious, but there has been a shift toward a greater balancing of the opposites. So we can say that if it continues to happen, over and over, then one day the balance may come about.

564   People also fall again and again into the same hole. They will seem to have gained a little ground, but then they fall in again. This goes on repeatedly — but there is always a little bit of the hole filled in, a few of the gains are retained. When they next fall into the trap, there is the feeling, "Oh! I've been here before, and I managed to get out before." One gains a little ground. It is a sort of secret confirmation of the personality. And so — a little change has happened, in spite of the sad end result.

Bibliography

Aarne, Antti. *The Types of the Folktale: A classification and bibliography*. Translated and enlarged by Stith Thompson. 2nd revision. Helsinki, 1964.

Aichele, Walther, and Martin Block. *Zigeunermärchen.* Die Märchen der Weltliteratur, edited by Friedrich von der Leyen. Munich: Diederichs, 1926.

Andersen, Hans Christian. "The Ugly Duckling." In *Complete Fairy Tales and Stories*, translated by Erik Christian Haugaard. Palatine: First Anchor Books, 1983.

Apuleius. *Cupid and Psyche*. Edited by Edward John Kenney. Cambridge: Cambridge University Press, 1997.

_____. *The Golden Ass: or the* Metamorphoses. Translated by W. Adlington. New York: Barnes & Noble Books, 2004.

Ardrey, Robert. *The Territorial Imperative, a personal inquiry into the animal origins of property and nations.* Königstein: Athenäum, 1997.

Bastian, Adolf. *Beiträge zur vergleichenden Psychologie: Die Seele und ihre Erscheinungsweisen in der Ethnographie.* Berlin: Nabu Press, 2010.

Beit, Hedwig von. *Symbolik des Märchens.* Vol. 2, *Gegensatz und Erneuerung im Märchen.* Bern: Francke, 1965.

Benfey, Theodor. *Kleinere Schriften zur Märchenforschung.* Berlin, 1894.

Berndt, Ronald M. *Kunapipi: A Study Of An Australian Aboriginal Religious Cult.* Melbourne: F.W. Cheshire, 1951.

Bettelheim, Bruno. *Psychanalyse des Contes de Fées.* Paris: Laffont, 1976.

_____. *The Uses of Enchantment: The Meaning and Importance of Fairy Tales*. New York: Vintage Books, 1975–1976.

Birkhäuser-Oeri, Sibylle. *The Mother: Archetypal Image in Fairy Tales*. Toronto: Inner City Books, 1988.

Bolte, Johannes und Georg Polivka. *Anmerkungen zu den Kinder- und Hausmärchen der Gebrüder Grimm*. 5 vols. Leipzig: Diederichs, 1913–1932.

Brothers Grimm. *Kinder- und Hausmärchen*.

Brunner-Traut, Emma. *Altägyptische Märchen*. Die Märchen der Weltliteratur, edited by

Bülow, Werner von. *Die Geheimsprache der deutschen Märchen*. Hellerau bei Dresden, 1925.

Burkhardt, Heinrich. "Psychologie der Erlebnissage." Dissertation. Zurich, 1951.

Campbell, Joseph. *The hero with a Thousand Faces*. New York: Joseph Campbell Foundation, 2008.

Chevalier, Jean, and Alain Gheerbrant, eds. *Dictionnaire des Symboles*. 20th ed. Paris: Robert Laffont, 1982.

Dante, Alighieri. "Hell." Part 1 in *The divine comedy*, translated by Henry Wadsworth Longfellow. San Diego: Canterbury Classics, 2013.

Dieckmann, Hans. *Märchen und Träume als Helfer des Menschen*. Stuttgart: Bonz, 1968.

_____. *Märchen und Symbole: Tiefenpsychologische Deutung orientalischer Märchen*. Psychologisch gesehen, no. 31. Stuttgart: Bonz, 1999.

_____. *Der Zauber aus 1001 Nacht*. Krummwisch: Königsfurt, 2000.

_____. *Gelebte Märchen: Lieblingsmärchen der Kindheit*. Stuttgart: Kreuz, 1993.

_____. *Methods in Analytical Psychology: An Introduction*. Asheville: Chiron Publications, 1991.

Durand, Gilbert. *The Anthropological Structures of the Imaginary*. Brisbane: Boombana Publishing, 1999.

Dostoevsky, Fjodor. *The Brothers Karamazov*. Translated by Richard Pevear and Larissa Volokhonksy. New York, Toronto: Alfred Knopf, 1992.

Eliade, Mircea. *Myths, Dreams, and Mysteries: The Encounter Between Contemporary Faiths and Archaic Realities*. London: Harper and Row, 1968.

_____. *Shamanism: Archaic Techniques of Ecstasy*. Princeton, NJ: Princeton University Press, 2020.

_____. *The Forge and the Crucible: The Origins and Structures of Alchemy*. Chicago: University of Chicago Press, 1978.

_____. *The Myth of the Eternal Return: Cosmos and History*. Princeton, NJ: Princeton University Press, 2018.

Franz, Marie-Louise von. "Active Imagination in the Psychology of C.G. Jung." In *Psychotherapy*. Boston: Shambhala, 1993. New edition in preparation by Chiron Publications, Asheville. Vol. 26, CW.

_____. *Archetypal Dimensions of the Psyche*. Boston: Shambhala, 1999. New edition in preparation by Chiron Publications, Asheville. Vol. 27, CW.

C.G. Jung: His Myth in Our Time. Vol. 9, CW. Asheville: Chiron Publications, 2023.

_____. *Creation Myths*. Revised Edition. Boston: Shambhala, 1995. New edition in preparation by Chiron Publications, Asheville. Vol. 20, CW.

_____. *Feminine in Fairy Tales*. Vol. 13, CW. Asheville: Chiron Publications, 2024.

_____. *Individuation in Fairy Tales*. Boston: Shambhala, 1990. New edition in preparation by Chiron Publications, Asheville. Vol. 17, CW.

_____. *Niklaus von Flue and Saint Perpetua*. Vol. 6, CW. Asheville: Chiron Publications, 2022.

_____. *Number and Time: Reflections Leading Towards a Unification of Depth Psychology and Physics*. Evanston: Evanston Northwestern University, 1974. New edition in preparation by Chiron Publications, Asheville. Vol. 21, CW.

"On Active Imagination." In *Psychotherapy*. Boston: Shambhala, 1993. New edition in preparation by Chiron Publications, Asheville. Vol. 26, CW.

_____. *Pattern of Creativity Mirrored in Creation Myths*. Dallas: Spring Publications, 1972. New edition in preparation by Chiron Publications, Asheville. Vol. 20, CW.

_____. *Psychotherapy*. Boston: Shambhala, 1993. New edition in preparation by Chiron Publications, Asheville. Vol. 26, CW.

_____. *Reflections of the Soul: Projection and Recollection in Jungian Psychology*. Chicago: Open Court, 1995. New edition in preparation by Chiron Publications, Asheville. Vol. 22, CW.

_____. *Shadow and Evil in Fairy Tales*. Boston: Shambhala, 2017. New edition in preparation by Chiron Publications, Asheville. Vol. 14. CW.

The Golden Ass. New edition in preparation by Chiron Publications, Asheville. Vol. 15, CW.

_____. *The Interpretation of Fairy Tales*. Revised Edition. Boston: Shambhala, 1996. New edition in preparation by Chiron Publications, Asheville. Vol. 8, CW, 2024.

_____. *The Problem of the Puer Aeternus*. Toronto: Inner City Books, 2000. New edition in preparation by Chiron Publications, Asheville. Vol. 10, CW, 2024.

Goethe, Johann Wolfgang von. *Faust. A Tragedy*. Translated by Walter Arndt. New York, London: W.W. Norton & Company, 1976.

Frazer, James George. *The Golden Bough*. Munich: BookRix, 2019.

Gehrts, Heino. *Das Märchen und das Opfer: Untersuchungen zum europäischen Brüdermärchen*. Bonn, 1967.

Gennep van, Arnold. *Les rites de passage*. Paris, 1909.

Grant, Michael, and John Hazel. *Who's who in Classical Mythology*. London: Routledge, 2002.

Grimm, Jacob, and Wilhelm Grimm. *The Complete Fairy Tales*. Translated by Jack Zipes. London: Vintage Books, 2007.

Gulya, János, and Ruth Futaky. *Sibirische Märchen*. Die Märchen der Weltliteratur, edited by Friedrich von der Leyen. München: Diederichs, 1995.

Handwörterbuch des deutschen Aberglaubens. Edited by Hanns Bächtold-Stäubli. 10 vols., reprint of the edition from 1927–1942. Berlin: Verlag de Gruyter, 2000.

Hannah, Barbara. *Encounters with the Soul.* Asheville: Chiron Publications, 2015.

_____. "On Active Imagination." In *The Inner Journey. Lectures and Essays on Jungian Psychology,* Toronto: Inner City Books, 2000.

Herrigel, Eugen. *Zen in the Art of Archery.* Eastford: Martino Fine Books, 2020.

Holy Bible. King James Version. Nashville: Thomas Nelson, 2016.

Huth, Otto. *Das Sonnen-, Mond- und Sternenkleid.* Unpublished, 1942.

_____. "Der Glasberg." In *Symbolon II.* 1961.

I Ching: The Book of Changes. New York: Dover Publications, 2012.

Innerschweizerisches Jahrbuch für Heimatkunde, Sagen und ihre seelischen Hintergründe. Lucerne, 1936–1960.

Isler, Gotthilf. *Die Sennenpuppe: Eine Untersuchung über die religiöse Funktion einiger Alpensagen.* Basel: Schweizerische Gesellschaft für Volkskunde, 1992.

Jacob, Georg. *Märchen und Traum.* Hannover: H. Lafaire, 1923.

Jaffé, Aniela. *Bilder und Symbole aus E. T. A. Hoffmanns Märchen "Der goldene Topf."* Einsiedeln: Daimon, 2003.

Jung, Carl Gustav. *Collected Works (=CW).* Vol. 1-20. Princeton, NJ: Princeton University Press, 1957.

_____. *Aion: Researches into the Phenomenology of the Self.* Vol. 9/II, CW.

_____. *Alchemical Studies.* Vol. 13, CW.

_____. *Archetypes and the Collective Unconscious.* Vol. 9/1, CW.

_____. *Civilization in Transition.* Vol. 10, CW.

_____. *Mysterium Coniunctionis: An Inquiry into the Separation and Synthesis of Psychic Opposites in Alchemy.* Vol. 14/II, CW.

_____. "On the Nature of the Psyche." In *The Dynamic of the Unconscious.* Vol. 8, CW.

_____. "On the Psychology of the Unconscious." In *Two Essays on Analytical Psychology.* Vol. 7, CW.

_____. "Psychological Commentary on The Tibetan Book of the Dead." In *Psychology and Religion: West and East*. Vol. 11, CW.

_____. *Psychological Types*. Vol. 6, CW.

_____. *Psychology and Alchemy. Vol. 12, CW.*

_____. Psychology and Religion: West and East. Vol. 11, CW.

_____. *Symbolic Life*. Vol. 18, CW.

_____. "Symbols and the Interpretation of Dreams." In *The Symbolic Life*. Vol. 18, CW.

_____. *Symbols of Transformation*. Vol. 5, CW.

_____. "Symbols of Transformation in Mass." In *Psychology and Religion*. Vol. 11, CW.

_____. *Synchronicity: An Acausal Connecting Principle*. Vol. 8, CW.

_____. *The Dynamic of the Unconscious*. Vol. 8, CW.

_____. "The Personification of the Opposites." In *Mysterium Coniunctionis: An Inquiry into the Separation and Synthesis of Psychic Opposites in Alchemy*. Vol. 14/I, CW.

_____. *The Practice of Psychotherapy. Essays on the Psychology of the Transference and Other Subjects*. Vol. 16, CW.

_____. "The Psychology of the Mass." In *Psychology and Religion: West and East*. Vol. 11, CW.

_____. "The Spirit of Mercury." In *Alchemical Studies*. Vol. 13, CW.

_____. "The Transcendent Function." In *The Dynamic of the Unconscious*. Vol. 8, CW.

_____. "The Visions of Zosimos." In *Alchemical Studies*. Vol. 13, CW.

_____. *Two Essays on Analytical Psychology*. Vol. 7, CW.

_____. "Wotan." In *Civilization in Transition*. Vol. 10, CW.

Jung, C.G. *Memories, Dreams, Reflections*. Edited by Aniela Jaffé. Translated by Richard Winston and Clara Winston. New York: Vintage Books, 1989.

Jung, C.G. *On Psychological and Visionary Art. Notes from C.G. Jung's Lecture on Gérard de Nerval's "Aurélia."* Edited by Craig E. Stephenson. Princeton, Oxford: Princeton University Press, 2015.

Jung C.G., and Wolfgang Pauli. *Atom and Archetype: The Pauli/Jung Letters 1932–1958.* Edited by C.A. Meier. Princeton: Princeton University Press, 2001.

The Interpretation of Nature and the Psyche. New York: Pantheon Books, 1955.

Jung, Emma. "Die Anima als Naturwesen." In *Festschrift zum 80. Geburtstag von C.G. Jung.* Zurich, 1955.

_____. *Animus und Anima: Two Essays.* New York: Spring Publications, 2004.

Jungbauer, Gustav. *Märchen aus Turkestan und Tibet.* Die Märchen der Weltliteratur. Jena: Diederichs, 1923.

Karlinger, Felix. *Grundzüge einer Geschichte des Märchens im deutschen Sprachraum.* Darmstadt: Wiss. Buchgesellschaft, 1983.

_____, ed. *Wege der Märchenforschung.* Darmstadt: Wiss. Buchgesellschaft, 1973.

Kerényi, Karl. *The Gods of the Greeks.* London: Thames and Hudson, 2010.

_____. *The heroes of the Greek.* London: Thames and Hudson, 1974.

Koch-Grünberg, Theodor. *Südamerikanische Indianermärchen.* Die Märchen der Weltliteratur, edited by Friedrich von der Leyen. Jena: Diederichs, 1921.

Kunike, Hugo. *Märchen aus Sibirien.* Jena: Diederichs, 1940.

Laiblin, Wilhelm. "Der goldene Vogel: Zur Symbolik der Individuation im Volksmärchen." In *Jugend gestern und heute.* Stuttgart: Klett, 1961.

_____. *Wachstum und Wandlung: Zur Phänomenologie und Symbolik menschlicher Reifung.* Darmstadt: Wiss. Buchgesellschaft, 1974.

Laistner, Ludwig. *The Sphinx's Riddle: Elements of a History of Mythology.* 2 vols. 1889.

Leskien, August, and Friedrich von der Leyen, eds. *Balkanmärchen: Aus Albanien, Bulgarien, Serbien und Kroatien.* Die Märchen der Weltliteratur. Jena: Diederichs, 1915.

Lévi-Strauss, Claude. *The Raw and the Cooked.* Translated by John Weightman and Doreen Weightman. Chicago: University of Chicago Press, 1996.

_____, ed. *Wege der Märchenforschung*. Darmstadt: Wiss. Buchgesellschaft, 1973.

Leyen, Friedrich von der, Jacob Grimm, and Wilhelm Grimm. "Die verwünschte Prinzessin." In *Das Deutsche Märchen und die Brüder Grimm*. Vol. 2. Jena: Diederichs, 1922 and 1923.

Leyen von der, Friedrich and Paul Zaunert. *Deutsche Märchen aus dem Donaulande*. Jena: Diederichs, 1926.

Lorenz, Konrad. *On Aggression*. Translated by Marjorie Kerr Wilson. London: Routledge, 2002.

Löwis of Menar, August von. *Russian Folktales*. Edited by Reinhold Olesch. London: Bell, 1971.

Lurker, Manfred. *Bibliographie zur Symbolkunde*. Baden-Baden: Heintz, 1964.

Lüthi, Max. *The European Folktale: Form and Nature*. Bloomington: Indiana University Press, 1986.

_____. "Die Gabe im Märchen und in der Sage: Ein Beitrag zur Wesenserfassung und Wesensscheidung der beiden Formen." Dissertation, Universität Bern, 1943.

Maier, Michael. *Atalanta Fugiens*. Manchester: Old Book Publishing, 2015.

_____. *Atalanta Fugiens: Hoc est Emblemata nova de secretis naturae chymica*. Facsimile-Druck der Oppenheimer Original-Ausgabe of 1618 with 52 engravings by Matthäus Merian d. Ae. Edited by Lucas Heinrich Wüthrich. Kassel and Basel: Bärenreiter, 1964.

Märchen der Weltliteratur, edited by Friedrich von der Leyen und P. Zaunert. Jena/Köln/Düsseldorf, 1912. New edition, Düsseldorf, Köln: Diederichs, 1983.

Meinhof, Carl. *Afrikanische Märchen*. Jena: Diederichs, 1921.

Neidhardt, John G. *Black Elk Speaks: Being the Life Story of a Holy Man of the Oglala Sioux*. Lincoln: University of Nebraska Press, 1988.

Nerval, Gérard de. *Œuvres complètes*. Edited by Jean-Nicolas Illouz. Vol. XIII: *Aurélia, ou, Le Rêve et la vie*. Paris: Classiques Garnier, 2013.

Olesch, Reinhold. *Russian Folktales*. Translated by E.C. Elstob and Richard Barber. London: G. Bell & Sons, 1971.

Onians, Richard Broxton. *The Origin of European Thought: About the Body, the Mind, the Soul, the World, Time and Fate*. Cambridge: Cambridge University Press, 1951.

Pauli, Wolfgang, see C.G. Jung and Wolfgang Pauli. *Atom and Archetype: The Pauli/Jung Letters 1932–1958*. Edited by C.A. Meier. Princeton: Princeton University Press, 2001.

_____. *The Interpretation of Nature and the Psyche*. New York: Pantheon Books, 1955.

Post, Laurens van der. *The Heart of the Hunter*. London: Vintage Book, 2010.

Propp, Vladimir. *Morphology of the Folktale*. Austin: University of Texas Press, 1975.

Pschmadt, Carl. "Die Sage von der Verfolgten Hinde." Dissertation. Greifswald, 1911.

Rasmussen, Knud. *Die Gabe des Adlers: Eskimoische Märchen aus Alaska*. Frankfurt: Societäts-Verlag, 1937.

Rhys, David. "Zur Geschichte des Radsymbols." In *Ostwestliche Symbolik und Seelenführung*. Eranos Jahrbuch 1934. Zurich: Rhein-Verlag, 1935.

Rilke, Rainer Maria. *Werke*. Annotated edition in four volumes with supplementary fifth volume. Edited by Manfred Engel and Ulrich Fülleborn. Vol. 1: *Gedichte 1895–1910*. Frankfurt a. M., Leipzig: Insel, 1996.

Rittershaus, Adeline. *Die Neuisländischen Volksmärchen: Ein Beitrag zur vergleichenden Märchenforschung*. Halle: Max Niemeyer, 1902.

Sartori, Paul. "Der Schuh im Volksglauben." *Zeitschrift des Vereins für Volkskunde*, 1894.

_____. "Sitte und Brauch." In *Handbücher der Volkskunde*. Vol. 5. Leipzig, 1910–1914.

Schmidt, Wilhelm. *Der Ursprung der Gottesidee*. Munster: Aschendorff, 1912–1955.

Schmidt, Johann Georg. *Die gestriegelte Rocken-Philosophie*. Chemnitz: Stössel, 1718-1722.

Schwabe, Julius. *Archetyp und Tierkreis: Grundlinien einer kosmischen Symbolik und Mythologie.* Basel: Schwabe, 1951.

Stauff, Philipp. *Märchendeutungen: Sinn und Deutung der deutschen Volksmärchen.* Leipzig: Dürr, 1935.

Steinen, Karl von den. *Unter den Naturvölkern Zentral-Brasiliens: Reiseschilderung und Ergebnisse der zweiten Schingu-Expedition 1887–1888.* Berlin: Severus Verlag, 2013.

Stroebe, Clara. *Nordische Volksmärchen: Norwegische Volksmärchen.* Vol 2. Jena: Diederichs, 1940.

_____. *The Norwegian Fairy Book.* Vol. 2. Whitefish: Kessinger Publishing, 2008.

Tegethoff, Ernst. *Französische Volksmärchen.* Die Märchen der Weltliteratur, edited by Friedrich von der Leyen. Vol. 2. Jena: Diederichs, 1923.

Thompson, Stith. *Motif-Index of Folk Literature: A Classification of Narrative Elements in Folktales, Ballads, Myths, Fables, Mediaeval Romances, Exempla, Fabliaux, Jest-Books and Local Legends.* 6 vols. Copenhagen: Rosenkilde and Bagger, 1955–1958.

Tolkien, John Ronald R. *The Lord of the Rings.* 3 vols. London: Harper Collins, 1993.

Tylor, Edward Burnett. *Primitive Culture: Researches into the Development of Mythology, Philosophy, Religion, Art and Custom.* London, 1891.

Vonessen, Franz. "Sich selbst bestehlen – von der symbolischen Natur des Eigentums." In *Symbolon: Jahrbuch für Symbolforschung.* Edited by Julius Schwabe. Vol. 5. Basel: Schwabe, 1966.

Vries, Jan de. *Forschungsgeschichte der Mythologie.* Freiburg: Alber, 1961.

Wilhelm, Richard. *I Ching or Book of Changes.* London: Penguin Books, 1995.

Wyrsch, Jakob. "Sagen und ihre seelischen Hintergründe." In *Innerschweizerisches Jahrbuch für Heimatkunde.* Vol. 7. Lucerne, 1943.

Index

G

◆

Index of Fairytales